DICK FITZGERALD

Dick Fitzgerald's signature

First published in 2008 by

CURRACH PRESS

55A Spruce Avenue, Stillorgan Industrial Park, Blackrock, Co. Dublin

www.currach.ie

1 3 5 4 2

Cover by bluett

Origination by Currach Press

Printed in Ireland by ColourBooks, Baldoyle Industrial Estate, Dublin 13

ISBN: 978-1-85607-962-4

DICK FITZGERALD

KING IN A KINGDOM OF KINGS

TOM LOONEY

CURRACH
PRESS

Dedicated to the memory of my late father Jack Looney,
one of the old stock,
and to folk like him,
who make the GAA the great movement it is

Acknowledgements

The genesis of this biography was Maurice Francis O'Leary's celebratory pamphlet for the Killarney Crokes seventieth birthday in 1956. I was eleven and demanded to meet the last surviving founder-member of the club, Martin Kissane. I acknowledge the generosity and contribution to culture of the people who have told the GAA story – writers, photographers, librarians, researchers, storytellers, broadcasters, supporters, critics, mentors and players. I thank them all. I also thank Antony Farrell of Lilliput Press for consent to use the phrase from Séamus de Faoite's short story which gives this book its evocative title and Con Houlihan's insight into the heart of Killarney taken from his introduction to de Faoite's short story collection.

I have drawn deeply from the rich well of many who recorded the Dick Fitzgerald and Kerry football story. I acknowledge their heritage and thank them all for their valued contribution. My cousins Kevin Coleman and Edmund Eagar provided key photographs, as did Valerie O'Sullivan, Seán Kelly, Paddy and Lil MacMonagle, Mary Ellen Spillane, the late Declan Horgan and his son Tim. The cooperation of Michael O'Leary and Margaret Piggott of Killarney UDC and of all the staff at Killarney and Tralee county libraries is much appreciated; also the help of Gerard J. Lyne and his National Library colleagues in Kildare Street. The staff at the National Archives in Bishop Street, Dublin, were most helpful, as were Dr Ciara Breathnach of UL and Ballymacelligott and RTE's archivist Dara O'Donoghue.

Paddy O'Shea and Eamonn Fitzgerald wrote to me in Peru in 1980 as they were about to research and publish their respective Dr Crokes club histories. Without their invitation and encouraging challenge much would have been lost. I thank them and all their fellow Crokes officers and members, in particular Tadhgie Fleming, Tom Healy, John Keogh, Jackie Looney, Brian O'Callaghan and Pa O'Brien. Jesuits Senan Timoney, Donal Neary and Brother John Maguire were helpful in relation to Dick Fitzgerald's Mungret days, as were Denis O'Donoghue of St Brendan's College, Killarney, Michael Hennessy and Declan Ó hÉaluithe of Presentation College Cork and Fathers John Cotter and Tom Deenihan from that 'beautiful city'. The advice and help given by two North Kerry priests in Dublin, J. Anthony Gaughan and Tom Kearney, is deeply appreciated. The late Fr John B. O'Sullivan provided some important information regarding his Fitzgerald relatives, as did Maeve O'Sullivan, Kenmare. I acknowledge the hospitality and help of Margaret and T. Ryle Dwyer, Tralee and the interest of Doctors Jim and Conor Brosnan, Dingle.

To all my family and friends *míle buíochas*. Thanks especially for the overseas encouragement of Fr Ken O'Riordan and Sheila Ward in England and Jim O'Sullivan in Hamburg. The hard work of Breda Sugrue, Killarney and Cathy Griffin, Lispole, got the text of this book to the ever-helpful Jo O'Donoghue and her Currach Press team.

When the harvesting *meitheal* is finished there's the Kerry custom of sitting on the ditch pondering on the wonder of it all.

Beir bua is beannacht
Tom Looney, Dingle, May 2008

Contents

King in a Kingdom of Kings

O God be good to you, Dickeen Fitz,
You king in a Kingdom of kings.

In a short story, 'Pictures in a Pawnshop', by Killarney writer Séamus de Faoite, Jack is walking with Joe Jack to a county football final in Tralee. The above comment is made by Jack when he sees a picture of the 1903 Kerry team on the wall of a Firies public house.

Dickeen Fitz was born to Michael and Bridget (née Healy) Fitzgerald of College Street, Killarney on 2 October 1882, although many subsequent references, including reports of football games he played, suggest that he was born in 1884 or even 1886. The Fitzgeralds were merchants, running a successful export business of eggs, poultry and butter from a rented premises in College Street, adjacent to the modern-day Scott's Hotel.

Their first child Catherine had died in infancy so they passed her name on to another daughter. Edmond, born in 1875, was ordained a priest for the Kerry diocese in 1900 but served all his ministry in Cork until his death in 1936. He played a key organisational role in the controversial Kerry US tour of 1927. Helena spent the most of her adult life as Sr Josepha in Cork's North Presentation Convent, where she died in 1968. (North

Presentation Convent was a hiding place for Irish Volunteer weapons during the War of Independence.) Other siblings included Patrick, Kathy (Mrs Gunning) and Bridget, who was unmarried and remained in the home place. Richard Fitzgerald was baptised on 3 October 1882 in St Mary's Cathedral, Killarney by Fr M. McCarthy. His godparents were Patrick Fitzgerald and Mary Fitzgerald.

Dick Fitzgerald was born into a Kerry that underwent massive upheaval, revolution and change during the course of his short lifetime. Within two years of his birth the Gaelic Athletic Association was founded in Thurles. During the three years leading to the secret foundation, in 1886, of Dr Crokes GAA Club in Killarney, some 1,600 Kerry tenant families were evicted on to the dykes and ditches of the Kingdom. Michael Davitt, founder of the Land League and GAA patron, highlighted this social dislocation during his 1886 visit to Castleisland. Davitt acknowledged Kerry to be 'the most lawless county in the struggles'[1]. At this very time Killarney was classified as 'a particularly disturbed district' according to the Public Records Office Memo.[2]

After early schooling at the local Presentation Convent primary school and the Presentation Brothers' Monastery school, Dick went on to attend three secondary schools in three counties. The first was St Brendan's Seminary, Killarney 'where he blossomed forth as a gifted footballer'[3]. This diocesan college, which became popularly known as 'the Sem', was founded in 1860. The register for September 1895 records the enrolment of student No. 1080, Richard Fitzgerald. In a school famed for classical studies, Richard did not 'blossom forth' as a classicist, however. The school archive reveals that his Junior B Greek exam result at Christmas 1898 was registered as 'very bad' and his Latin paper at Christmas 1899 merited another 'very bad' rating.

Fitzgerald made many Munster friends during his teenage years in a country experiencing the Land War, the Parnell split, the campaign for Home Rule and the determined idealism emerging from a new national consciousness. The Home Rule Bills of 1886, 1893 and 1912 offered hope of greater autonomy to Irish nationalists, although these hopes took a severe downturn with Parnell's early death in 1891 and the ensuing split in the national movement. Dúglas de hÍde and Eoin Mac Néill founded Conradh na Gaeilge in 1893 and by 1903 Craobh na nÁirne (the 'sloes' of the Irish version of the town's name) of the Gaelic League in Killarney was well established.

In 1901 Dick Fitzgerald entered the Jesuit-run Mungret College in Limerick, 'where he became a proficient hurler'[4]. Finally, in 1902, he attended the Presentation Brothers' commercial school in the Mardyke in Cork City with his former 'Sem' classmate and life-long friend Jerry O'Leary. At this time he became a member of the famed Nils Football Club. This city club was formed in 1887 when the members of the unsuccessful Berwick Rangers Rugby Club disbanded and shortly afterwards decided to re-group as a GAA club. They adopted the Latin name 'Nil Desperandum' meaning 'Do not despair', which was abbreviated to 'Nils'. As well as Dick Fitzgerald, who played with them as a sixteen-year-old while attending Presentation Brothers' College[5], Dingle's Batt O'Connor, who spent four years as apprentice boot maker in Leeside, played for Nils. The high-fielding O'Connor lined out for Kerry on the winning 1907 Croke Cup side captained by Dickeen Fitz and on the victorious 1909 All Ireland team.[6]

Jim Cronin's 2005 publication, *Making Connections – A Cork*

GAA Miscellany, gives a good account of the Nils club. Cronin concludes with a poem that might well describe the young Dick Fitzgerald taking the train back to his native Killarney. There he registered with his local Dr Crokes club, which was facing its fifteenth season. It was a move that yielded a great harvest for the GAA.

NIL DESPERANDUM

In the morning of life with bosom elate
The youth leaves the home of his heart
To seek on the treacherous ocean his fate
And in life's busy scene he takes part.
Oh then sailing along 'midst trouble and care
He sings, 'Nil Desperandum, I'll never despair.'

At length when the perilous voyage is o'er
And the vessel at anchor safe lies
How gladly he springs on his dear native shore
And quickly then homewards he flies.
Oh then throwing off his trouble and care
He sings, 'Nil Desperandum, I'll never despair.'[7]

2

'Fit to Carry the Game You Shaped for Them, Dickeen Boy'

MacGearailt-versus-Mgarilt,M'Gerald, Fitzgerald; 'son of Gerald'; the Irish form of the Norman surname Fitzgerald. The Fitzgeralds rank with the Burkes and Butlers as one of the most illustrious of the Anglo-Norman families in Ireland. They derive their name and descent from Gerald, Constable of Pembroke, whose wife was Nest, daughter of Rhys Ap Tewdwyr, King of South Wales. Gerald flourished in the early part of the twelfth century. His son, Maurice Fitzgerald, was one of the companions of Strongbow, and from him are descended all the families of the name in Ireland. He received large grants of land, which continued in the possession of his descendants down to recent times. Members of the family frequently filled the highest offices under the English Crown. The head of the Leinster branch of the family for centuries bore the title of Earl of Kildare, later Duke of Leinster, while the head of the Fitzgeralds of Munster was Earl of

Desmond.[1]
Fr Patrick Woulfe, *Sloinnte Gael is Gall*, 1923

At the turn of the twentieth century Killarney was a small, sleepy tourist town. The 1901 Census reported that Michael and Bridget Fitzgerald, listed as export merchants, along with Ellie, Kathy, Richard, Bridget and Patrick Fitzgerald, were resident in College Street on census night.[2] (Fr Edmond –Ned – ordained for Kerry Diocese in 1900, was on loan to the Diocese of Cork by this time.)

College Street takes its name from the classical school located there in Penal times, from which 'following its constitution as a seminary, students went through their complete course for ordination.'[3] Although this college was transferred to New Street it was replaced by another important education centre when, in 1838, the Presentation Brothers took up residence where the Arbutus Hotel now stands. They took over the existing school at Fair Hill before moving to their current location at Falvey's Inch, which was to the west of the town in 1841. In 1860 the Belgian Franciscans arrived at the invitation of Bishop David Moriarty and founded their Friary on Martyrs' Hill at the eastern end of College Street. (The name Martyrs' Hill dates back to Penal times and the execution there in 1653 of Fr Thaddeus Moriarty OP from Castlemaine and Baile an Fheirtéaraigh's chieftain Piaras Feirtéar.)

The RIC barracks stood close to the Friary on the site where Árus Phádraig now stands. Local folklore has preserved the apocryphal story that the barracks had originally been designed and intended for construction in India but was mistakenly built in Killarney!

Killarney GAA club was founded in secrecy in 1886. The

spark was ignited in O'Mahoney's public house in College Street, now known as Squire's Pub, on Sunday the Eve of All Saints. 'Nineteen dangerous dreamers' convened in secret in the Railway Company's Gashouse near the Iron Bridge at Fair Hill on Tuesday 2 November 1886. A Kilkenny railway official named Andy Mulcahy had offered the gathering a place to found the GAA Club. 'The first chairman was Con Courtney, a merchant who was accompanied by his College Street neighbours, Jim O'Leary, Denny Courtney and French polishers Martin and Jack Kissane. They elected Dan Guerin as vice-chairman; Dan's brother Con of Mangerton View was also present. High Street was represented by Michael Moriarty, a draper, who was elected secretary and Mike Looney, a railway man like Paddy and Jack Crowe. Maurice Moynihan and Bob Roberts of Pound Lane were present, also Mick Gleeson, a boatman, Tim Gallagher who worked in Bowman's hardware shop, Jim Gallivan, a clerk, Michael O'Sullivan, brother of Bishop O'Sullivan, Jim McGuinness, a carpenter from Henn Street, and John Langford, who managed O'Sullivan's farm at Killeen and who was to contribute much to the development of the GAA in Kerry.'[4] The club received a letter from GAA patron Archbishop Thomas Croke of Cashel and Emly agreeing to become its patron.

Mark Tierney OSB, GAA historian and biographer of Dr Croke of Cashel, has researched the infiltration of the GAA by Dublin Castle authorities. He notes the concentration of both Fenians and Irish Republican Brotherhood (IRB) activists in the Kerry County Board by 1890 and the concerns expressed by District Inspector A. Gambell on 12 April 1890. The Tralee informer code-named 'Emerald' corroborated Gambell's worst fears as GAA County President Maurice Moynihan 'swore me as a member of the IRB.'[5] Tierney shows that by 1895 the police had successfully penetrated every GAA club in the country by planting two informants who regularly reported to Dublin Castle.

Three years later Dr Crokes lost the very first Kerry Senior County Championship final to Laune Rangers of Killorglin on a score of 0-6 to 0-3. Four Dr Crokes footballers, Dr William O'Sullivan, Mike Hayes, Tom 'Crosstown' Looney and John Langford, won Munster senior medals as members of the Laune Rangers side representing Kerry in 1892.[6] Dublin's Young Irelanders won the All Ireland in Clonturk Park in the capital on 26 March 1893 on the score 1-4 to 0-3 (when one goal equalled 5 points). Team captain J.P. O'Sullivan publicly posted a challenge for a re-match in the press on 5 April. He felt aggrieved, arguing that the unsporting play, incapable refereeing and the uncivilised behaviour of the rival fans necessitated a re-match at a neutral venue. The Dublin champions ignored J.P.'s challenge and a full decade was to pass before the Kingdom became serious challengers for national honours. J.P.'s son, Dr Eamonn, later coached eight Kerry teams to All-Ireland glory between 1924 and 1962.

Teenager Dick Fitzgerald did not figure on the Crokes panel. The club again lost the 1900 Senior County Football Final to Laune Rangers. Despite trailing the Killarney team by two points to one at half-time the men from Killorglin won their fifth senior title on a score of 3-4 to 0-3. The first known published photograph of Dick Fitzgerald shows him as a slim curly-haired youth with the successful Dr Crokes county finalists of 1901. The championship of 1901, which continued into 1902, was plagued with objections and counter-objections all the way to the Munster Council, which backed the Crokes against Tralee Mitchels on 19 July 1902. Tralee had enjoyed the favour of the

Kerry County Board in their objection to Dr Crokes semi-final victory. But former Kerry star, rugby international Dr William O'Sullivan, defiantly and successfully led the Killarney appeals and cleared the way for Dr Crokes county-final appearance against Caherciveen in Tralee on 3 August 1902. 'Each side was appearing in its third senior county final.'[7]

> The ground was full as the teams came on the field. A new face was seen on the Crokes line-out, a face that was to become a household name over the next three decades and that face belonged to a sixteen-year old boy from College Street by the name of Richard Fitzgerald. In every sense of the word he was indeed a boy and he was playing with household names, men of great stature, but he was not overawed by the occasion. In a very competent team performance 'the men from the Lakes' carried the day on a score of 1-2 to 2 points. Back at home the team were paraded through the town by two bands. Celebrating went on into the night and the following few days.[8]

The definitive reference book to all Kerry senior hurling and football county finals, *Records of the Kerry County Senior Championships 1889–1998, Face the Ball*, was compiled by Pat O'Shea of the Tralee Kerins O'Rahilly club and published by Coiste Chontae Chiarraí in 1998. The title is set on a background of two crossed camáns surmounted by a football. The top right image highlights the Kerry County Board's distinctive logo featuring our national games, the three peninsulae of Kerry, an Irish wolfhound and Ballyduff's Rattoo Round Tower under the triple-crown shield of Munster.

Twenty-two clubs contested the 1901 championship, including two Dr Crokes teams as well as two each from both Firies and Ballymacelligott parishes. *Face the Ball* concludes its report on that year's campaign: 'At "no time" Crokes were a goal clear and so clinched their first championship. Included in their team was the sixteen-year old Dick Fitzgerald.'[9] 'He would go on to win three further senior county medals in the following decades.'[10] Team: E. O'Sullivan (Captain), Paddy Dillon (goal), P.E. Valkenburg, R. Fitzgerald, W. Lynch, J. Myers, D. O'Keeffe, T. O'Keeffe, J. O'Sullivan, D. O'Meara, D. Kissane, J. Kissane, T. Clifford, T. Looney, M. Horgan, M. Murray.

All through his football career Dick Fitzgerald was hailed (inaccurately) as a child prodigy who won County Championship and All-Ireland medals in his mid-teens. En route to a county final in Tralee, many years later, Séamus de Faoite's protagonist Jack eulogises the ghost of his hero of 1903:

> *Fit to carry the game you shaped for them, Dickeen Boy…*
> *Dickeen, you king in a Kingdom of kings.*[11]

'The Memorable Meetings of Kerry and Kildare'[1]: All-Ireland 1903

As reigning County Champions Killarney's Dr Crokes enjoyed captaincy of the Kerry team in the 1902 season. Eugene O'Sullivan captained the side in the earlier games. Later in the season (28 March 1904) he became head of the Kerry County Board and served as MP for a fleeting period in 1907. On 10 May 1903 Kerry defeated Waterford in Cork by four points to three. Their semi-final victory over Cork was in Millstreet on 10 August on a score 2-7 to 0-3. The Munster final against Tipperary ended in a draw at 1-4 each on 4 October 1903. The replay on 1 November 1903 saw the Kerry side, captained by Tom 'Crosstown' Looney, defeated by one point, 1-6 to 1-5. Both finals were hosted at Turner's Cross in Cork. Under the heading 'Seven Kerry Crokes, Con Clifford writes: 'Dr Croke men on the team were: Eugene O'Sullivan, Dick Fitzgerald, Paddy Dillon, Denny Kissane, Tom Sullivan, Dan McCarthy and Tom Looney.'[1] Greater things were in store for the next season.

But chaos reigned in the Kerry County Championship programme of 1902. During 1903 the GAA backed the successful national campaign to declare St Patrick's Day a public holiday. *Face the Ball* spells out the conclusion of a sorry sporting year:

'…the County Board awarded Tralee Mitchels the County Championship at a meeting held on 25 July 1903. Mitchels had won the title by getting three walk-overs and winning just one game.'[2]

Dick Fitzgerald's second club season came to a controversial and abrupt end at Kenmare on 24 August 1902 when Tralee Mitchels, who were leading Dr Crokes by seven points to four, 'left the field'.[3] Famed referee J.P. O'Sullivan 'was treated with disrespect' as fighting continued after the walk-off: he 'then awarded the match to Killarney'. The *Kerry Sentinel* reported that the unruly scenes during and following this game worsened at Kenmare railway station: 'The County Board ordered the match to be replayed in Listowel, but Killarney refused to play and Mitchels were awarded the game.' Laune Rangers conceded to Mitchels, who next defeated Listowel on 3 May 1903 before enjoying their third walk-over from four-time finalists South Kerry.

Despite Fitzgerald's unsatisfactory club season he was maturing as a player and taking steps towards a place on the Kerry senior county panel. During the next thirteen seasons he intermittently occupied this place, during which time he played in nine All-Ireland senior finals, winning five – including three Croke Cups – and he later won three County Championships in a row. The intermittent aspect was due to the fact that the Kerry County Board was not always affiliated to the Central Council of the GAA owing to organisational and political situations which were to arise in the interim. (The famous ban on imported games which was mooted by resolution at Congress in 1901 became law in 1902.)

Round 1 of the 1903 Senior Munster championship was played in Cork on 12 June 1904. This was the first in a series of matches over the next two years which deepened the hold of the twenty-year-old GAA on the Irish psyche. Kerry defeated Waterford 4-8 to 1-3 and won the semi-final against Clare in the Market's Field, Limerick, on 7 August 1904 on a score of 2-7 to 2-0. The same venue hosted the provincial final on 31 October 1904, with Waterford's J.F. O'Donnell appointed as referee. Kerry easily won this final, 1-7 to 0-3, and qualified to meet the Connacht representatives Mayo. 'Even though Mayo contested the 1903 All-Ireland semi-final they were not Connacht champions. Galway were awarded the Connacht title without kicking a ball, when Mayo and Roscommon were both found to be illegal.'[4] The men from the Kingdom enjoyed a victory over the Westerners by 2-7 to 0-4. Leinster champions Kildare easily defeated Cavan in the other semi-final.

The 1903 All Ireland Senior Football Final day – Sunday 23 July 1905 – is a red-letter day in the annals of the GAA and of Irish sport. Confusion abounded as almost 15,000 supporters travelled to Tipperary town, where the sporting and spectator facilities proved completely inadequate. The Kerry rail system failed the Kingdom fans who were seriously delayed in a breakdown between Ballybrack and Killarney. Another delay occurred at Limerick Junction, where the Quane Brothers supplied a brake to convey the Kerry team to the game. Many decided to walk to Tipperary town from Limerick Junction. Eventually, the train arrived at its destination at 3.20 pm with the game already in progress. 'Their belated arrival increased the congestion, made confusion worse confounded.'[5]

Kildare, popularly known as 'the Lily-Whites', lined out in an all-white strip. Furthermore, they painted their boots white: the Kingdom togged out in red with green cuffs and collars. These were the club colours of Tralee Mitchels, current County goalwards, unopposed, and flashed the ball past Dillon! Kerry disputed the score, but the referee allowed it. Wild excitement! Kildare two points in front with 10 minutes left. Before the Kerrymen recovered their full senses Kildare notched another point – three now ahead. With defeat staring them in the face Kerry roused themselves to supreme efforts. Grand catching and powerful kicks enabled them to take play into Kildare ground. The ball went wide. Again, the Kerrymen bore down on the Kildare sticks. They had a free. Kildare packed the posts and cleared. Back came Kerry again, J.T. Fitzgerald sending up the white flag.

Play became vigorous and exciting. Stack was injured, but to the relief of the Munster followers he resumed. Two minutes to go! Kerry attack in desperation. Up the wing they came. A Kerryman was fouled in possession and his side got an angle free. Time almost up! Dick Fitzgerald kicked the ball as his Kildare namesake, Leinster's greatest goalman, stood astride the goal-line. The leather sped straight and true to the mark. It seemed as if the ball would drop on the bar, but it fell underneath. The Kildare goalman held it safely, but in so doing, pulled the second leg behind the line! He caught the ball and kicked clear to the wing. But the goal umpire raised the fatal green flag.

Kildare disputed the score. The referee (late Pat McGrath) abided by the umpire's decision and allowed the goal. The spectators' pent-up feelings broke all bounds. Kerrymen, in the wildest

Champions, who also provided Thade Gorman as team captain. The recent fervour of a successful Kerry County Council electioneering poster and slogan, 'Up Baily', crossed over into the immortal 'Up Kerry' from that day onwards. (James Baily from Ballymacelligott was a man of the people campaigning for a seat in the 1903 local elections. His supporters coined the rallying cry 'Up Baily' and he subsequently headed the poll.)

Tipperary's Pat McGrath was both referee and host as he was the owner of the All-Ireland playing field. His was an almost impossible task as the roped sideline barriers could not contain encroaching fans during a pulsating and controversial match. 'Kerry won the toss and decided to play against a slight wind and incline of ground.'[6] Kildare led at half-time by two points to Kerry's one, scored by Dick Fitzgerald. Then as Kerry enjoyed wind and incline advantage they pressed their challenge. Soon they levelled and went ahead with another point from the boot of 'the legendary Dick Fitzgerald, who was only seventeen at the time…'[7] 'Part of the attack was a tall lanky lad of seventeen [sic], perfect feet and hands, most deadly marksman of all time – Dick Fitzgerald.'[8]

Next came a bizarre event which was to have a major influence on the future life of the GAA. Acclaimed sports journalist Paddy Foley – 'P.F.' as he signed his avidly-read *Kerryman* columns – included this graphic account some forty years later in his book, *Kerry's Football Story*:

> Then came an extraordinary incident. A line of people had encroached up on the field. Kildare came along the left wing, up behind the crowd. The Kerry defenders, thinking the ball was dead, had ceased play, but the 'All White' men swept

abandon, rushed in over the pitch, throwing up hats and coats and hugging the players. Pandemonium ruled. The referee blew and blew the whistle unavailingly to get the ground cleared, with the Kildare players and followers protesting against the score. As the referee could not get the game restarted he awarded the match to Kerry, declaring the score: – Kerry 1 goal 4 points; Kildare, 1 goal 3 points.[9]

This was the largest crowd to view any sporting encounter in Ireland to date and the record gate receipts amounted to £123/13s/4d. The Kerry train arrived home to Tralee at 4.20 am on Monday morning, its passengers thinking that the Kingdom were All Ireland champions! Further cause for comment was the fact that most of the Killarney contingent was left behind as they missed their 6.15 pm special. P.F. relates how Kildare rightly objected to the goal decision at a hearing of Central Council held immediately after the game.

The Kerry County Board had not been notified and was not represented at this hearing, where Pat McGrath and his goal umpire, Mr Lundon, stood by their decisions of earlier that afternoon. However, Central Council overruled these officials and ordered a replay on 13 August 1905 at the same venue. Once more Pat McGrath was to be in charge of the whistle. The Kerry County Board protested, demanding an emergency Central Council meeting. Both Austin Stack and T.F. O'Sullivan made an impassioned appeal, quoting the rules: 'No appeal can be entertained against a referee's decision on a score.' But by now Pat McGrath was admitting personal doubt and confusion about Dick Fitzgerald's last-second goal. Goal umpire Mr Lundon stood by his green-flag decision. The Central Council insisted on the replay but was undecided about the venue. Letters to the editors of the Dublin papers suggested a variety of locations including Belfast, Limerick and even London's Crystal Palace. Cork was the appointed venue, with Dublin's M.F. Crowe to act as referee, not the already nominated Pat McGrath. And no wonder!

Kerry agreed to contest the final. The Killarney panellists trained in Killarney and Tralee's players in the county town. On Sunday 27 August 1905, trains departed Caherciveen, Listowel, Tralee, Castleisland and Killarney stations bound for Cork, where 12,000 spectators gathered. 'This was the largest official attendance ever assembled at any game in Ireland.'[10]

In a close and foul-ridden opening half Dick Fitzgerald scored three points of Kerry's five. The Kingdom led the Lily-Whites by two points at half time. Kildare played a much more effective second half and drew level with a Kerry side that was coasting to victory. 'Four minutes from the end Conlon, after gaining possession on the wing, beat McCarthy, Kirwan and Dillon for a great equalising goal but Kerry hung on grimly, despite intense pressure, to make it a draw.'[11] *The Kerryman* of 1 September 2005 harshly criticised the Kerry seventeen for their inability to exhibit 'clever tactics by kicking the ball out to touch' while leading. 'The *Kerry Sentinel* reporter, however, was more generous – Kerry had the match won and won well, when through their own carelessness and over confidence, this goal was scored. We trust it will be a lesson to them in future matches…It was a great match – a splendid match and what we are proud to state a well-conducted one. The utmost good order prevailed among players and spectators. The referee, Mr M.F. Crowe, Dublin was the fairest we have ever seen. Those who stood out conspicuously on the Kerry side were: The brothers

Gorman, A. Stack, M. McCarthy, R. Fitzgerald, Kirwan, J. Fitzgerald, Curran, Myers and D. McCarthy.'[12]

A happy Central Council set about arranging the second replay of the 1903 final. Kildare set their sights on Jones's Road, Dublin, while Kerry favoured any central location. Once again Cork was chosen with Sunday 15 October 1905 as the big day. Both teams trained assiduously for 'the rubber' [the third game] The Kildare was were then known as 'Sons of Sarsfields' or 'Roseberry', after the birthplace of Patrick Sarsfield. They enjoyed a central location for joint training sessions as they mainly resided and worked in the Newbridge and Clane areas. Kerry trained in two separate group sessions but arranged practice or challenge matches to serve as joint squad preparation in Tralee and the Cricket Field, Killarney.

'Fifteen special trains brought the fans to Cork'[13] and among them were the 4,000 Kerry fans. 'The crowd was estimated at from twenty to thirty thousand.'[14] Takings at the Cork Athletic Grounds amounted to £270 as 25,000 paid thruppence a head at the turnstiles making it 'the biggest taken at a GAA game up to then'.[15]

'A drizzling rain still fell as the teams lined out. Kerry won the toss and opened with a soft wind behind them.' M.F. Crowe called 'Backs back', blew the whistle and threw in the pigskin to decide the 1903 All-Ireland Home championship. P.F. takes up the story of the game:

> After Kildare had pressed to send wide, Kerry took up the running. Dick Fitzgerald crashed a hard ball for the goal, but his Kildare namesake, Jack, brought off a marvellous save, which evoked thunderous applause from the crowd. Kerry

maintained pressure, efforts from the Gormans, Dan McCarthy and Dick Fitzgerald being well cleared by the Kildare defenders. Kerry continued to press, and trying for goals lost certain points. At length O'Neill changed the scene of action. Dick Fitzgerald crossed to John Thomas and the Tralee player drove over the bar for the opening point after fourteen minutes of lively football. Ned O'Neill, in a hard tackle dislocated his shoulder, and was replaced by F. O'Sullivan (Killarney). Cribbín, a great Kildare back, under pressure gave a free, Dick Fitzgerald sent to his namesake John Thomas and up went the white flag, putting Kerry in front (three points to two) and so the scores remained at the half time.

Shortly after the restart Dillon brought off a magnificent save from Kennedy and Kerry, then swept to the attack, Jim Gorman driving over a point. Grand, combined play among the Kerrymen was the next feature. The Gormans, Curran, Myers, Kissane, Stack and Dan McCarthy distinguished themselves before Billy Lynch got possession and added a point to Kerry's mounting tally. From a very difficult angle Dick Fitzgerald screwed between the uprights for Kerry's sixth point and Lynch quickly followed with another.

Kildare seemed to go to pieces as Kerry warmed to their work. The 'Kingdom ' men again tried for goals with minors [points] there for the taking. They got neither. A lengthy clearance by Con Healy was secured by D. Fitzgerald. He left with Jim Gorman and the Boherbee sharpshooter sent up another white flag. Shortly after came the final whistle and the great Kerry-Kildare struggles were at an end. The Kingdom men were All-Ireland Football Champions for the first time on the scores: Kerry 8 points; Kildare 2 points. Kerry: T. Gorman (Capt.), J. Gorman, D. Curran, Mce. McCarthy, J. Buckley, C. Healy, J.T. Fitzgerald. A. Stack (Tralee), R. Fitzgerald, P. Dillon (goal), W. Lynch, Dan McCarthy, J. Myers, D. Kissane (Killarney), R. Kirwan, D. Breen (Castleisland), E.O'Neill (Caherciveen), F. O'Sullivan (Killarney) replaced E. O'Neill (injured). Mr M.F. Crowe refereed'.[16]

Kerry were fêted as Home Champions. They had proved their critics wrong – those who held they could not play in the rain. An encounter with the London and Irish exiles was required to decide who would merit the All-Ireland crown. The All-Ireland final was fixed for Clonturk Park, Dublin, on Sunday 12 November 1905. Twelve years before, on 26 March 1893, this had been the venue for Kerry's disappointing 1892 All-Ireland final display against Dublin, who won 1-4 to 0-3. That day Kerry's Laune Rangers were intimidated by 'the constant hissing of the Metropolitans', as reported in the local press. The *Kerry Sentinel* of 29 March 1893 explained in its post-match analysis: 'they did not attempt violence, but they hooted and groaned the Kerrymen in the midst of play in a manner that was not alone discreditable to those guilty of it but calculated to take the spirit and heart out of the Killorglin men in their play which it did most effectively.'[17]

The men of 1903 were more tempered for the fray. Sam Maguire was captain of a London-Hibernian side that proved no match for the 1903 Kingdom seventeen:

> The match was by no means a good one, Kerry's superiority being apparent. For the first few minutes, London-Irish made a plucky fight, but their chances from the outset appeared hopeless. Kerry led by eight points clear at the short whistle and won their first All Ireland by eleven points to three. The Kerry team was the same as that which won at Cork. London-Irish were captained by a noted Cork Gael Sam Maguire, from whom the All-Ireland Championship Cup got its title.[18]

The Kerry hurlers with the 21-a-side Ballyduff selection had won the 1891 All-Ireland title. Enter the senior footballers of Kerry, who by 2007 had won their thirty-fifth senior football title. The foundations laid since 1891 helped to fan a tradition, which has yielded a golden Celtic Cross harvest for GAA players from every parish in the Kingdom.

'On Sunday night a banquet was given to the victorious team by residents of the metropolis. Dr Coffey, President UCD (a Tralee man) was Chairman at the function.'[19]

Two photographs survive of the victorious 1903 side. As the campaign took place over two years and eight games I have endeavoured to identify and name every player and substitute associated with this inaugural national football victory. I first undertook this task at the express request of John O'Leary of the East Kerry Board, himself a Spa GAA official who was helping the Kerry County Board Centenary Committee to prepare for a fitting celebration. The *Kerryman* supplement, which was a major feature in the special Kerry GAA Centenary Commemoration of 1903, listed all known panellists as follows: Thady Gorman (captain), James Gorman, Denny Curran, Maurice McCarthy, John Buckley, Con Healy, Austin Stack, John Thomas Fitzgerald (Tralee Mitchels), Dick Fitzgerald, Paddy Dillon, Billy Lynch, Dan McCarthy, Denny Kissane, Florence O'Sullivan, Jack Myers (Killarney Crokes). Denny Breen, Roddy Kirwan (Castleisland). During the course of this game Kerry used two substitutes, P.J. Cahill and Con Ryan of Tralee Mitchels.

In the games against Kildare Charlie Duggan (Mitchels), Tom O'Sullivan (Crokes) and Éamon O'Neill (Cahirciveen) played. In the All-Ireland semi-final T. Sugrue, who played for both Tralee Mitchels and Castleisland, lined out. During the Munster Championship Jim O'Connell and E. Hanafin (Mitchels), Eugene O'Sullivan (Crokes), Mike Joy (Laune Rangers), and Paul F. Hayes (Tarbert) played on the Kerry team.

The following players were listed as substitutes but did not take part in any game: Mike Pendy (Mitchels), J. Walsh (Ballylongford), Larry Buckley, Denis O'Keeffe, Tom Looney (Crokes), Pat Joy (Laune Rangers), Tom Murphy (Listowel).[20]

Dr Crokes club honoured some of its winning panellists by hosting a centenary gathering in their clubhouse on 13 May 2003. Their sub-committee issued framed photographic tributes to the next-of-kin of some of the Crokes representatives on Kerry's first victorious Gaelic football team.

'Small' Jer O'Leary of Main Street, Killarney, was the supreme authority on Killarney and Kerry GAA As the man reputed to have helped to make the deal to purchase Croke Park he is rightly held in high esteem. On that occasion in Wynn's

Hotel, Dublin, he urged seller and buyer to 'split the difference'. Jones's Road was bought. Crokes historian, Con Clifford, shared 'Small' Jer's memory of the 1903 campaign.

'Did you know,' said he, 'that a free kick made the GAA?"

'No.'

'Well,'said Jer, 'Dick Fitzgerald took a free in the last seconds of the 1903 All-Ireland final to draw the game, which led to the subsequent games which in turn, laid the foundation of the nationwide popularity of Gaelic football. His kick sped straight and true towards the goal. His namesake, the Kildare goalie, caught the ball but was adjudged to have stepped over the goal line and the umpire allowed the goal and from that incident on football became the number one sport in Ireland.'[21]

The compilers of *The Munster GAA Story* sum up the Kingdom's breakthrough and 'rise to greatness – which caught the imagination of the public.'[22] They also highlight both the dramatic contribution of the Lily-Whites and the unexpected gesture of Central Council in awarding them gold medals as gallant runners-up.

> These contests which were played in the most friendly spirit did more to popularise and develop Gaelic football than anything that had happened previously. The standard of skill displayed, in particular in the second and third contests, raised the game to a new level. In addition the extra revenue raised from the gate receipts put the Central Council on a firm financial footing for the first time. The Association had a surplus of £377 which was a considerable sum in those days. Central Council presented a special set of gold medals to Kildare in recognition of the part

they had played in the series.[22]

Dick Fitzgerald, commenting on the Kerry-Kildare games, wrote in *The Sunburst*, a weekly of the time:

In the Leinster representation of 1903 we found foemen worthy of our steel. Kildare were splendid footballers, every one. In contrast I would say they were more polished than Kerry, but any drawbacks there may have been in our finish was more than compensated for in fire and dash. The spirit of victory had set us aflame.

In my long career I never remember to have seen more determined games. It was do or die with Kerry and when we won in a third test there was wild rejoicing in our Munster home. Football took a turn for the better about this period. I must be pardoned for claiming that this was mainly due to the memorable meetings of Kerry and Kildare. Certain it is that both counties gave football a fillip that marked, as it were, the starting point of the game as we know it today. To Kilkenny also must go a share of the credit for their battles with Kildare had already helped to do in Leinster what Kerry and Kildare later did for all Ireland.[23]

KERRY VERSUS LONDON (ALL-IRELAND, 1903)
(Air: 'God Save Ireland': chorus after each stanza)

See our conquering heroes come
To the strains of fife and drum,
See the cheering crowds, who greet them at the train
Bearing proudly back the shield
From the foemen's hard-fought field,
Thundering forth old Kerry's grand refrain.

Chorus
Hurrah, Up Kerry, Sing we proudly!
Hurrah, Up Kerry, Might and main!
Three times for green and gold,
For our boys both brave and bold –
Hi Hurrah! Up Kerry once again!

Foemen, worthy of your steel,
Once again you're made to feel
Kerry's prowess, Kerry's nerve and Kerry's brain!
Irish teams from Louth to Cork,
All your states, e'en proud New York,
Strike your colours to the Kingdom's grand refrain.

Never shall our grand old game
Lose in prestige or in fame
While the gallant sons of Kerry shall remain –
Theirs to keep the old flag flying,
All imported games decrying,
Cheered along by Kerry's proud refrain.

TQ[24] (Source: *Kerry GAA Year Book*, 1980)

All-Ireland Title Defence, 1904

The All-Ireland champions easily accounted for their Cork neighbours in the 1904 Munster senior semi-final in the Market's Field, Limerick, on 29 October 1905. The score was 1-4 to nil. This was the year Thomas F. O'Sullivan, Kerry's Munster Council delegate, was elected Provincial Chairman. It was decided to erect a monument to the late Dr Croke, Archbishop of Cashel and Emly and GAA patron, who had died three years earlier. It was significant that the Association opted to rent permanent office accommodation on Sackville Street (O'Connell Street) Dublin, thus centralising GAA business and shifting the hub of control from Munster to the metropolis.

Waterford proved a more difficult opposition in the Munster Football Final. The game was played in Cork's Athletic Grounds on Sunday 10 December 1905. 'Waterford were well worth their narrow interval lead, and when they went ahead by 0-3 to 0-1 early in the second half Kerry appeared to be in very serious trouble. A tremendous battle was waged for the remainder of the game and Kerry salvaged a draw through points by Dick Fitzgerald and Billy Lynch.'[1] Cork declined Kerry's offer to play extra time to decide the tie. The day after Nollaig na mBan (7 January) Kerry travelled to defend their Munster crown on a wet Dungarvan pitch. Kerry ran out easy replay winners 2-3 to

0-2. 'Feature of Kerry's play was their great combination. Myers and Lynch excelled and Dick Fitzgerald availed of nearly every opportunity presented. On the beaten Waterford team was a brother of Roddy Kirwan.'[2]

The Kerry County Chairman was Eugene O'Sullivan of Firies, former senior county captain who had led Dr Crokes to their 1901 county title. He sought and received the complete backing of the Kerry panel in his attempt to win the Westminster parliamentary seat. 'A short time before polling day, the Kerry footballers travelled to Dungarvan to replay Waterford in the 1904 Munster final. Before the match a meeting of the Kerry team adopted a resolution of best wishes to Eugene O'Sullivan for his success in the forthcoming contest for the representation of East Kerry.' 'The resolution', says the report, 'was signed by all the members. Kerry won the match but John Murphy MP won the election.'[3]

Eugene O'Sullivan did, however, become MP for a brief period in 1907 after a colourful and acrimonious election campaign. He and his arch-rival John Murphy organised rallies in support of their candidacy, which included the extensive use of marching bands and popular rhymes. The Murphyites chanted:

Up Murphy: Up Murphy
Get out of the way!

The O'Sullivanites used a more local chant:

Up Eugene:
Up Eugene:
Up Eugene from Firies

and

> *The band played in*
> *The band played out*
> *The band played in from Firies!*

O'Sullivan carried the day but lost his seat when a court upheld objections on the grounds of intimidation and personation. The decision of the presiding judges, who praised both Murphy and the unseated O'Sullivan, gave rise to a by-election. The MP of three days was replaced in Westminster by his own cousin Michael Tim O'Sullivan. Eugene would prove a key administrator and local politician and played a leadership role in the realisation of Fitzgerald Stadium, Killarney in 1936. He died in 1942. His brother John Marcus O'Sullivan became the first Minister for Education in the Irish Free State.

Before playing the penultimate games in the 1904 championship Kerry contested the Croke Cup, which had been initiated that year as a memorial to the late Archbishop Thomas Croke. They drew the final with the Mayo Stephenites at Tuam and lost the replay in the Market's Field, Limerick, on 4 March 1905, by 1-2 to 0-4. Dick Fitz represented his county on that Munster-based selection and went on to captain the victorious Croke Cup side of 1906.

Kildare was surprisingly defeated in the 1904 Leinster Championship. Dublin defeated a good Kilkenny side to win the provincial title. Upon defeating the Connacht champions, Dublin qualified to meet Kerry, who had defeated Ulster champions Cavan 4-10 to 0-4 in the semi-final played at Jones's Road, Dublin, on 6 May 1906.

The All-Ireland was once again played in Cork's Athletic

Grounds, on Sunday 1 July 1906. Dublin got off to a lively start but Kerry led 0-4 to 0-2 at half time. 'At the start of the second half, Dublin, with the aid of the breeze went all out to pull back their arrears and a mighty battle ensued. Kerry never looked like losing control, however, with Kirwan and Cahill towers of strength in the centre, and it was left to Dick Fitzgerald to get the only score of the second half – a well-taken point. This left Kerry winners by 0-5 to 0-2.'[4] 'It was a dour game, Kerry's masterly high fielding and perfect positioning close to goal outshone a polished Dublin side. The Dublin line-out included Paddy Casey of Lispole, Richard Fitzgerald played a particularly brilliant game for Kerry.'[5]

The Kerry seventeen responsible for that 1904 triumph were: A. Stack (Capt.), Mce. McCarthy, D. Curran, J. O'Gorman, J.T. Fitzgerald, J. Buckley, C. Healy, P.J. Cahill, J. O'Sullivan (Tralee); D. Fitzgerald, P. Dillon (goal), J. Myers, D. McCarthy, F. O'Sullivan, T. O'Sullivan, C. Murphy (Killarney); R. Kirwan (Castleisland). The Dublin team, which included P. Casey, of Lispole, was: P. McCann, M. Kelly, P. Daly (Geraldines); J. Brennan (Keatings); J. Dempsey, D. Brady (Emmetts); J. Lynch, Capt., J. Grace, M. Keane, P. O'Callaghan, T. Murphy, M. Barry, J. Chadwick, L. Sheehan, T. Walsh, P. Casey, J. Fahy (Kickhams).[6]

THE ROSE OF CIARRAÍ
(Air: The Rose of Tralee)

The men from the Kingdom have always been famous.
In Dublin, or Galway, or Cork by the Lee;
But the best one to cherish, or sing of their praises,
Our own darling colleen, the Rose of Ciarraí.

She may come from Killarney or famed Parknasilla,
Iveragh nó Daingean nó Cathair Saibhín;
Bí sí Máire, nó Caitlin, nó Eibhlín nó Síle,
She's proud of the heart of the Rose of Ciarraí.

She will tell you of deeds done on fields far and yonder
And of trophies won for her far over the sea;
How O'Keeffe and Murt Kelly, Tadhgie Lyne and the
*   Landers,*
Brought pride to the heart of the Rose of Ciarraí.

She will also relate to a team that was mighty
Joe Barrett and Sheehy, Mac Gearailt from Sneem,
Joe Sullivan and Brosnan, Paul Russell and Whitty
We'll never have better says the Rose of Ciarraí.

Then with tears in her eyes she will praise Dick Fitzgerald
The darling-est footballer ever was seen,
Austin Stack and Tom Ashe, brave martyrs for Ireland,
Their memories shall live says the Rose of Ciarraí.[7]

Trans-Atlantic Trio and Kildare's Final 1906

The 1905 Senior Munster season was prolonged over a three-year span. Kerry met and defeated Tipperary in the neutral Cork Athletic Grounds on 27 August 1905 on the score 5-8 to 1-4. The semi-final against Cork was hosted at the same venue on 21 January 1906 and Kerry won by double scores, 1-7 to 0-5. The Athletic Grounds were proving to be happy hunting grounds for the visiting Kingdom sides!

There was a lengthy wait for the Munster Senior Final, which was held in Tralee. Kerry defeated Limerick 2-10 to 1-6 on 8 April 1907. During 1906, three prominent GAA personalities died. Patron of the Association Michael Davitt died on 1 June 1906. In November GAA founder Michael Cusack from Clare died, as did J. K. Bracken, who had attended the inaugural foundation meeting in Hayes's Hotel in Thurles on 1 November 1884.

For three Dr Crokes players the winter months of 1906 brought an unexpected and exciting international link. 'Small' Jer O'Leary related the surprise arrival of a transatlantic cable in early August 1906. It literally came out of the blue and read 'To Jerry O'Leary, GAA, Killarney send Dick Fitzgerald, Paddy Dillon and another player.' Signed: Denis Buckley.[1] The bemused 'Small' Jer turned the corner from his Main Street home, travelled up Henn Street to inform Dick Fitzgerald and then down Brewery Lane to the Dillon Lace Industry household. The decision was made to invite Dan McCarthy of Rathcomane, Ballyhar, to make up the travelling trio. Former Kerry and Dr Crokes player, Florry O'Sullivan, who had recently emigrated to the US, is credited with advancing this pioneering invitation.

We are fortunate that records survive in Con Counihan's travel agency in High Street Killarney to tell the tale of a positive response. When the passage money arrived for the three players to go to the USA, the news spread like wildfire through the Killarney district. Tickets were booked through Con Counihan. The record states that 'Richard Fitzgerald (age 23), Donie McCarthy (age 24) and Patrick Dillon (age 24) sailed to New York on the S.S. *Lucania* of the Cunard Line from Queenstown on 14 October 1906.'[2]

From start to finish this telegram and the subsequent football tour spawned a host of folktales and stories long remembered in Killarney. At Cobh the trio encountered a hapless fellow-townsman, a blacksmith named Ryan who was, for the third time, to be denied permission to board the steamer on health grounds. Astute Dick Fitzgerald made a famous switch which worked a miracle. The story was told by Con Clifford: "At embarkation the officer in charge called out the three players' names to embark. Dickeen pushed the man forward as one of the three players, having previously switched some papers and the plan worked without detection.'[3] Ellis Island was the next port of call where Barthold's 300-foot bronze Statue of Liberty welcomed the Killarney athletes and their ailing neighbour who planned a longer stay.

The log of the *Lucania* on file in the Ellis Island archive tells the story of the arrival of the All-Ireland stars. The trio are listed as 'labourers' with '$30' in their wallets. The worried Ryan, who declared his own $25, planned to lodge with his New York-based brother Daniel. As both Fitzgerald and Dillon stood 5'11" tall they could not fool the immigration officers' scrutiny and pass for a 5'6" blacksmith. Dan McCarthy was only two inches taller and showed no signs of the unacceptable conjunctivitis, the eye ailment listed against the official Ryan entry. The substitution worked a dream and Dan McCarthy, impersonating the worried Ryan, passed all tests with flying colours. The four Killarney bachelors answered 'No' to questions put to them on the subject of anarchy, polygamy and imprisonment. The corresponding entry for Dick Fitzgerald's 1927 return visit would report his five jail terms during 1916.)

Host Denis Buckley and his fellow Kerry GAA exiles arranged a huge reception to welcome the footballers at the port of entry. The 1906 touring party were fêted both home and away. Their Christmas Eve welcome back to Ireland has happily been recorded. A group from Killarney travelled to Queenstown to receive the all-conquering homecomers. The car broke down at the county bounds. While it was being repaired two of the party, who were members of the Killarney Pipe Band, took out their pipes and to keep warm began a parade drill for passengers and footballers. Unknown to them a wake was taking place for an old piper in his home cottage down in the valley. Con Clifford takes up the story:

> The house was full and the drink was flowing. Eventually the sound of the pipes filtered through the cold night air to the cottage and when the mourners heard the shrill eerie music there was panic. Some of them scattered. Some fell on their knees and prayed like they never prayed before, and of course most of

the men just kept on drinking, celebrating the passing of a great piper. One of them commented, 'that the great man hadn't ever lost his touch.'[4]

The travelling party made their way west to a huge 'Christmas in Killarney' homecoming. The footballers were paraded through the town behind the Killarney Pipe Band to a College Square inn where ale and tales flowed. Goalkeeper Paddy Dillon, who came from a family involved in the tourist trade and was himself a jarvey, was asked how he liked New York and New Yorkers. He shared a tale about disenchantment and an unfulfilled ambition. Apparently he had hoped to visit Long Island and 'all his requests for directions were ignored by rushing New Yorkers. He gave up the ghost and said to Dickeen, "All my life I have been showing Yanks the way to Muckross and Ross Castle but never again!"'[5]

As the 1905 championship continued we note Roscommon emerging as Western champions, having defeated Mayo in Tuam by 0-7 to 0-5. The semi-final was hosted at the Market's Field, Limerick, where after a tough first half Kerry led Roscommon 2-4 to 1-3. Kerry added six points in the second half and held Roscommon scoreless, qualifying to meet the Lily-Whites, who had easily accounted for Cavan in the other semi-final by 4-15 to 1-6.

'There were protracted negotiations before Thurles was decided as the venue,'[6] on Sunday 16 June 1907. The running battle about the venue waged from late spring into June. Meanwhile the debate continued in the letters to the editor's column in local and national newspapers. However the long delay did not favour Kerry, whose County Board ceased to exist. Two All-Ireland medallists, Dan McCarthy and Johnny Buckley, had emigrated to USA. A Roseberry/Sarsfields selection represented contenders Kildare. Back-to-back champions Kerry were represented by a Tralee John Mitchels line-out. (Until about 1914 the club that won the County Championship went on to represent their county in the All-Ireland series. They had the right to co-opt players from other clubs if they wished. For instance Ballyduff represented Kerry in 1891, Laune Rangers were defeated finalists in 1892 and John Mitchels lined out for Kerry in 1903 as well as 1906.) The complacent Kingdom side decided that there was no need for special training.

Seventeen special trains converged on Thurles on 16 June. An estimated 18,000 filled the terraces in expectation of a classic encounter. Many broke in to gain free entry. Kerry won the toss and, surprisingly, took the decision to play against the wind. This proved fatal as Kildare took the game to the champions, leading 0-6 to 0-1 at half-time despite Kerry's midfield dominance. In the second half the expected wind advantage brought no favours to the defending champions. Disaster struck early when a fisted ball into the Kerry penalty area was deflected by a Kerry player and pounced upon by Jack Connolly of Clane for the final's only goal. Kildare now led 1-7 to 0-1. Kerry rallied to add four points to their total but it was not enough and Kildare became All-Ireland Senior Champions for the first time on the score 1-7 to 0-5.

The recriminations that followed are recorded in the local papers. Blame is laid on the 'woefully deteriorated' Kerry display as against Kildare's 'decided improvement'. The *Kerryman* writer declared: 'We cannot but deplore the carelessness, which lost our team the match. No attempt was made to improve the form of the players by united training.'[7] Correspondence was published in the same newspaper faulting the performance of acclaimed referee M.F. Crowe. This powerful rebuttal came from Austin Stack, who had captained the successful 1904 side:

I am sure I am voicing the opinions of the whole of the Kerry team when I say the referee's decisions at Thurles were, as they have always been, absolutely impartial. I shall not endeavour to make excuses for the team's defeat, for they were beaten fairly and squarely on the day's play.

In the absence of a Kerry County Board Stack adopted an honourable stance in the public domain. He went on to decry the performance of 75 per cent of his colleagues but affirmed: 'Kerry can still beat Kildare.'[8] 'Few people in Kerry begrudged Kildare their victory.'[9] The Lily-White-Kingdom saga had helped the GAA blossom and bloom in the popular mind nationally.

The Association, which was growing in confidence, launched its first *Gaelic Athletic Annual* edited by Frank B. Dineen during 1907. The *Annual* reflects a confident organisation advancing

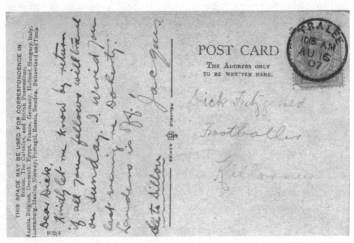

Postcard sent to Dick Fitzgerald by Jacques McDonnell, Secretary of the non-existent Kerry County Board, in 1907. The postcard carried a view of Blennerville Bridge, Tralee.

the 1884 ideals of Cusack, Croke and like-minded supporters of native games.[10] Consolation for Kerry came with the 1906 Croke Memorial Final victory against Mayo in Ennis on 17 November 1907. Dick Fitz captained this side, representing Munster.

The departure of the influential County Secretary, Thomas F. Sullivan, to Dublin proved a major loss to the GAA in Kerry. He was chairman of the Munster Council of the GAA in 1907. Kerry County Board did not exist from Autumn 1906 until it was reformed in September 1907 and the County Championship in both hurling and football had fallen into disarray. A 1906 decision ruled that the hurling competition would be played on a league rather than knock-out basis, meriting Kilmoyley another county senior title. A second directive insisted on the parish rule. This decision was to serve the Association well but led to many fearsome debates and legal wrangling. After the Kerry County Board was reconstituted Killarney's Eugene O'Sullivan retained the presidency, which in those early days included chairmanship power and obligations. He was opposed and deposed by Austin Stack in the 1908 leadership tussle.

THE KERRY DANCES

Oh the days of the Kerry dancing
Oh the ring of the piper's tune
Oh for one of those hours of gladness
Gone alas! Like our youth, too soon
When the boys began to gather in the glen, of a summer night
And the Kerry piper's tuning made us long with wild
delight.

Chorus
Oh to think of it, oh to dream of it,
Fills my heart with tears
Oh the days of the Kerry dancing,
Oh the ring of the Piper's tune
Oh for one of those hours of gladness
Gone alas! Like our youth, too soon.

Was there ever a sweeter colleen
In the dance than Eily Moore
Or a prouder lad than Thady
As he boldly took the floor
'Lads and lasses to your places
Up the middle and down again'
Ah the merry hearted laughter
Ringing through the happy glen.
Chorus
Time goes on and the happy years are dead
And one by one the merry hearts have fled
Silent now is the wild and lonely glen
Where the bright glad laugh will echo ne'er again
Only dreaming of days gone by fills my heart with tears
Loving voices of old companions
Stealing out of the past once more
And the sound of the dear old music
Soft and sweet as in days of yore
When the boys began to gather in the glen, of a summer night
And the Kerry piper's tuning made us long with wild
    delight.
Chorus[11]

Morale of Club and County, 1907–1908

The confusion reigning in Kerry GAA during the latter half of the first decade of the twentieth century crept into club life as well. But P.J. Devlin wrote in *The Irish Year Book 1908* that the 'years of serious disorganisation, endless disputes, illegalities and friction' were passing.[1] He might well have been referring to the curious ongoing 'see-saw' tensions between the Dingle Gascons and Killarney's Dr Crokes!

Dingle defeated a depleted Killarney side by 1-9 to 0-2 in a friendly on Sunday 25 August 1907. Meanwhile, Eugene O'Sullivan, who retained the County Board presidency and was delegate to GAA Central Council, observed that, apart from the two major towns, Kerry football was on the wane. The fact that the recently depleted county panel was largely based on Tralee and Killarney clubmen did not help to foster the game across the Kingdom. As the Dr Crokes club examined its low morale, Kerry goalkeeper Pat Dillon spoke at a club meeting on 10 March about a new determination to reorganise their players and bring back some glory for their club. Their subsequent championship run brought them to the county semi-final stages after a curious series of encounters with Dingle Gascons.

The opening round of the 1907 County Championship began for these two teams on the Church holiday of 8 December

1907. The slick and speedy Lakesiders met a stubborn western defence in an exciting encounter that ended in a draw. Followers eagerly anticipated the replay, fixed for Sunday 26 January 1908 by the County Board. Dingle refused to play and Dr Crokes were awarded the match but the Killarney club declined to claim the game, which was then rescheduled for Sunday 9 February 1908, in Tralee. A huge crowd attended the match, which was played in ideal conditions. The game ended in a draw 0-6 to 0-6. The replay was again arranged for Tralee on Sunday 9 March. The packed Killarney special Great Southern train arrived and a large crowd entered the Sportsfield on a day of heavy rains. Dr Crokes togged out but their Dingle rivals failed to show. The referee awarded the game to the Crokes, who then challenged a local Tralee side to entertain the rain-soaked spectators.

Dingle objected to the referee's decision, claiming that some of their panel were unwell on Sunday. The County Board officers backed the referee's report and awarded the game to 'the Clear Air Boys'. Dick Fitzgerald addressed this County Board meeting in a personal capacity. He undertook to bring the whole matter to his club and report back. At the Dr Crokes EGM it was solemnly decided not to claim the game. A third replay was arranged for the same venue on Sunday 24 May 1908. In the meantime Crokes had lost some key players to the emigrant ship, and another, James Sheehan had died. Dick Fitzgerald paid tribute to Sheehan as one of the club's 'foremost players'.[2]

On 24 May special trains from the west and the east steamed into Tralee's railway station. A depleted Killarney team was forced to line out with some new younger players given the recent loss of James Sheehan and the ankle injury suffered in training by Dick Fitz. After a tough struggle Dr Crokes won the game and Dingle objected once again. This time they claimed that two team members – Cahill and Fitzmaurice, students from St Brendan's Seminary, Killarney – were illegal. The County Board would have none of it and Crokes qualified to meet another team from the same Dingle parish in the semi-final. Lispole went on to win this match, played in Listowel on Sunday 18 July 1908, on a score of 0-7 to 0-4. Crokes stated that being unable to field several of their best players proved their downfall. Pat Dillon was not between the posts; nor did Dick Fitzgerald line out against Lispole.

The *Kerryman*, under a 'Bravo Lispole' headline, reported on 'a fine game…roughness and fouls were numerous on both sides. The teams should study their rule books a little more and learn that any attempt to hold, catch, kick, trip or jump is contrary to the laws of Gaelic football.'[3] The 1907 County Final fixed for Listowel on a rainy Sunday 23 August 1908 did not materialise as only half the Lispole team travelled. Tralee Mitchels agreed to a replay which they easily won on Sunday 13 September, by 0-11 to 0-1 'Remarkably, it was the first time that they had won a final on the field of play.'[4]

Face the Ball shows a head-and-shoulders photograph of a cap-wearing 'Thomas Ashe, trainer/player Lispole, 1907.' This Black Raven piper and schoolteacher was to meet Pope Leo XIII and successfully lead the Ashbourne Volunteers during Easter Week 1916. He died in Mountjoy Jail on 25 September 1917 after forced feeding during his hunger strike. Michael Collins addressed the estimated 30,000 people who attended his funeral in Glasnevin, Dublin.

A Kerry selection represented Munster in a special Railway Shield and won the trophy outright with victories two years in a row. Munster-Kerry versus Connacht-Roscommon played in Tipperary on 17 February 1906 and Munster-Kerry won by 2-10 to 0-2. Munster-Kerry versus Leinster-selected played at Jones's Road, Dublin, on 22 September 1907 and Munster-Kerry won 1-7 to 1-6. The Munster Croke Cup team captained by Dick Fitzgerald defeated Connacht (Mayo) in Ennis, winning the 1906 title by 2-6 to 2-3 on 17 November 1907.

Kerry's 1906 Munster campaign ended in a provincial final defeat. They accounted for Clare on Sunday 12 May by 2-8 to 0-1 and for Tipperary on 20 May by 0-7 to 0-6. Both early games were played in the Market's Field, Limerick. Cork was victorious in the Munster final in Tipperary on Sunday 10 August 1907 by a large margin of 1-10 to 0-3. Kerry's 1907 provincial run resulted in an easy victory over Clare on 15 March 1908 in the Market's Field, Limerick. The semi-final at the same venue ended in a double-score defeat at the hands of Cork on 29 March 1908, 1-9 to 0-6.

There are many instances of fundraising competitions in the early annals of the GAA. Some of these were for the Association's own needs but many had a strong community dimension, for example to fund schools, libraries, historical monuments and parish projects. During 1908 two games were organised to help fund the spire of St Mary's Cathedral, Killarney. The local Cricket Field on the banks of the Flesk hosted the Cork versus Kilkenny hurling challenge and the Kerry versus Cork football game. That autumn Johnny Hayes of Nenagh, who had just won the most famous Olympic Marathon of recent history in London, sporting the USA colours, ran an exhibition race in Lord Kenmare's Half-Moon Demesne Field for the same cause. Fundraising for an appropriate monument to the memory of Archbishop Croke involved Kerry's active participation in the Croke Memorial competition. Kerry were easily defeated by Ballina Stephenites, representing Mayo, in the 1907 Croke

Memorial Final played in Jones's Road on Sunday 22 November 1908. The score was 1-8 to 0-5, a result that reversed the previous year's final outcome.

Dick Fitzgerald was clearly emerging as a player and administrator whose status in the Dr Crokes club was highly rated and respected. In late December, 1908, on the occasion of the death of the young Denny Kissane – another playing colleague and All-Ireland winning hero – Dickeen said: 'For the club to lose two of its most prominent players in one year was indeed a tremendous [loss] but a far bigger loss to their respective families.'[5] Fitzgerald, the double-All-Ireland winner who was active on the playing fields for county and club, assumed club secretarial duties for 1908.

Dick Fitzgerald was none too pleased to see the his friend and former team-mate Eugene O'Sullivan ousted from leadership of the County Board. Tralee's Austin Stack assumed the chairmanship role following a successful campaign to outvote O'Sullivan. Dick Fitzgerald suggested that there had been 'a preconceived plan to remove Mr O'Sullivan from the chair'.[6] The ensuing suspicion and disaffection had a negative effect on the Killarney club's participation in the championship. 'Killarney Crokes were at loggerheads with the County Board over the chairmanship and refused to enter a team this year.'[7] Kerry were determined to assert their football prowess and proved their ability by winning the 1908 All-Ireland Semi-Final.

At county, provincial and national levels, the Association continued to evolve. Congress would in future meet in Dublin and not in a Munster venue and from now on chartered accountants would audit the GAA's accounts. The Munster Council was at last in a favourable financial position with assets at £53/19s/10d. In recognition of the fact that Kerry had won the Railway Shield for two years in a row the Provincial Council voted to allow Kerry to retain the trophy in perpetuity as reward.

Kerry's first round of the 1908 Senior championship opened in Listowel on Sunday 26 July 1908, when they defeated Clare 0-11 to 0-3. Back-to-back champions Cork were defeated by Waterford, whom Kerry easily accounted for in Cork's Athletic Grounds on 6 December 1908, 0-7 to 0-2. The All-Ireland Semi-Final was rescheduled for 14 February 1909 in Limerick, against respected Connacht champions Ballina Stephenites representing Mayo. 'The Stephenites took to the field in neat white jerseys and also sported blue caps. It was a sensational first half. Backs beat forwards throughout, and the only score was a solitary Kerry point. The Kerryman were in their element in the concluding stages, during which Mayo completely collapsed, Kerry winning by 2 goals 4 points to 1 point.'[8] Two Killarney forwards scored the goals – Dick Fitzgerald at the start of the second half and Con 'of the Hundred Battles' Murphy later on. Kerry were in their fifth All-Ireland Senior football final, to be played in Thurles against Dublin.

The record shows that in two previous All-Ireland encounters, each team had one victory – Dublin in 1892 and Kerry in 1904. By this time Dublin had amassed ten All Ireland titles to Kerry's two. On 9 May 1909, some 10,000 supporters made their way to Thurles for the final. The game went well for the first forty-five minutes. Dublin led by 0-3 to 0-2 at half time after a close game. Con Murphy scored Kerry's only second half-point but could not match the Metropolitans' 0-10. Dublin progressed from their decisive home final win to an easy final proper victory over London by 1-10 to 0-4 on Sunday 1 August 1909.

'The result was regarded with considerable disgust in Kerry. The team was strongly criticised in the local press...The 1908 defeat, coupled with criticism which followed acted as a tonic to the players. *Beidh lá eile ag an bPaorach* was their firm resolve when the new season opened.'[9] Dublin had by now won their second three-in-a-row set of All-Ireland crowns. At last, after years of frustrating rows and objections – for instance the 1903 football championship was played over the period 1903–5 – the chronological order was about to be restored as the 1909 championship began and concluded during its own calendar year.

'THE IRREPRESSIBLE DICK'
1909 CHAMPIONS AND OBJECTIONS GALORE

The year 1909, which saw the unexpected death of J. P. O'Sullivan, was to be a good year for the Kingdom. On 1 August 1909, Kerry travelled to Limerick's Market's Field to oppose the host county in the first round of the Munster series. The first half was a closely-contested affair with the visitors leading 1-3 to 1-2 facing into the second period. Kerry ran out easy winners on a score of 2-18 to 1-2 and qualified to meet Cork in the Munster Final in Limerick on Sunday 19 September 1909.

This match led to controversy both on and off the Market's Field. There was huge Kerry dissatisfaction with the referee, whose forte was hurling!

> Players caught and obstructed each other to their hearts' content. Kerry were leading at the interval (1-6 to 1-3). The second half became rough, the referee allowing every latitude. A Corkman lifted the ball from the ground and kicked between the posts. The referee allowed the score. Kerry protested and walked off the field. They were persuaded to return... under protest.[1]

As the men from Macroom, the County Champions representing Cork, won 2-8 to 1-7, Kerry objected to Jerry Beckett, the Kilgarvan native – who had lined out illegally for Kilgarvan during a holiday visit – being on the Cork team. He was deemed illegal by the Munster Council, who then awarded the provincial title to Kerry. Dick Fitzgerald and Jacques McDonnell, who were the Kerry delegates at the hearing of the Munster Council on 17 October, requested a replay instead of a 'paper' title. Cork consented.

A huge crowd attended the re-match in Cork's Athletic Grounds on 7 November 1909. 'They were treated to a splendid exhibition of football, fought at a dazzling place. A Kerryman, Jerry Beckett, played with Cork. To show there were no hard feelings, a Corkman, Johnny Skinner, played with Kerry. A former rugby player, Skinner had secured employment at the Killarney Mental Hospital and under the capable tuition of Dick Fitzgerald, developed into one of the greatest Gaelic forwards of the day. After half an hour's play Cork were leading by three points to one. After half-time they went further ahead. The sides exchanged points and with ten minutes left the home side was still two points to the good. Then came a whirlwind Kingdom finish. A masterly move between Dick Fitzgerald and his protégé, Skinner, produced a goal. It was all Kerry thereafter', the match ending 1-6 to 0-6.[2] Cork's objection was overruled by the Munster Council on a vote of 5-3. The gate of £116 was donated to the bereaved family of the late Bob Duane, a former Tipperary footballer who had died in October.

Kerry faced Mayo's Ballina Stephenites once again in the semi-final game arranged for Ennis, County Clare, on Sunday 21 November 1909. Michael F. Crowe was in charge of a game where Kerry led by 2-5 to 0-4 at half time and 2-12 to 0-6 at the final whistle.

Louth reached their first ever All-Ireland Final by defeating Kilkenny in Leinster and then Ulster champions, Antrim. 15,000 gathered in wintry conditions at Jones's Road, Dublin on Sunday 5 December 1909. The gate realised £307/3s/6d although many impatient supporters forced their entrance into the grounds. An intriguing clash of styles emerged as Louth excelled using ground football.

> Louth attacked at once along the ground. Cleverly placed passes, burning the sod, kept the Kerry defenders pinned to their post…A lengthy ball from O'Connor at midfield was clutched securely by Fitzgerald. Two Louth backs pounced on him, but the irrepressible Dick swerved clear and short passed to Skinner whose shot shook the net. Half time Kerry 1-3 to Louth 0-3.[3] In a second half played at frenetic pace the Kingdom contained and defeated the Wee County 1-9 to 0-6. Mitchelstown native John Skinner scored 1-7 of Kerry's total.

However, further objections were raised at Central Council level.

The six grounds were:

1. That M.J. Quinlan played foreign games
2. That F.J. Cronin played in the Dublin football league
3. That J. Casey played under the assumed name of Healy after transfer from Valentia Football club

4. That Mullane played against Ballybunion, an unaffiliated club
5. That J. Kennelly committed a similar breach
6. That J. McCarthy took part in an 'illegal match'

The Central Council meeting on 2 January 1910 heard the objection. Austin Stack and A.J. Smith of Valentia represented Kerry. Three of the points in the objection were answered successfully and Louth then withdrew the other three. So, in an eventful year, Kerry finished as All-Ireland champions, and the men who made it possible were: T. Costello (Capt.), M. McCarthy, F.J. Cronin, C. Healy, J. O'Sullivan, M.J. Quinlan (Tralee), T. Rice (Abbeydorney), D. Breen (Castleisland), R. Fitzgerald, P. Dillon (goal), C. Murphy, E. Spillane, J. Skinner (Killarney); J. Mullane, J. Kennelly (Listowel); B. O'Connor (Dingle); J. McCarthy (Valentia).[4]

The GAA's silver jubilee year proved a very successful one as championships in both major codes were at last up to date and completed before year's end. The Association's financial situation was finally placed on a more secure foundation as it entered the second decade of the twentieth century.

Leather Medals
for Paper Champions Louth, 1910

The All-Ireland champions began their title defence in Cork's Athletic Grounds on Sunday 12 June when they accounted for Waterford 2-13 to 0-1. The semi-final against Clare took place at Limerick's Market's Field on 2 October 1910. This was a very one-sided affair, ending 3-1 to 0-0.

A strong Macroom selection represented the Rebel County as Munster Final contenders on Sunday 30 October by the banks of the Lee. It was a vigorous low-scoring battle. The half-time score read one point each and the Kingdom retained its provincial crown 0-4 to 0-2. A *Kerryman* critic reported: 'The match was contested with terrific determination. Cork were made up of a splendid lot of vigorous athletic men and excellent fielders. But contrasted with Kerry's science their style showed them to be merely a hardworking, strong, bustling lot of players'.[1] A huge crowd attended a bravely contested final, which helped to build up the long tradition of footballing rivalry between the two neighbours.

It was a long train journey to Tuam in County Galway for another semi-final encounter with Mayo on Sunday 21 August 1910. Kerry won this tilt against the Westerners 1-7 to 0-4 to qualify for a repeat final showdown with Louth. But the subsequent debate, withdrawal and awarding of the All-Ireland crown to the Wee County led to much bitterness and recrimination.

Central Council scheduled the 1910 All-Ireland Final for Sunday 13 November 1910 at Jones's Road, Dublin. It was to be a unfortunate thirteenth because of railway stock and a Kerry point of principle. While the growth of the GAA is linked to an impressive national railway infrastructure it must be noted that the Great Southern Railway Company of the time or 'The Great Sourface Railway', as the Dublin *Leader* used to call it – was regarded in Gaelic circles as hostile to national games. 'County Boards…were severely handicapped when arranging matches… by the lack of co-operation on the part of the railway authorities. Excessive fares were often charged and proper travelling facilities were not provided.'[2] Apparently no concessions were afforded to players who were consigned to slower trains departing Tralee Station where:

> Players, in twos or threes, were mixed up with the ordinary passengers. Confusion was increased at Killarney where Saturday was market day and country shoppers boarded the train with baskets, bags and parcels.
>
> These conditions were not pleasant for players facing a lengthy journey with an All-Ireland on the morrow…On 10 November 1910 Mr N.M. Stack, Honorary Secretary, Kerry County Board, asked for concessions and tickets at excursion rates be allowed for ten officials, who would travel with the team.

The speedy but discouraging reply from Mr S. Cooper Chadwick read: 'There will be sufficient room in the 3.20 pm train for the Kerry team to Dublin on Saturday next, and it will not be necessary to provide a through coach…I regret that cheap tickets cannot be issued generally…The company have arranged a special fast train at a reasonable fare on Sunday for Kerry people anxious to witness the match'.[3] This reply outraged the County Board, who were 'conversant with the railway company's hostile attitude. They decided not to travel, preferring to sacrifice the All-Ireland rather than submit to the scandalous treatment meted out to them by the railway company.'[4]

A contentious national debate followed Kerry's decision, which was strongly penalised by the resolution of GAA Central Council: 'By seven votes to six Central Council awarded the title to Louth.'[5] The defending champions received widespread support from all the Munster counties, along with Kilkenny, and a host of nationalist groupings including the Ennis branch of the Gaelic League. On 4 December the Dublin County Board harshly criticised Kerry, who faced a Central Council resolution of expulsion for a five-year period. Belfast moved a motion to ban Kerry for the shorter term of six months. Louth County Board delegate Mr Ward abstained from voting on a decision strongly opposed by Austin Stack. The resolution to reschedule the match was defeated by seven votes to six.

Tralee's John Mitchels GAA club published the following challenge: 'Kerry to play Louth in Dublin, the championship to be at issue; the gate receipts to go to the Dr Croke, Wolfe Tone and Parnell Memorials; if Louth refuse to accept a walk-over as Kerry did in the 1905 final against Kildare, that Kerry forego claim to the All-Ireland medals in the event of winning'.[6] Louth replied that they were 'under no obligation to accept a bombastic challenge from Tralee'.[7] A Kerry County Board challenge was similarly dismissed. Mr Ward made a facetious offer that Kerry might play Louth's second-string team. Kerry agreed with the proviso that the Wee County's first team also play them on the same date. Louth ignored the challenge.

Luke O'Toole of the Central Council stated 'that as the final was not played there were no funds on hand so the Council could not buy All-Ireland medals for Louth. Wherefore Mr P. J. O'C., writer of the GAA notes in the *Kerryman*, sarcastically suggested that the Central Council should buy leather medals and present them to Louth because 'paper champions' richly deserved such trophies!'[8]

Suggestions were made that a Munster GAA body independent of Central Council should be formed and that Kerry withdraw from the Association. This drastic suggestion did not become a reality. It is important to know that Kerry's first All-Ireland victors had to pay their own fares for poor rail service in 1891. Ballyduff's Paddy Carr who played in the Kerry hurlers' 1891 winning side 'told John D. (Hickey) that the team went by train to Dublin and each player had to pay his own expenses, which were then sixteen shillings, a considerable sum at that time. "When we got back to Tralee on Sunday night at 3 am there was no one to meet us. We went up to Tom Slattery's of Rock Street where we killed the time until 11 am and then took the train to Lixnaw. And indeed there was no day off when we got home, we all had to turn into work as if nothing had happened.'"[9] The vanquished football team of the following year arrived into Dublin on the ghost train at 5 am. The twelve-hour journey from Killorglin in an overcrowded box carriage did little for their performance in Clonturk Park against their Dublin hosts.

Kerry's confrontation with the railway authorities in 1910

achieved greatly improved travelling comforts for teams and supporters alike. 'The publicity also generated better travelling facilities for teams on long train journeys, although for Kerry the giving away of a great chance to win another title was a heavy price to pay.'[10]

Despite the loss of revenue that year Luke O'Toole of GAA Central Council adopted a novel approach when promoting the Limerick versus Wexford All-Ireland Hurling Final. Advance publicity invited patrons to enter Jones's Road grounds at the Canal or Clonliffe Road ends for sixpence; it cost twice that fee for the enclosure and stands. Entrance to the balcony cost two shillings and the sideline seating cost half a crown. However, 'the promoters regret that they cannot give free admission to ladies owing to the demand for seats.'[11] As the GAA's age of chivalry waned Wexford became hurling champions for the very first time on Sunday 20 November on a score of 7-0 to 6-2.

An eventful GAA year came to an end following much football controversy. The throw-in rule 'backs back' was introduced for the first time, also the change from the old goal and point posts arrangement (à la Australian rules today) to a set twenty-one feet between posts. Belgium was treated to the novel visit of the Cork and Tipperary hurling teams for exhibition games in Malines, Brussels and famed Fontenoy. This unique September window on hurling, which was not well promoted by the host country, was organised in conjunction with the Pan-Celtic Congress. Tipperary won the series by two games to one.

9

A Glorious Decade for Club and County, 1910-20

The decade of the First World War and the War of Independence was to prove a golden age for Dick Fitzgerald, both at county and club level. During 1911 Dick Fitzgerald served his club as a member of Dr Crokes committee, having relinquished his secretarial post. Their sporting year was undistinguished but marred by contention. As there had been no football County Championship in 1909 the County Board opted to combine the following two years as one. Having easily defeated Valentia (Young Islanders) in the 1910-11 County Senior Quarter-Final by 5-8 to 0-4 on 10 August 1909 Dr Crokes waited two years to play a tempestuous semi-final against traditional rivals Tralee Mitchels.

Tralee was the venue on Sunday 19 March 1911 where: 'Crokes won the toss and elected to play against the wind. There was no score for the first twenty minutes but before half time Tralee had scored 1-2. In the second half the Mitchels' defence held out against a terrible bombardment from the Crokes forwards. Play was give and take until six minutes from full-time when a dispute arose between prominent members of the teams. The Killarney team left the field and Tralee were awarded the match.'[1] A new Congress ruling put paid both to Crokes objection and the club's participation in Gaelic sport for the following six months. 'Crokes were suspended for six months – a new rule had been added, making it a mandatory suspension for any team that walked off the field during the course of a game.'[2]

The fall-out was enormous and was to have repercussions at both club and county levels. 'There was consternation…Imagine the consequences. It meant that not alone were Crokes out of action but it also meant that Dick Fitzgerald, Con Murphy, John Skinner, Denis Doyle, Paddy Breen, Paddy Healy and any other county prospect could not play with Kerry for the next six months. So the objection was thrown out and Dr Crokes were out of action for almost the rest of the year (1911).'[3]

Club delegate Dick Fitzgerald addressed the County Board meeting in May 1911 as the draws were being made for the championship. 'Fitzgerald requested that they delay the draw. The chairman (Austin Stack) said "that it was by their (Crokes) own action that they could not compete and if they had to wait until September when they would be reinstated the championship would run late again." Dickeen used his persuasive powers and it was agreed that whoever came out of the draw to meet Dr Crokes would play the game on any date after 18 September.'[4] A Kerry solution to a Kerry problem!

The good old days of abandoning the playing field had come to an abrupt end. Local humour recalls the great Tom Costello once jokingly taunting the even greater Dick Fitzgerald, his great friend, on the matter:

> 'Whenever ye are getting beaten, you had only to whistle and the Killarney lads followed you like small boys, as you left the field.'

Dick smilingly answered, 'We always had some trick to be equal to ye fellows.'

Dickeen was a past master in the art of repartee.[5]

Because of the six-month suspension meted out to Dr Crokes, Kerry lined out without their Killarney contingent against Limerick in the home side's Market's Field on Sunday 2 July 1911 and won 2-4 to 0-1 to qualify to meet Waterford in the Munster semi-final scheduled for Mallow on Sunday 27 August. Kerry were confident that they would defeat the Decies men and go on to the final and All-Ireland series once the six-month Crokes suspension had passed. They lined out without lately retired Tralee stalwart Maurice McCarthy and Valentia Islander Jack McCarthy who had recently departed for America. 'Kerry had always defeated Waterford and were expected to do so again. But, in the absence of the Killarney men, the Kingdom outfit was like a rudderless ship. Waterford won by 1-2 to 1 goal. These were the half-time scores and there was no scoring in the concluding period. The Killarney walk-off at Tralee the previous March proved very costly for Kerry'.[6] Cork won the 1911 Munster and All-Ireland titles.

The year of the *Titanic* was to be a disaster year for the now complete Kingdom panel. They came through a victorious three-game 1912 Munster campaign. The opening test against All-Ireland champions and neighbours Cork drew a bumper crowd and gate of £191 at Tralee's grounds on Sunday 23 June 1912 when the Rebels lost their crown 2-3 to 0-1. In the Fermoy semi-final Kerry easily accounted for their victorious opponents of the previous year by 1-4 to 0-1 on Sunday 15 September. Clare were both hosts and opponents at Ennis on Sunday 10 October with Cork's famed Willie Mackessy in charge of the whistle. 'In the Munster final, Clare put up a brave show before going under 0-3 to 0-1.'[7]

P.F. penned a humorous account of Kerry's All-Ireland Semi-final visit to the capital on Saturday 24 August, 1912:

> In the All-Ireland semi-final Kerry were drawn against Antrim at Dublin. It will be recalled that the Ulster men were no match for Cork in the previous year's All-Ireland and that Kerry beat Cork comfortably. Therefore, as Mr Euclid would say, Kerry should have no difficulty in beating Antrim! On the Saturday evening before the match the Kerry players arrived in Dublin. A notable son of the 'Kingdom' had got married that morning in the Metropolis. The Kerry team were invited to the wedding. What was more natural than that they should accept. They merely had a 'matter of form' game on the morrow. So the boys went and enjoyed themselves thoroughly.
>
> But the road to football, or any success, is the hard and narrow path. The day following the nuptials the Kerry boys could not play football. Antrim won 3-5 to 2 points perhaps the most sensational GAA result of all time. To add gall to the already bitter Kerry draught, Louth beat Antrim in a the ensuing All-Ireland Final, by 1-7 to 1-2.[8]

10

Three-in-a-Row County Champions 1912–14

After their disastrous suspension two years earlier and subsequent defeat at the hands of Tralee Mitchels, Dick Fitzgerald and his Croke colleagues were firmly resolved to win their second County title. Their first outing was in Rathmore against defending champions Laune Rangers on Sunday 4 August, 1912. The Killorglin team was 'eliminated in the first round by Killarney Crokes.'[1] The team which left Killorglin station that morning at 11 am arrived full of eager supporters via Farranfore, Ballybrack, Killarney and Headford to an en-fête Rathmore.

Crokes, who won the 3 pm toss, elected to play with wind and hill and were down 0-1 to nil by half-time. 'Dick Fitzgerald was the dominant figure in the second half getting all his side's scores, 2 goals and 2 points.'[2] Dickeen, who was busily training for the Munster Senior Championship early rounds, found time to referee two second-round football matches in Killarney on Sunday 1 September – Cahirciveen 1-1 to Listowel's 0-2 and Rathmore 1-1 to Valentia's nil. The fact that the referee had a vested interest in the 1912 championship competition did not seem to bother any of the teams or their supporters.

Crokes second-round engagement was against Ballydonoghue in Listowel on Sunday 20 October. The *Kerryman* reported: 'The contest was both exciting and interesting from start to finish.

But of course it was a foregone conclusion that the Crokes, having such men as Dick Fitzgerald, Con Murphy and John Skinner, should come out on top. However, the Ballydonoghue boys played well in spite of the power of their opponents'[3,], who won 2-3 to 0-1. The semi-final was set for Castleisland on Sunday 15 December, when Crokes faced Sliabh Luachra neighbours Rathmore from the foot of the Paps. Seán Stiofán Ó Súilleabháin in his *Aililiú Rathmore* gives a brief account of this encounter: 'We were defeated by a six-goal margin 7-2 to 1-2.'[4]

A new Tralee team called Parnells emerged as county finalists to meet Dr Crokes in Listowel on Sunday 22 December. Two brief press accounts sum up a poor Tralee display against the Lakesiders. The *Kerryman*'s Christmas edition boosted the Tralee challengers: 'Very rarely did the ball enter Killarney's territory and when it did the visits were extremely brief. In short it was a one-sided game with the winners playing superb football and the losers working heroically to make their defeat as light as possible.'[5] The Monday edition of the *Kerry Evening Star* stated: 'There was a good attendance of spectators. Play was rather one-sided, the Killarney men having the best of matters all through the game and the final score came as a big surprise to the Parnell followers. Half-time 1-2 to nil – Full-time Killarney Crokes 1-6 to Parnells' nil'.[6] Killarney were elated as they returned home with their second county title.

The County Board Convention was outraged at the lack of reportage. Of the thirty matches organised and played, 'scarcely one third of them had been reported. The county final got a grand total of four lines, but a soccer match in Waterville received a full report. The Convention regrets that the Association is not receiving its due share of support from the Kerry press – a deputation be appointed to interview the various newspaper proprietors and failing a satisfactory assurance of improvement the county committee are instructed to take whatever steps they deem necessary in the matter.'[7] It is relevant to note that during this decade: 'Tralee had, at one time, fourteen different weekly newspapers. In a world where television and radio were not yet available and travel was relatively difficult, newspaper editors were key influences of public opinion. In Kerry, the editors of the main Kerry newspapers certainly held positions of power.'[8]

During 1913 all teams would line out with fifteen players and not seventeen as heretofore. 'Dick Fitzgerald presided over a County Board meeting where nineteen clubs affiliated for the 1913 County Championship...Also at the meeting Dick Fitzgerald was presented with the 1912 County Championship medals won by Dr Crokes. It was proposed at the meeting that the new county colours would be green with a gold hoop across the chest and sleeves.'[9]

In the spring Dick Fitzgerald refereed the Currow versus Rathmore game. These sides would later meet in the County Championship. This resulted in a series of objections including Currow's stating that their opponents had had four Cork players over the previous four years. A Rathmore official admitted to 'the names of the non-registered men, and said they were registered last year but not in their own Christian names.'[10] Rathmore's counter-objection revealed 'that, contrary to rule 9B, the players and an officer from Currow attended as spectators at the international rugby match at Cork on Easter Monday last.'[11] Currow admitted that those named were in Cork but not for rugby! Both sides were suspended for one month.

Killarney won their first-round title defence against Valentia Island on Sunday 20 April and encountered both Tralee teams in the succeeding qualifying rounds. On Sunday 17 August they met and defeated Tralee Parnells 3-3 to 0-3. They emerged winners against traditional rivals Tralee Mitchels in the quarter final on 21 September, with a score of 2-4 to 1-1. Tralee got off to a lively start by scoring a point but Crokes 'with Con Murphy, Skinner and Dick Fitzgerald showing remarkable cleverness equalising after nine minutes...In a hectic finish the Tralee men mounted fierce pressure but the Killarney defence wouldn't budge.'[12]

The infamous semi-final day in Tralee on Sunday 16 November consisted of a double bill as Castleisland took on a Kilcummin side who 'ran out worthy winners after a close struggle and in spite of having a young team appearing in the closing stages of a major competition, they were very impressive.'[13] The score was 0-1 to nil.

The reigning County Champions received a warm reception as they took the field against Castlegregory, who won the toss and with their wind advantage led by 1-1 to 0-1 at half-time. As Crokes stormed into the second period and laid constant siege to their challengers' posts a section of the crowd began persistent booing against the Lakesiders. Undaunted, the champions 'kept their heads, playing the ball at all times. Dick Fitzgerald scored two great points and Denis Doyle, after a searing dribble, gave the Castlegregory goalkeeper no chance...Some of the Castle team were getting over robust at that stage, mainly from the promptings of the unruly mob...Paddy Healy displayed his prowess when he saved another goal and Dickeen closed the scoring with a point to put his side into another County final. The final score: 2-3 to 1-1.'[14]

The trouble began as 'the game finished in fading light and on their way off the field, the team were hassled by the agitators but members of Tralee Parnells' and Mitchels' club came to the assistance and rescued them to their cars.'[15] The *Kerryman* headlines read: 'Brilliant display marred by spectators' rowdy display...regrettable scenes in Tralee Sportsfield.'[16] Castlegregory, Mitchels and Parnells held three club meetings to condemn the actions of the agitators. Parnells suggested that Dr Crokes would be in their rights to resign from the Association given the verbal abuse and violence meted out to them. To add further fuel to the smouldering crisis John Clifford, Chairman and W. McCarthy, Secretary, published a letter of intent to resign in the *Kerryman* of Friday 22 November 1913 (Home Rulers FC was a Dr Crokes junior side):

> Main Street,
> Home Rulers F.C.,
> Killarney.
>
> Resolved, that we, the members of the above club, uphold the decision of our Senior Club in severing their connection with the GAA as a result of Sunday's scenes in Tralee, and that we condemn the action of the Tralee individuals who carried on such cowardly tactics, as Tralee clubs always got a fair reception in Killarney.

But at a special meeting of the Dr Crokes club it was decided to contest the county final despite strong calls from the body of the meeting for immediate withdrawal from the Association.'[17]

Former Kerry goalkeeper Pat Dillon, who had won three All-Irelands, led his clubmen as he won his third County Championship medal on Sunday 18 January 1914. 'The Killarney versus Kilcummin football final, as anticipated, turned out an easy win for the Clear Air Boys. During the first half Kilcummin gave a good display and kept the champions at bay. Score was one goal each. During the second half, however, the champions let themselves go and although the Kilcummin team did all they could to stem the tide of victory they had to go under to the tune of the Killarney 3-1, Kilcummin 1-0, leaving the Killarney team once more champions of Kerry, an honour they deserved and fought hard to attain. The runners-up are to be congratulated on reaching the final in their first year.'

> *Killarney* Crokes: Paddy Dillon (captain), Edward Spillane, Jim O'Connell, Jack Cronin, John Skinner, Con Murphy, Jim Cronin, Tim O'Sullivan, Paddy Healy, John O'Donoghue, John F. Carney, John Collins, Dick Fitzgerald, Denis Doyle, Maurice Donovan, Paddy Breen, John O'Mahony. Subs: Tim Breen, Mick Scannell.

> *Kilcummin:* L. Kelly, D. Counihan, J. Price, E. McCarthy, William Fleming, Paddy Moriarty, J. Grady, J. Gallivan, C. Murphy, Con Healy, Eugene Moriarty, J. Murphy, Tim Doherty, P. Herlihy, D. McSweeney, M. O'Callaghan.[18]

Dick Fitzgerald would continue to captain the Kingdom as a result of this back-to-back county senior double.

The First World War and
How to Play Gaelic Football, 1914

Dick Fitzgerald, Jacques McDonnell of Ardfert and Tralee and Diarmuid Cronin of Rathmore were delegated to attend the Munster Council meeting in the UDC Offices, Tipperary, on 29 March 1914. The provincial mood was upbeat as the well-attended games – Kerry versus Cork netted £308 – had resulted in a profit of £369/8s/3d. From this amount £200 was granted to the proposed Croke Memorial in Thurles and £100 divided between all Munster counties. 285 clubs were affiliated, forty-nine more than in 1913. Dick's two companions were full Munster Council members during 1914, while he was busy writing and preparing for publication the first-ever GAA instructional manual. His authoritative coaching manual, *How to Play Gaelic Football* was printed and published by Guy and Co. of 70 Patrick Street, Cork. The seventy-eight-page illustrated volume went on sale for one shilling during October 1914. Galway's renowned footballer Seán Purcell, selected as centre-forward on the Team of the Millennium, later recalled how 'St Jarlath's football was based on a book by the late great Dick Fitzgerald and it was more or less the *Koran* as they called it in Jarlath's of how to play football.'[1]

The 1914 County Championship, which opened with a Tralee Mitchels win over Valentia Island on 24 May, was to continue over a three-year span until early January 1916. During this period the First World War caused massive social upheaval in Kerry as many young men perished in the fields of France and on the beaches of Gallipoli in faraway Turkey. Castleisland historian Thomas F. Martin has researched the story of *The Kingdom in the Empire* and catalogued the names of some 548 Kerry men killed in action. When you consider that the average Gaelic team consisted of a panel of twenty-one, that would be the equivalent of some twenty-six club teams in Kerry alone. I personally knew and remember some Killarney First World War survivors who were the walking wounded of our community. When I spoke to him in 1974 the late John Murphy of Mitchel's Crescent, Tralee responded to my query about his regiment, the Munster Fusiliers, whose HQ was in Kerry's capital:

'John, do you mind me asking you how many of you from Tralee went on to the beaches at Gallipoli?'

'No, Father, twenty-one of us from Tralee went on to the beaches and I left nineteen of them behind.'

There was international outrage when the German U-boat the *U-20* torpedoed the *Lusitania* off the Old Head of Kinsale on 7 May 1915, with the loss of 1,198 crew and passengers This atrocity against a passenger liner impelled the United States to enter the campaign against the Germans.

As defending champions Crokes received a bye to the County Championship semi-final against Currow, who gave a walkover on 13 December 1914. Crokes were greatly weakened by the departure to Clonmel of All-Ireland medallist John Skinner. Johnny Mahony, also a loss to both club and county teams, emigrated to New York in March 1915. He is the footballer featured in many of the action photographs published by Dick Fitzgerald in *How to Play Gaelic Football*. 'He immediately joined the US army and during World War I the man whose abdominal muscles were strengthened in the Cricket Field, Killarney, became the boxing champion of his battalion in two weights. When he returned to Ireland he captained Kerry through the 1923 championship and played in the All-Ireland semi-final win of 1-3 to 1-2 over Cavan on 27 April 1924. He had to return to New York to his job in the Fire Department and thus missed the final versus Dublin'[2] – which Kerry won.

Tralee Mitchels played three games in all and qualified for the final by holding Caherciveen scoreless on Sunday 14 March 1915. The only final clash ever between traditional rivals Mitchels and Crokes took place in Listowel on Sunday 11 April 1915. The first, disputed, encounter witnessed by a huge crowd led to a three-match saga over the following two years.

The Kerryman reported that 'the match was the fastest and best contested county final ever played in the Kingdom. Every man of the thirty players worked as if his personal life depended on it. The exchanges on both sides were excellent and were up to the high standards of the teams. It was a fast scientific game from the start and at times the football was absolutely thrilling.'[3] Mitchels won by a late disputed point in a game which led to disparaging comments about the refereeing performance of P. Landers from Listowel. The sporting Tralee club convened a special meeting requesting Kerry County Board to re-fix the game 'owing to the unsatisfactory ending. I hope the Crokes will with their usual sporting spirit appreciate the action of the Mitchels and meet them in friendly rivalry.'[4]

The three-in-a-row contenders readily consented. 'But fixing the venue was not so simple. On 24 April a Board meeting fixed the game for Rathmore on 16 May 1915 with Mr Landers as referee. The *Kerryman* of 1 May commented adversely on the Board's choice of venue…not an enclosed one and consequently is at the mercy of money-shy and tight-shirted individuals'.[5] Diarmuid Cronin, who as fixtures' chairman had secured his own native Rathmore as host venue, fought a losing battle to convince the County Board. His published letter defending 'the Lawn' as a favourable and proven money-making venue coincided with the breaking of the major news story of the sinking of the *Lusitania* off the Cork coast.

'Crokes asked for a postponement of the final and this was granted. At a meeting on 29 May the replay was fixed for 11 July in Listowel. The change of venue was 'a matter of £.s.d. to the Board,' said the Chairman. The *Kerryman* of 3 July offered a prize of one guinea (£1/1s) for correctly forecasting the score.'[6] Mr Landers was once again in charge of the replayed County Final in Listowel on Sunday 11 July 1915. Crokes led at half-time 0-5 to 0-3. Mitchels rallied early in the second half and scored two quick goals. Dick Fitzgerald scored the equalising point. Mr P. Landers refereed in a manner that gave great satisfaction to both sides. Final score: Killarney Dr Crokes 1-6, Tralee Mitchels 2-3. Gate receipts were £66.

It was at this time that many prominent GAA players enlisted in the Volunteers who were reviewed by Eoin Mac Néill in Killarney in May 1915. 'When a challenge match in Drogheda on Easter Sunday 1916 ended with the Louth players calling for three cheers for Kerry, Dick Fitzgerald called for 'Three cheers for Eoin Mac Néill instead.'[7]

The manner in which the venue and date of the second replay were settled gives a fascinating insight into the workings of the County Board and the deciding role of Dick Fitzgerald in bringing closure. Diarmuid Cronin of Rathmore presided at a meeting on 7 August which scheduled the second replay for a fortnight later. As Killarney were not represented a County Board meeting was held in the Railway Hotel, Tralee, on 14 August. Cronin switched the venue to the Lawn with himself as referee for Sunday 12 September. Two subsequent County Board meetings of 4 and 11 September struggled with the complex issue of venue. Battle lines were drawn and Rathmore was swinging into favour as greater numbers of club delegates were flocking to these meetings. It was even proposed that the matter be put before the Munster Council for resolution but without follow-through.

Winter approached and on 27 November a solution was found with Crokes captain Dick Fitzgerald in the chair. 'Again there was a long discussion and both Rathmore and Listowel were proposed. The voting was three-all. Rathmore got the votes of the Chairman, of our old friend John Lawlor (Ballyheigue), and of D.J. Griffin (Castlemaine) who in August had been pro-Listowel. Dick Fitzgerald's casting vote gave it to Rathmore. The date was finally fixed. The match was played in the Lawn on the second Sunday in January 1916.'[8]

A special train brought a huge crowd to a village which was now highly organised. The see-saw game proved most entertaining, if low-scoring. Jack McGaley scored an early Tralee goal but 'Con of the 100 Battles' Murphy unexpectedly equalised, with Denis Doyle adding a point before half-time. Con Murphy scored the second half's only score resulting in captain Dick Fitzgerald 'bearing the laurels' on a score of 1-2 to 1-0. The referee was Limerickman Michael Crowe, who had refereed nine All-Ireland Finals, including both codes in 1909 and 1913.

It proved a gala day for Rathmore, whose GAA Club and community pulled out all the stops to host the visiting teams and supporters. A band led the marching Volunteers to the Lawn. The RIC's Sergeant Enright reportedly 'paid tribute to the Volunteers, saying, 'They were the best conducted and most helpful people in Rathmore that day.'[9] Only two arrests, for minor incidents, were made by himself and his colleague Sergeant Greany. All the shopkeepers and publicans were very pleased, none more so than the GAA County Board delegate Diarmuid Cronin. 'So it was over. The 1914 championship had taken a long time but it had been completed.' 'Meanwhile the Allies and the Central Powers fought it out on a global scale. The Gallipoli Expedition (Dardanelles Campaign) against the Turks went on all during the months that the County Board was trying to arrange the Crokes versus Mitchels replays. Allied forces finally extricated themselves from this disastrous campaign the day the Crokes retained the title.'[10]

Crokes were triple champions 1912–14 but in effect were Champions of the Kingdom until the conclusion of the 1917 campaign when Tralee Mitchels defeated Farranfore after three games on an unrecorded date some time in 1918. That six-year span was a blue riband time for the captain, Dick Fitzgerald: seeing the launch of his original *How to Play Gaelic Football* in 1914, his three county titles and two All-Irelands /Croke Cups. This period also saw the hosting of the Oireachtas in Killarney in both 1914 and 1918 and Dick spending a lengthy footballing holiday as a guest of His Royal Highness at the dreary Frongoch camp in Wales – a prisoner of war following the Easter Rising.

'MUNSTER'S ILLUSTRIOUS AND PATRIOTIC ARCHBISHOP': THE CROKE CUPS

From 1896 to 1915 a series of hurling and football competitions were intermittently organised under the broad title of 'Croke Cups'. Some competitions were played on a county basis and others on a provincial one similar to the Railway Cup competition. Dr Thomas Croke, Archbishop of Cashel and Emly, who was Patron of the GAA, died in Thurles in 1902. Dick Fitzgerald rated him so highly that he dedicated his own 1914 publication to Dr Croke:

TO THE MEMORY
Munster's Illustrious and Patriotic Archbishop,
THE MOST REVEREND DR. CROKE,
One of the First Founders of the GAA,
and
Patron of the Killarney Football Club,
With which the Author of this little work has had the honour of being associated as Member and Captain.'[1]

Furthermore, he includes Dr Croke's famous letter to Michael Cusack of 18 December 1884, accepting the invitation to become GAA patron, along with a portrait of the encouraging and challenging Cork-born cleric.

Dick Fitzgerald lined out for the Munster teams participating in the 1907 and 1908 Croke Cup competitions. 'The Croke Cup football final was played at Ennis on 17 November, 1907, between Munster (Kerry) and Connaught (Mayo). Mr L.J. O'Toole, secretary of the Association, refereed. Munster won, the final score being: KERRY...2 goals 6 points, MAYO...2 goals 3 points. The teams were:

Kerry – R. Fitzgerald (capt.); P. Dillon (goal), Costello, Spillane, Houlihan, King, Breen, O'Shea, Cronin, O'Connor, Murphy, Sullivan (2), Barry, Mullins, Cahill, and Fitzgerald.

Mayo – A. Corcoran (Capt), D. Ryder, R. Boshell, W. Boshell, P. Farmer, J. Deevy, T. Barrett, J. Moran, L. Casey, T. Murray, J. Gilmartin, M. McHugh, M. Rafter, B. Ferguson, P. Murray, and P. Sweeney (goal).'[2]

Dick Fitzgerald's successful captaining role must be unique as he also captained the winning Croke Cup Kerry teams of 1913 and 1914.

Munster's 1908 campaign proved the reverse of the previous year's results:

> The final ties for the Croke Cup hurling and football competitions, which were conducted on inter-provincial lines, were played in Jones's Road on 22 November 1908, in the presence of a large number of spectators. Kerry and Clare, representing Munster in football and hurling respectively, defeated the representatives of Ulster, – Monaghan in football and Antrim in hurling: while Galway (hurling) and Mayo (football)

representing Connacht, beat Dublin in both games. The finals then were between Clare and Galway in hurling and Mayo and Kerry in football, Clare won the hurling match easily on the following score: Clare…3 goals 14 points. Galway…1 goal 4 points. Mr George Martin, Belfast, refereed.

In football Mayo beat Kerry on the following score: Mayo…3 goals 8 points, Kerry…5 points. Mr M. F. Crowe, Dublin, refereed. The teams were: Mayo – A. Corcoran (Capt), W. Boshell, T. Gilmartin, M. McHugh, B. Ferguson, L. Casey, P. Farmer, D. F. O'Connell, Thos. Barrett, J. Moran, P. Kilduff, G. Fitzgerald, E. Boshell, T. Boshell, D. Ryder, M. Rafter, P. Sweeney (Ballina Stephenites).

Kerry – M. McCarthy, (Capt. Tralee), P. Dillon (goal), R. Fitzgerald, A. Murphy, (Killarney), W. Reardon, J. Sullivan, D. Mullins, T. Costello, W. Lawlor, C. Healy, A. McElhinney, P. Scully, P. Cahill, P. Casey, T. Cronin, W. Mahony, E. Spillane, (Tralee).[3]

Kerry's previous appearance in a Munster Senior Hurling Final had been on 6 December 1908. However, as only fourteen of the seventeen- a-side Kingdom panel arrived, Kerry conceded a walk-over to Tipperary. Bad weather prevented the whole panel's presence on the day. Despite this the men from Kilmoyley treated patrons to an exhibition of their hurling skills for fifteen minutes. The following year they featured as runners-up in a national hurling final, as reported in the 'Kerry GAA Centenary' *Kerryman* supplement of 17 November 1988:

On 31 October 1909, Kerry played Leix in the final of the Croke Cup. The game was held in the Market's Field, Limerick and was refereed by Mr T. Kenny of Galway. Leix won by 3-11 to 3-7 and Kerry lined out as follows: Matt Corridan (Capt.), Michael Meehan, Daniel Ashe, Tom Lawlor, Jack Rice, Jimmy Harris, Tim Quane, Jeremiah Davis, Thade Corridan, John Deenihan, Moss Evans, Paddy Mahony, P. Moloney, Tim Meehan, William Cotter, Paddy Walsh, John Byrne.[4]

In 1910 leading referee Michael Crowe of Limerick and Dublin mooted the concept of organising a fundraising tournament to establish a fitting memorial to GAA Patron Dr Croke of Cashel and Emly who had died eight years earlier. Nobody knew in which direction this suggestion would take the Association. Nor did anybody visualise that it would be Dublin and not Thurles that would be home of the greater memorial to Dr Croke. The Easter Congress of 1913, noting that the fund stood at a mere £308, resolved to hold the Croke Memorial Final under new rules. It is important to acknowledge that earlier competitions dating back to 1896 paved the way for greater achievements. The Irish proverb '*Bíonn gach tosnú lag*' (Each beginning is weak) seems apt when we observe the final result. The daring Congress decision of 1913 realised the dream of purchasing a national stadium within two years. Kerry and captain Dick Fitzgerald played central roles in achieving this goal.

'MORE VICTORY AND FAME' 1913–14

History and folklore entwine to bring high glamour to the accounts of the Louth versus Kerry Croke Memorial Final of 1913. To qualify, Kerry defeated Cork at the Athletic Grounds in February 1913. Louth first beat Dublin and then Antrim en route to the final. Old rivalries surfaced as the 'Paper Champions' of 1910 faced the 'Stand Down' Kingdom team. Kerry, who had fielded a weak side against Cork, decided to begin a collection towards a training fund and initiate serious trials and selection matches in Tralee, Killarney and Listowel. As the monies poured in, including dollars from Holyoke, Pittsburg and San Francisco, balladeers were preparing their tributes. Louth too was in serious preparation mood for what was to be an epic encounter.

Kerry arrived in Dublin on the Saturday, accompanied by almost 6,000 fans. On Sunday 3 May 1913 the red-clad Louthmen faced the men in green and gold at Jones's Road, the pitch still in the ownership of Limerickman Frank Brazil Dineen. 26,000 spectators witnessed an engrossing struggle as veteran Maurice McCarthy came out of retirement for Kerry. Louth scored an early goal but Donovan, Murphy and Moriarty pointed to equalise before half-time. Kerry dominated the second half but could not penetrate the Wee County's solid back line. 'With ten minutes to go Dick Fitzgerald sent Kerry a point in front,'5 then Johnston levelled and when referee McCarthy from Cork blew the final whistle the score was level: Kerry 0-4 to Louth's 1-1. The gate came to £750, a record.

Central Council fixed the replay for the same venue on 29 June 1913 although Kerry requested Cork's Athletic Grounds. Intensive preparation swung into gear with Louth contracting professional help from soccer coaches from Glasgow and Belfast. Excitement mounted in anticipation. Traleeman Jack O'Reilly, who was a teacher in the South Seas, travelled home via San Francisco for the game. He visited many cities across the US, giving lectures and collecting for the training fund. Dan McCarthy, the 1903 veteran, made the trip to Dublin from New York.

Jack McCarthy in Dunboyne, County Meath, provided hospitality and accommodation for the Kerry team on the eve of the replay. The 40,000 who crammed into Jones's Road saw a clash of style between Kerry's catch and kick and Louth's clever ground football. But this time it was all Kerry as Breen and Skinner goaled and colleagues tacked on four points to Louth's total 0-5. 'Dick Fitzgerald (captain and centre-forward) was the brains of the attack'.[6] The gate receipts, which reached £1,183, put the GAA on a strong financial footing and they purchased the stadium at Jones's Road for £3,641 later that year, 1913.

Huge throngs welcomed home the conquering heroes, who were greeted in Killarney by the local Fife and Drum as well as the Brass and Reed Bands. Dickeen was shouldered to the Town Hall, displaying the magnificent Croke Memorial Trophy presented by the same Great Southern and Western Railway Company with whom Kerry GAA had had a serious dispute during the 'Stand Down' of 1910. The winners' medals show a head-and-shoulders likeness of Dr Croke with the legend 'Memorial Competition' and, deeply engraved on the other side, 'Victory Kerry'. The original medal shows the Archbishop's mitre with the crossed keys of Peter surrounded by shamrocks, and with a pigskin football atop.

On this occasion Killarney UDC Chairman and 1903 veteran Eugene O'Sullivan addressed the crowd. He referred to 'an interesting coincidence that this coveted trophy should be won by Killarney, who on this occasion, formally represented Kerry and who twenty-seven years earlier adopted the name of Dr Croke as the distinctive title of their club'.[7] Johnny Skinner and Dick Fitzgerald responded on behalf of the panel and thanked the UDC for their 'splendid reception'. Patrons at Tralee's Theatre Royal were able to watch the match highlights on silent film, another way of bringing Gaelic sport to broader national and, in time, international viewership.

Congress decreed that the Croke Memorial games be contested under the new rules: teams of fifteen a side, not seventeen.

KERRY VERSUS LOUTH TOURNAMENT FINAL, 1913

You ask shall they win when they meet the Boyne waters,
Or if they shall fail against brave sons of Louth –
Though 'tis Gael against Gael near my musings there hovers
A belief that the honours shall come to the south.

Although Louth stands for all that we stand for in Kerry –
The games and the tongue and the hopes of our land –
Yet strengthens the faith in the sad mood or merry,
When local pride calls we can trust in our land.

When Dick Fitz leads his men to the scene of the battle,
All anxious as he for dear Kerry's fair name,
And his shouts like a war-cry from fields where guns rattle
There can be but one echo: 'More victory and fame!'

He has fought hard and long for his team and his country,
And humbled his rivals full often I ween –
For the sake of the games and without fee or bounty,
He'll revel again 'neath the old gold and green![8]

Back-to-Back All-Ireland Titles 1913–14

Kerry's defence of the Munster title began in Ennis against the previous year's vanquished Claremen. The Kingdom won easily on Sunday 25 May 1913, by 2-2 to 0-1. The semi-final clash against Tipperary ended level at two points a side in the Athletic Grounds, Cork on Sunday 31 August 1913 with 'Carbery', the well-known sporting journalist P.D. Mehigan, also known as 'Pato', as referee. On Sunday 12 October 1913 'in the replay at Fermoy, Kerry led by one point to nil at half-time. A goal by Davy Stapleton raised Tipperary's hopes but Dick Fitzgerald's men finished stronger to win 0-5 to 1-0'.[1] The Kingdom had a convincing win over Cork in the Munster Final 'Dick Fitzgerald opened the scoring for Kerry with a point from a free and then he put his name on a beautifully taken goal…Points by Fitzgerald (2).'[2] Score: Kerry 1-6 to Cork's 0-1. 'An attendance of 10,000 paid £308'[3], to go through Cork's Athletic Grounds' turnstiles on Sunday 26 October 1913. Kerry also defeated Limerick in the Munster Junior Final that afternoon 1-3 to 1-2.

Galway were Kerry's semi-final opponents at Maryborough (Portlaoise) on Sunday 9 November 1913. The western champions managed to raise one white flag to 1-8 from the men of the south. The Kerry juniors drew with Mayo 1-2, Kerry 0-5.

Kerry were to play Leinster champions Wexford in the All-

Ireland Final. Training was top priority for both camps with Jerry Collins and Willie Connor guiding Kerry and world heavyweight boxing contender Jem Roche coaching Wexford.

A crowd of 20,000 converged on Croke Park on Sunday 14 December for the very first Wexford versus Kerry football final. Wexford made an early entry on to the pitch led by the Kilkenny Pipe Band. The Killarney mascot Jackie Wade led out the Kerry team. A photograph of him, resplendent in his green and gold, can be seen in the Bricín Restaurant in High Street, Killarney, which is run by his two nephews Johnny and Paddy Maguire.

Wexford proved worthy contestants as they took an early lead from the boot of Seán Kennedy, who was later to figure as their legendary leader of four wins in a row, 1915–18. But it was the Kingdom captain who put his seal on another famous Kerry victory:

> The forwards combined cleverly, and Dick Fitz, with a splendid shot, found the net…Fitzgerald had a minor [a point] in lively play. Kerry were doing better and had a free near the corner flag. Dick Fitz screwed the leather into the square and the ball was forced into the net, but the score was disallowed. Half-time: Kerry 1-1, Wexford 0-1. Dick Fitz added a minor to the Kerry total after they resumed.[4]

The Kerry back line excelled in repelling all attacks. Johnny Skinner added another goal as Pat 'Aeroplane' O'Shea completely dominated midfield play. 'Dick Fitzgerald, in an interview after the match, said it was the hardest match Kerry ever played.'[5] The referee was Harry Boland, the final score 2-2 to 0-3. The *Irish Independent* reported that Kerry won 'the greatest encounter ever witnessed at the headquarters of the Gael'.[6] 'Dick Fitzgerald, the team captain, was carried shoulder-high from the train in Killarney to a brake and there was a torchlight procession through the town headed by the local Brass and Reed and Fife and Drum Bands. Tar barrels and bonfires blazed everywhere.'[7] Eugene O'Sullivan, UDC Chairman again welcomed the victors and addressed the receiving assembly. Next stop was Tralee where:

> ...the celebrations were renewed. Thousands of people went to the Railway Station...The Boherbee and Strand Street Bands playing spirited airs headed a torchlight procession conveying the players to their homes. There were rejoicings also in the other Kerry towns. The All-Ireland Championship Cup was exhibited in the windows of Mr T. O'Sullivan MP (cousin of Eugene O'Sullivan UDC), Main Street, Killarney.[8]

The 1914 Kerry Team: Dan Mullins, Maurice McCarthy, Jack Lawlor, Tom Costello, Tom Rice, P. Healy, P. Kennelly, Con Murphy, Pat 'Aeroplane' O'Shea, Con Clifford, Dick Fitzgerald (captain), J. Moriarty, Jack Skinner, Paddy Breen, Denis Doyle.[9]

Amateur sport helps to forge community spirit and lasting friendship among rival players, mentors, clubs and counties. During the early part of 1914 we see evidence of this with the playing of friendly home and away challenge games. Kerry got a royal welcome when they participated in Feis Carman in New Ross. The Model County won the first leg. A return game to raise funds for Tralee's Sportsfield was organised for July 1914, 'in aid of the local Sportsfield, which had just been acquired by the County Board, and on which £600 was spent on improvements.'[11] The Wexford visitors arrived at Killarney Railway Station and 'received a great ovation. But Tralee excelled itself on the occasion. A huge crowd assembled at the railway station, the approaches to which were decorated with bunting bearing suitable slogans. Boherbee and Strand Street bands were in attendance and about 700 Volunteers…the bands struck up 'The Boys of Wexford'…and headed by torchlight procession…to their hotel.'[11] The guests were shown the beauty spots of Ardfert and Ballyheigue on Sunday morning before the well-attended challenge match, which turned out to be a fiasco for Kerry.

Lining out without regulars, the Model County men scored 3-5 to Kerry's 2 points. The touring party were treated to a 'drive around Killarney Lakes on Monday, and a return by boat. Among the oarsmen was 1903 Kerry goalkeeper Pat Dillon.'[12] Many Gaelic sport observers reckoned that 1914 would be Wexford's year of glory. The *Kerryman*'s GAA writer opined of the Kerry players: 'A team of old age pensioners would have given a better exhibition of football'.[13]

The recriminations and 'Paper Champions' rows of 1910 were well forgotten when Louth accepted Kerry's invitation to play a challenge game in aid of Tralee Sportsfield on Sunday 2 August 1914. Once again huge crowds welcomed the train and in torchlight paraded their honoured guests to the Central Hotel, Tralee:

> Excursion trains were run from all parts of Kerry for the game and the attendance (gate £110) exceeded that at the Wexford-Kerry match. A clinking exhibition of football resulted between two well-

matched teams, the home side being returned the winners 2-5 to 2-1. The game, which was played in a fine sporting spirit, amid tremendous enthusiasm, was one of the best ever seen in Tralee Sportsfield.[14]

The long road in defence of their fifth All-Ireland crown began for Kerry in Ennis on Sunday 15 June 1914 when Clare suffered a three-goal defeat at the hands and feet of their cross-Shannon visitors: Kerry 3-6, Clare 2-0. The provincial semi-final against Tipperary was hosted by the Waterford County Board at Dungarvan on Sunday 13 September 1914. Contemporary reports tell that this was a hard game contested in a drizzle. John Skinner, Dick Fitzgerald and the two-goal star forward Denis Doyle scored a tally of 2-3 to the Premier County's 0-2. 'Tipperary's rough tactics proved unavailing', according to the *Kerryman* report of 18 September 1914, as the Kingdom progressed to meet the challenge of Cork. Mr A. Quillinan of Limerick, who had refereed both qualifiers, was appointed to preside at the Munster Senior Final in Tralee Sportsfield on Sunday 4 October 1914.

Supporters travelled by rail from all over Kerry (Kenmare, Castleisland, Castlegregory and Valentia) and Munster (Limerick, Waterford, Mitchelstown, Youghal and Cork). Another bumper gate resulted as fans paid sixpence into the Sportsfield and a shilling for sideline or stand. The only first-half score came from the boot of Johnny Mahony, whose action photographs feature in Dickeen's *How to Play Gaelic Football* published that same month. In May 1915 he emigrated to New York. For years he played with the Kerry New York team and from 1931 strongly supported the fundraising campaign in aid of the Fitzgerald Stadium. Kerry's first All-Star, Donie

O'Sullivan of Spa, frequently met him in New York during the 1960s. John Skinner, Denis Doyle and Dick Fitzgerald added second half points to help the Kingdom retain their Munster crown and advance to another All-Ireland final, on a score 0-5 to 0-1. Again Kerry's opponents were Wexford.

'The game went ahead at Croke Park on 1 November (1914) with Harry Boland as referee.'[15] Twenty-six trains brought a crowd of 15,000 from Wexford and Kerry to support their beloved teams in a re-run of the 1913 final. Wexford's Kennedy goaled mid-way in the first half and despite wind and rain Aidan Doyle added a second goal for the Leinstermen to Kerry's lone point from Con Clifford. The sensational second half saw 'Aeroplane' O'Shea's high-fielded delivery to Dickeen and on to Paddy Breen who goaled. Con 'of the 100 Battles' Murphy pointed from long range. Kerry's defenders closed down the opposing forwards. P.F. gives a graphic account of the equalising score in the present tense:

> Dick Fitz has the ball close to the Wexford sticks. He is thrown down. Pop goes the referee's whistle! Dick takes steady aim, gauges the crosswind, and gets his boot squarely under the greasy ball. He lets fly as the spectators gaze with bated breath. Like the arrow from the bow the ball leaves his boot and crosses just above the bar. The scores are level and one of the most thrilling encounters for All-Ireland honours is at an end. Kerry 1-3; Wexford 2-0.[16]

Wexford's Gus Kennedy criticised Harry Boland's last-minute decision 'The referee, rather harshly I thought, gave a free to Kerry and Dick Fitzgerald sent it over the bar.'[17] That was the equalising score. Captain Dickeen was rated by Gus Kennedy as 'the most dangerous forward of them all'.[18]

J.D. Nolan, a Dublin commentator, in a letter published on the front page of the *Kerryman* on 5 November 1914 claimed: 'those Kerry "crocks" should stand down of their own accord to younger and better men and save the honour of the county'. I wonder if this was one of the reasons Jerry O'Leary and his fellow selectors begged retiree Maurice McCarthy of Tralee to make yet another comeback?

The same referee, Harry Boland, soon to make a major contribution to Ireland's struggle for Independence, was appointed to take charge of the All-Ireland Senior Football Final replay on Sunday 29 November 1914 in Croke Park. 20,000 paid to witness a tremendous match between two well prepared sides on a sunny, dry but very windy afternoon. Kerry made two changes, introducing Tom Rice's brother Jack from Abbeydorney and old-stager Maurice McCarthy.

Wexford got away to a flying first-half start. They scored six points – Byrne two, S. Kennedy two, G. Kennedy and Aidan Doyle one each – to lead the defending champions 0-6 to nil at half-time. Both Paddy Breen and Johnny Mahony goaled as 'Kerry resumed like a whirlwind…scores were even after five minutes. Up and down play followed…Dick Fitzgerald gave Kerry a point lead about midway in the period and he soon repeated…Kerry slowly but surely asserted superiority. Wexford's backs were bearing the brunt. A long drop by McCarthy was well held by Skinner. He swung clear of a Wexford back and the leather curled high between the posts. It is the last score of the game: Kerry 2-3; Wexford 0-6.'[19] For a game and sporting Wexford it was a case of 'Their day would come', in 1915, 1916, 1917 and 1918 but this was Kerry's fine double.

The Great Southern and Western Railway Company presented the Croke Cup for the competition with the stipulation that any team to won it two years in a row became its perpetual possessors. The Kingdom's captain, nominated by three-in-a-row Kerry County Champions Dr Crokes, accepted the valuable trophy and with his colleagues brought it south for another glorious homecoming. The 'crocks' were hailed as an exceptional team of worthy champions: Kerry had won their fifth senior title and: 'Two players, Maurice McCarthy and Dick Fitzgerald took part in all five victories.'[20]

One month later P.D. Mehigan published a special tribute in the Christmas edition of his *Gaelic Athlete*. Using his pen-name 'Carbery', he lauded players, officers and loyal fans:

> That they are a wonderful lot, no one who ever saw them perform will deny. They have evolved a method of football which is ever a pleasure to watch and have brought the game to a pitch of popularity and perfection which looked an impossibility prior to their advent. And the beauty of it all is that they are sportsmen every one. Never have foul, dishonest, nor ungraceful tactics been associated with their name. On and off the field they behave themselves in a style which does credit to their county and the game they play. There was long and anxious organisation and training before the present finished article was put up for public admiration. The Tralee and Killarney clubs had officers whose enthusiasm and energy were largely responsible for their men's advancement. When a county has men of the stamp of Austin Stack, J. McDonnell, the Brothers Collins,

Eugene O'Sullivan, Jerry O'Leary, etc., in control of a team's welfare, it spells success for the team. The perfect system of the trial games, with regular training practised by the Kerrymen, has given the lead to Ireland. Behind all that and perhaps the main factor in winning victory after victory is this great moral force – a big enthusiastic county's whole-hearted support. Never has a team been so loved by their county, by rich and poor alike, as these Kerry men are. What Gael is not familiar with the teeming train loads from valley, field and glen who throng to the finals; and what Dubliner is dead to the wild war-whoop which greets the Kerry flags. With their county men's heart behind them, Kerry will long keep near the top of Irish Football.'[21]

KERRY VERSUS WEXFORD (ALL-IRELAND, 1913)

Ho! They swing up from Dingle and in past Lixnaw,
Over the mountains from proud Iveragh;
Just mark how they rally from gallant Tralee,
In charming Killarney to muster with glee!
Hurrah for the Crokes! *Lo, the Mitchels are here;*
Give the Rangers, O'Connells and Gascons a cheer;
God bless them and weld them, success to the team
That has raised the old game to its place of esteem.

To strive for their sire-land, their honour to shield,
The champions of Ireland they face on the field;
With swoop like a swallow's the ball rends the air,
'Tis back like an arrow – McCarthy was there,

With Lawlor and Costello, Murphy and Rice!
Then O'Shea shoots the leather to Fitz in a thrice –
Dick passes to Skinner, 'tis netted by Breen,
And a cheer rends the air for the Kingdom's fifteen.

Let us cheer once again for the green and the gold,
For Kerry's fair daughters, her sons ever bold –
By the Bann and the Lagan, the Liffey and Lee,
Their names are as famed as in peerless Tralee!
A cheer for the dear ones, who've strayed o'er the foam;
A prayer for the brave ones, whose dust rests at home –
One final hurrah for the dauntless fifteen
Who vanquished all Ireland in nineteen-thirteen!

Up Kerry! Hurrah for her fighting fifteen.[22]

The Irish Volunteers, 1913

The Irish Volunteers were founded in Dublin on Saturday 25 November 1913. It was Conradh na Gaeilge *timire* (organiser), Irish teacher Pádraig Ó Siochfhradha who established a Company of the Irish Volunteers in Killarney on 28 November 1913. He adopted the *ainm cleite* or pen-name of 'An Seabhac' meaning 'the hawk' and is remembered by generations of Irish schoolchildren as author of *Jimín*, the story of the impish son of Máire Thadhg. The contribution of this Ventry born writer to the literary, cultural and revolutionary consciousness of Ireland is immense. It was he who, in 1916, directed the young Brian Kelly (Brian Ó Ceallaigh) from the Hall, Park Road, Killarney to stay at the Blasket Island home of Tomás Ó Criomhthain with a view to improving Kelly's Irish. Kelly, by encouraging Ó Criomhthain to write and 'An Seabhac' by editing his work, facilitated the publication firstly of *Allagar na hInise* (1928) and Ó Criomhthain's masterpiece *An tOileánach* (1929).

Gaelic League founder Eoin Mac Néill published an article entitled 'The North Began' in the organisation's journal *An Claidheamh Soluis* on 1 November 1913. As a direct result the Irish Volunteers came into being in the Rotunda Rooms, Dublin on 25 November at a meeting convened by The O'Rahilly of Ballylongford in north Kerry and by a Northerner, Bulmer

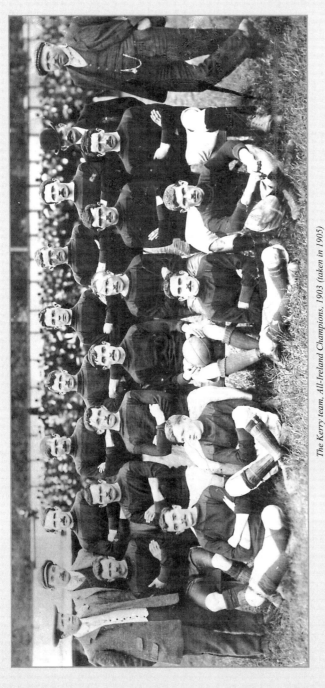

The Kerry team, All-Ireland Champions, 1903 (taken in 1905)

Back row from left: T. F. O'Sullivan, Hon. Sec. County Board; E. O'Sullivan, President, County Board; R. Kirwan; A. Stack; C. Healy; M. McCarthy;

T. Looney; J. P. O'Sullivan

Centre row from left: D.Curran; C. Duggan, D. McCarthy; T. O'Gorman, J. Buckley; W. Lynch, P. Dillon

Front row from left: J. O'Gorman; R. (Dick) Fitzgerald; J. T. Fitzgerald; D. Breen

(Photo courtesy Kevin Coleman)

The Dr Crokes team, Kerry County Champions, 1912–14.
Dick Fitzgerald is fourth from the right, back row.
(Photo courtesy MacMonagle)

The 1914 Kerry team, taken at a championship match in Fethard, County Tipperary.
Dick Fitgerald is sixth from the left, back row. Dr Eamonn O'Sullivan is third from the left, middle row
and 'Small' Jer Leary is on the extreme right, front row.
(Photo courtesy Mary Ellen Spillane, Kenmare)

The 1914 Kerry team (All-Ireland champions) photographed at the Cricket Field, Flesk Bridge, Killarney Back row from left: John Moriarty (Ballydonoghue); Denis Mullins (Tralee); Con Clifford (Tralee); Tom Costello (Tralee); Paddy Healy (Dr Crokes); Jack Lawlor (Kilmoyley); Paddy Kennelly (Laune Rangers); John Skinner (Dr Crokes) Front row from left: Tom Rice (Abbeydorney); Pat (Aeroplane) O'Shea (Castlegregory); Denis Doyle (Dr Crokes); Dick Fitzgerald (Dr Crokes); Jimmy O'Connell (Dr Crokes); Con Murphy (Dr Crokes); Jack Rice (Abbeydorney) (Photo courtesy of the late Denis Horgan, Killarney and Tralee)

Officers' training camp, Coosan Point, Athlone, 1915. Dick Fitzgerald is second from the left, back row:
(Photo courtesy of Kerry's Eye, Tralee)

The Clare senior football team, runners-up in the 1917 All-Ireland final, trained by Dick Fitzgerald
(Photo courtesy of T.J. Flynn and Joe Ó Muircheartaigh)

Micheal Collins at Inch House, New Street, Killarney on 22 April 1922

Back row from left: P.D. Moynihan, C. Courtney, D.C. Counihan, Hon. Sec., M. Courtney, C. Moriarty, E. Tangney, Brother Hugoline OFM, P. Horgan.

Brother Juniper OFM, J. Twomey, J. Dolan, Captain H. Spring, Reverend Father Mark OFM, J. Langford

Front row from left (seated): Kevin O'Higgins TD, Reverend Father Fidelius OFM, Mrs W. O'Sullivan, General Seán Mac Eoin TD, with Master Wm. O'Sullivan

(holding revolver) on his lap, General Michael Collins TD, Mrs P.D. Moynihan, Dr Wm. O'Sullivan, Reverend D.F. O'Sullivan, CC, M. O'Sullivan

(Picture courtesy of Marcus and Vincent Counihan, High St, Killarney)

The Dillon sisters, Bee (Bridget) and Kitty (on right).
Bee was Kitty's bridesmaid when she married Dick Fitzgerald in 1925.
(Picture courtesy Edmund Eagar)

Brewery Lane, Kenmare Place, Killarney, home of Dick Fitzgerald's wife, Kitty Dillon.
Dillon's lace industries were based here.
(Picture: Tom Looney)

The wedding of Dick Fitzgerald and Kitty Dillon on 17 October 1925
Back row from left: Michael Murray, Town Clerk, Killarney UDC;
Pat Dillon, Brewery Lane, Killarney, brother of the bride
Centre from left: Rita Looney, niece of the bride; Din Joe Bailey, Secretary, Kerry County Board,
bride and groom, Danny Jim O'Donoghue, NT, Barraduff, Cono Healy, solicitor, Killarney, best man
Seated: Fr Edmund (Ned) Fitzgerald, Kinsale, and Bridget Dillon, sister of the bride (bridesmaid)
(Picture courtesy of the Looney family)

Hobson, a member of the Irish Republican Brotherhood (IRB). The meeting resolved 'to secure and maintain the rights and liberties common to all the people of Ireland.'[1] Later that same month Cumann na mBan, the women's auxiliary movement of the Volunteers, was established.

IRB member and Kerry GAA Chairman Austin Stack joined the Volunteers in the County Hall in Tralee on 13 December 1913. Many leading Volunteers were closely linked with the GAA – Paddy Cahill of Tralee, Dick Fitzgerald of Killarney and Pat 'Aeroplane' O'Shea of Castlegregory.[2]

'An Seabhac attended the Volunteers' inaugural meeting on 25 November and established a company in Killarney three days later. He interrupted his Irish class for a lesson in military drill, and that night a company of Volunteers was formed:

> On 28 November, 1913, when a meeting of the Gaelic League was in progress in An Dún, High Street, Killarney, a stranger arrived and was met by An Seabhac (Mr P. Sugrue), who was one of the Irish teachers at the classes. The stranger was, we believe, a Donegal man, but we do not know his name. An Seabhac knew him and introduced him to those present. He said that he came on behalf of the Headquarters of the Irish Volunteers to ask that a Company be formed in Killarney. He said it was their object to have one formed in every town and village in Ireland. There and then all present decided to join and the Company was formed.

Michael Spillane and Michael J. O'Sullivan are first-hand witnesses who scripted this joint report for the Bureau of Military

History. They name thirty-six of the approximately forty who enlisted. Dick Fitzgerald is named No. 32. 'Appointed section commanders were 'An Seabhac', Michael Spillane, Michael J. O'Sullivan, Seán O'Casey, Pat Horgan and Tadhg Horgan. Secretary was Jim Counihan, post office official, and the treasurer was William D. F. O'Sullivan, from Killarney. Further branches were organised in Ballyhar, Fossa, Listry, Beaufort, Glenflesk, Firies and other parts of East Kerry.'[3]

During the Winter months after the start drills were held on two nights a week, and on another night a class for the instruction of officers was held. Instruction was given by Sergeant John McGovern, an ex-serviceman who has been appointed drill instructor. In the Spring of 1914 the officers visited the surrounding districts Ballyhar, Fossa, Beaufort, Listry, Glenflesk, Firies, Muckross, Barraduff and Rathmore. Companies were formed in all these districts except Barraduff. The organisation grew apace and many new members joined up in Killarney following public parades by the original body. There was no sudden large influx of men into the Volunteers, but a steady increase in strength up to September, 1914.

In June, 1914, Killarney Company was about 120 strong, in August it was unchanged, at the end of 1914 strength had fallen to about 60, by the end of 1915 it was about 120, and at Easter 1916, about 70.

The following officers were elected soon after the formation of the Company:

Michael Spillane; Captain.
Michael J. O'Sullivan; 1st Lieutenant.
Richard (Dick) Fitzgerald; 2nd Lieutenant.
Michael (Honey) O'Donoghue; Adjutant.
Section Commanders; Johnnie Clifford, Maurice Horgan, Willie McCarthy, Seán O'Casey. They continued in office until re-elected in May, 1915.[4]

Within three years Dick Fitzgerald and two of his above-mentioned neighbours, harness-maker Michael Spillane of Bohereencaol and New Street shopkeeper Michael J. O'Sullivan, were interned in Frongoch Prisoner of War Camp in North Wales. Meantime, there was much sporting and revolutionary activity in the Killarney area.

More branches were set up in the East Kerry district including Rathmore, Scartaglin and Currans. 2,000 Volunteers paraded and were reviewed in the Market, Tralee, on Sunday 14 June 1914. Following an excellent game of hurling in the Cricket Field: 'Several thousand Volunteers drawn from all parts of Kerry and from various centres in Munster, including the cities of Limerick and Cork, marched all through Killarney amid scenes of tremendous enthusiasm'[5] on the day the Oireachtas was held in Killarney, 26 July 1914. The volunteers were accommodated in various locations including the East Avenue and Old Town Halls, the Courthouse and the Half-Moon Demesne Field on the Kenmare Estate.

This was the very day of the Howth Gun-Running when three civilians were shot dead by British soldiers and thirty eight wounded on Bachelor's Walk, Dublin. The Volunteers were outraged that no retaliatory action had been taken against the Northern Unionists when they ran guns into Larne in April 1914.

Dúglas de hÍde, joint founder of the Gaelic League, was present as Uachtarán (President) of the Oireachtas. His late great-grandfather had served as Church of Ireland Minister in Killarney for twenty-five years (1809–34). De hÍde, who was later President of Ireland (1938–45), made a major contribution to Irish literature and the language revival.

A crowd of 10,000 attended Killarney's first Oireachtas 'one of the most successful festivals ever held by the Gaelic League in point of new entries and attendance at the competitions'.[6] 'It is worthy of special mention that the Killarney Company carried rifles openly, a fact which evoked loud cheering' in Lord Kenmare's Estate.[7] Famed Sliabh Luachra music master Pádraig Ó Caoimh, now commemorated by a statue in Scartaglin, won first prize in the fiddle competition, listed as 'Violin Solo' on the 1914 programme.

SPLIT IN THE IRISH VOLUNTEERS

John Redmond, leader of the Irish Party, had lobbied hard and apparently successfully for Home Rule: 'By the summer of 1914, with Home Rule to become law by September, Redmond was worried that any action by the Irish Volunteers might increase tension.'[8] At the Buckingham Palace Conference of July 1914 he rejected partition while the Unionists dissented. The Great War broke out on the 1 August 1914, when Germany declared war on Russia and two days later on France. The call to defend small nations echoed across Europe and many Kerrymen enlisted. It was at this juncture that Kerry achieved their Croke Cup and two in a row All-Ireland Senior Final victories and Dick Fitzgerald wrote and published *How to Play Gaelic Football*.

John Redmond, feeling that Home Rule was now a guaranteed reality, 'called on the Volunteers to assist Britain by joining the

British army. The great majority – some 170,000 – answered his call; the minority, dominated by the IRB retained the title Irish Volunteers, while Redmond's followers became known as the National Volunteers. In May 1915 Redmond declined a seat in the war cabinet, in which Carson became Attorney General.'⁹

During September 1914 dissent with Redmond's decision came to a head in Kerry. Tralee sided with the newly-formed Irish Volunteers as against Redmond's National Volunteers by 100 to 20 and the pattern was repeated across the county: Listowel 139 to 7, Caherciveen 37 to 27, Cordal 68 to 2. Both Ballyferriter and Castlegregory were unanimously for the Irish Volunteers while Dingle was 80 per cent for. The split scarcely affected the Rathmore district, which remained overwhelmingly pro-Irish Volunteer. As for Killarney it remained neutral, having 'made use of the diplomatic act to steer itself through the rift. Its purse was in a Redmondite pocket. But on the night of 7 May 1915, the whole Volunteer force in Killarney shed its neutrality and declared for the Irish Volunteers.'¹⁰ (The 'Redmondite pocket' is a reference to the pro-Redmond leanings of the Treasurer, William D.F. O'Sullivan. His own brother, an army chaplain, was killed and buried in France.)

Dick Fitzgerald proved proactive in guiding this decision:

> Killarney Volunteers…held a meeting in the Volunteer Hall in High Street to reorganise in favour of Mac Néill. Speakers…included Michael Spillane, Michael J. O'Connor, Tralee, Dick Fitzgerald of Killarney and Ernest Blythe. Fitzgerald asked those in favour of affiliating with the Irish Volunteers to move to the right side of the hall. There was then a cheer as every man present went to that side, Michael

Spillane was elected Captain of the company, Michael J. O'Sullivan was elected First Lieutenant and Dick Fitzgerald Second Lieutenant with M. F. O'Donoghue honorary treasurer and Seán O'Casey honorary secretary. Eleven new members were enrolled and the proceedings concluded with the singing of 'A Nation Once Again'.[11]

Tralee's former football star and GAA authority figure 'Austin Stack was the recognised leader for all Kerry. It was he who took the salute at a review of Volunteers and of colours at Killarney on Whit Sunday, 1915...An account of the Killarney parade tells us that on "...Whit Sunday, 1915...Killarney's old Cricket Field was the scene of a great display of national advancement and solidarity. In a momentous and tense atmosphere several thousand volunteers from every nook and corner were reviewed by Eoin Mac Néill, the leader of the movement, and presented with their colours, which were blessed by Rev. Father Ferris. Under the command of Austin Stack, the vast, assembled force of Kerry's marshalled manhood, fully armed with rifles... strength and resolution resounded from these marching feet. The atmosphere at the saluting base was electric. 'We have no fear, we have no doubt that the sun is rising for Ireland.' There was a tense and awe-inspiring hush as these prophetic words floated over the vast assemblage."'[12]

A Whit Saturday telegram from Sir Morgan O'Connell, a loyal and concerned citizen, to the Lord Lieutenant in Dublin failed to halt proceedings: 'A meeting under the auspices of Sinn Féin is to be held tomorrow calling itself a football match, but with the perfectly open and avowed intention of being turned into an anti-recruiting meeting. Will your Excellency do anything to stop it'?[13] Evidently, his Excellency did not!

As Dick Fitzgerald and fellow-Irish Volunteers from Killarney paraded, their neighbours were being killed and injured in the trenches of France. Anecdotal evidence states that thirty-four men from Well Lane, off Killarney's Main Street, were recruited for the cause of Britain and its allies. A commemorative monument, naming local men killed in action overseas, is planned for on the site at the Ha Ha, Kenmare Place, where the impressive Royal Munster Fusiliers Memorial stands. *Kerry's Eye* of 28 February 2008 quoted local UDC Councillor Michael Courtney:

> When the Great War broke out, many joined the British Army, many for the pay to feed their families. More joined because of the inducement to see the world...All that happened to the majority was that they paid with their lives. Nearly all who enlisted were killed or sent home badly disabled. Many are buried today in the poppy fields of Flanders. Others were blown to bits with no trace of burial or account of where they died. History tells us that thirty-four people from the lanes of Killarney fought in the Dardanelles and only a few came back. A book of names of the war dead...will be available to the public for inclusion and inspection at Killarney Town Hall and in the Killarney Library. To date a few hundred names have been enlisted in the book.[14]

Since 1895 every cell of the GAA had been successfully penetrated by two informers reporting back to Dublin Castle. Thus, the Crown authorities were well informed of the true allegiance of all GAA members. Local historian and footballer Donie O'Sullivan has researched this tense era in Kerry's sporting and political story. In *Dr Crokes Gaelic Century* he notes:

> Dick Fitzgerald was a prominent member of the Volunteers. Membership of the Dr Crokes and the Volunteers often overlapped. On 1 August 1915 the Kerry senior team, controlled by the County Champions Dr Crokes, was to play Cork at Fermoy. When it was learned that the game clashed with the funeral of O'Donovan Rossa, Kerry refused to play. Dick Fitzgerald (captain) and Jer O'Leary (selector) sent the following telegram to the Munster Council: 'Kerry still loyal Irishmen, will not play.' Remember O'Donovan Rossa addressed the Dr Croke club in Killarney in 1894.[15]

('The *Kerry Sentinel* of 27 June 1894 published the address of Dr Crokes Chairman John Corcoran together with the response of Jeremiah O'Donovan Rossa, the veteran Fenian, just returned from his enforced American exile.'[16])

Austin Stack was summoned by Pádraic Pearse to his school, St Enda's in Rathfarnham, Dublin, during the autumn of 1915. Pearse informed him that the Rising would take place the following Easter and that Stack would take responsibility for the distribution of arms for the Rising to be imported from Germany into Tralee bay. Strict secrecy was imposed on Stack, who welcomed Pearse to Tralee on 26 February 1916 for a review in the Tralee Sportsfield of 500 North Kerry Volunteers from Tralee, Listellick, Abbeydorney and Ballymacelligott. The Volunteers were on a war footing as plans for the Rising were in place and Kerry was meant to play a crucial role.

Towards the end of 1915 Michael Collins, a former London hurler who was a member of the Geraldines GAA Club, was ordered by his IRB superiors to return to Ireland. Collins found employment with Craig Gardners Accountants in Dame Street, Dublin. Austin Stack, an income tax collector for the Cahirciveen and Dingle areas, got into difficulties with his own government employers because of his open Volunteer profile. Dublin Castle reports describe Stack as 'an advanced GAA man and a pro-German'.[17] The Volunteers were utilising many GAA grounds for drilling purposes although in January 1914 Luke O'Toole of Central Council refused them permission to avail of the newly purchased Croke Park for this purpose. But later that month GAA President James Nowlan called upon Association members to 'join the Volunteers and learn to shoot straight'.[18] Dublin Castle had good reason to watch the sporting organisation they had comprehensively infiltrated.

Kerry had three Volunteer brigades and the No. 2 Brigade was centred in Killarney, covering east Kerry from Castleisland and the district north of it, all the way south to Kenmare. It was sub-divided into five battalions by 1919. 'The Third Battalion was in Killarney with Michael Spillane in charge, Michael J. O'Sullivan was his deputy, Pat O'Shea his adjutant and Jim Coffey the quartermaster.'[19]

The Coosan Point Training Camp, held near Athlone, County Westmeath, in September 1915, one of four such camps held during that period, 'turned out to be a real education in military tactics' according to Tralee Volunteer Billy Mullins. 'Training Officer was OC Ginger O'Connell...He gave us useful tips, that were to stand to us many years later, during the fight for freedom.'[20] O'Connell wittily describes lengthy cross-country treks into County Galway and how a training group the previous month was hastily moved on by a fellow east-Galway Volunteer who feared he would lose his tenancy because they attempted to set up camp on his landlord's estate in Ballinasloe without permission. The trainers who consented to undergo these special courses during 1915 included Austin Stack of Tralee, Dave Griffin of Castleisland, Seán Kerins of Scartaglin, Killarney's Michael Spillane and Dick Fitzgerald, and Terence MacSwiney, later Lord Mayor of Cork. In the Ballinasloe camp 'dinner was to be boiled ham, cabbage and other vegetables'.21

Colonel O'Connell evaluated that September course as 'the most successful from the military point of view of the four camps'.[22] O'Connell's unpublished historical memoir finds fault with the GAA for not being dedicated to the Volunteers:

> It seems the commitment of the GAA to the Volunteers is far from total…while noting that many of his best officers were captains of hurling and football teams. Unfortunately the athletic activities of such men conflicted with their military duties and when a match conflicted with a parade or field day too often the parade or field day was put into the background.[23]

However, some Kerry GAA personnel did cooperate with Pearse's pre-Rising plans. 'Soon after his return home Stack was visited in Tralee by Pearse who formally appointed him Brigadier over the Kerry Volunteers and intimated that a rising had been decided upon. Stack arranged for a substantial consignment of rifles and ammunition to be collected at the residence of The O'Rahilly at 40 Herbert Park, Dublin and to be transported to

Tralee on the train bringing home the supporters of the Kerry football team'[24] on Sunday 7 November 1915, the day Wexford defeated defending champions Kerry.

WEXFORD VERSUS KERRY (ALL-IRELAND, 1915)

In Croke Park in Dublin town,
On the brilliant sward so green,
Those thirty thousand Irish men
Will ne'er forget the scene,
When the gallant Gaels from Kerry,
Who ne'er a conqueror knew
Lined up to save their title brave
From the boys in gold and blue.

The champions from the Kingdom
Long held the Gaelic sway,
There couldn't be found in our island round
Their equals in the fray.
But mark old Wexford's furious charge,
Their lines pierce them through –
Ah, Kerrymen you've met your peers,
The boys in gold and blue!

The Kingdom's sons are sturdy ones
By victory twice were crowned.
But to see brave Paddy Mackey
Careering down the line,
While cheers from five thousand throats
Ring for the Geraldine!
Long may their glory brightly shine

In story and in song!
Long may their prowess be upheld –
Our heroes true and strong.
To Wexford's name they've added fame –
I'll sing their praise anew,
Who won All-Ireland honours,
The boys in gold and blue![25]

Pádraig Kehoe, Enniscorthy

'Bringing German Rifles
to the Lonely Banna Strand', 1916

The Munster GAA Story records: 'The year 1916 was not alone a memorable one for the GAA, it was a memorable one for the Irish Nation.'[1] By late July Kerry County Board had withdrawn from the All-Ireland Championship. Dick Fitzgerald, Austin Stack and many GAA players and mentors were by then imprisoned in Frongoch, North Wales, and other British holding centres.

The 'terrible beauty'[2] identified by W.B. Yeats in his poem 'Easter 1916' had come at a terrible cost to the Irish people and Kerry was not spared, as terrific might met fierce resistance, 'in bloody protest for a glorious thing', in the words of Pádraic Pearse. Different GAA members took a broad variety of positions through this testing revolutionary period and it was a challenging time for the GAA leadership.

Kerry suffered some inglorious setbacks and failures in its pre-Rising activities. The débâcle of Roger Casement's ill-fated Banna Strand landing and capture on Good Friday 1916 was compounded by the Ballykissane Pier tragedy. The Easter Sunday order of Eoin Mac Néill calling off Volunteer manoeuvres exacerbated a complex and confusing situation for all Irish Volunteers on standby.

Dick Fitzgerald and his Killarney Company were armed and ready for action:

> At Easter, 1916, the arms of the Company consisted of:
> 52 Martini Enfield single shot rifles
> 3 magazine rifles
> 10 shotguns
> 15 revolvers
> 1,700 rounds of .303 ammunition
> 500 rounds of revolver ammunition
> 300 ball cartridges
> 4 miniature rifles
> All the above arms had been purchased from The O'Rahilly, 40, Herbert Park, Dublin, in 1915, for £200. Michael Spillane, Michael J. O'Sullivan, An Seabhac and William D.F. O'Sullivan went to Dublin to effect the purchase of the armaments. Arthur Hill went also to pass judgment on the purchases. On that occasion The O'Rahilly told the deputation there was no area he was more pleased with than East Kerry, because the area did not cost Headquarters a penny to organise or drill.[3]

The *Aud*, commanded by Captain Karl Spindler, departed Lubeck Docks in north Germany on 9 April 1916. It contained a cargo of '20,000 rifles, 10 machine guns, some millions of rounds of ammunitions as well as a supply of bombs, land mines and grenades'.[4] This former British cruise ship was now at sea under a Norwegian flag and due into Tralee Bay between 20 and 23 April, with Karl Spindler at the helm. Sir Roger

Casement, Robert Monteith and Daniel Bailey were aboard the U19 German submarine accompanying the *Aud*, which did not have wireless equipment. The plan was that Austin Stack, upon receiving delivery of the arms at Fenit, would commandeer a train to despatch and deliver weapons for the Rising to the Kerry, Cork, Limerick and Galway rebels.

Austin Stack and trusted companions expected to take delivery of the arms on Easter Sunday night or early Easter Monday as the Rising date had been altered by the Dublin leaders who decided 'that arms must not be landed before the night of Sunday 23'.[5] Spindler and his twenty-one-man crew lay offshore on Holy Thursday night and came to within 600 yards of Fenit Pier on Good Friday morning. Spindler risked detection by flashing green signals landwards to the anticipated Stack reception party but as the ballad puts it 'no answering signal came from the lonely Banna Strand'. Being incommunicado, he was unaware of the new deferred dates.

The U19 discharged its three passengers on to Banna Strand on the morning of Good Friday, 20 April. They too were unaware of the deferred dates and the wet and weary Casement took refuge at McKenna's Fort. Monteith and Bailey evaded capture and went to Spicer's shop in Tralee where they made contact with Stack. Monteith informed him of Casement's predicament but Stack and his fellow searchers failed to locate Casement as Monteith's directions were imprecise. A local Ardfert man had notified the RIC about the collapsible boat on the strand and the police took in the bearded stranger for questioning and detention.

Meanwhile, the *Aud* sailed away from the North Kerry coastline and at 6pm was spotted and captured by the British Navy's *Bluebell* patrol boat. While the *Aud* was being escorted into Cork harbour Spindler commanded that his ship be scuttled at dawn on 22 April. He and his crew took to the lifeboat and were captured and interned for the duration of the war.

It now has emerged that the whole venture was already doomed. 'In his memoir *The Mystery of the Casement Ship* (1931) Spindler claimed that copies of documents containing the entire plans of the Irish venture were stolen from the office of Wolf von Igel, a secretary of the German Embassy in Washington, and that President Wilson personally appraised British officials of the plans.'[6] Bailey, the captured British Army soldier recruited by Casement into the Irish Brigade, turned out to be one Sergeant Beverley. This Irishman and British agent soon disappeared, having informed the authorities about Casement.

Monteith made his escape to a safe house in the Ballymacelligott/Glounageentha area and home to Limerick before his escape to the USA. He made a nostalgic trip to Banna Strand at dawn on Good Friday 1948, in the company of the late Nonie O'Briain of Dublin, daughter of Cathal Brugha, who told me about it. Donal O'Sullivan's biography of John Kearney, head of the RIC in Tralee, shows that Kearney was kind to Casement and kept his prisoner on a low-security overnight stay in Tralee. The grateful prisoner presented his jailer with his watch as a gift. Why Austin Stack and his fellow activists made no attempt to rescue Casement remains one of the many enigmas surrounding the Rising in Kerry.

The archive of the Irish Bureau of Military History records the testimony of Austin Stack's widow, who attempted to clarify her husband's position: 'Austin was blamed by some for not trying to organise the rescue of Sir Roger Casement and I know he felt sore about it, but (he) always said his orders were definite that no shot should be fired before the start of general hostilities on Easter Sunday and he knew well that any fracas that might take place in Tralee would frustrate all the plans for the Rising.'[7]

Limerick historian Mainchín Seoighe describes the ill-fated Holy Week Kerry car journey from Limerick to Cahirciveen. The purpose of the expedition was 'to dismantle the wireless station at Caherciveen and set up a transmitter in Tralee with which it was hoped to make contact with the arms ship and submarine'.[8] (Unknown to the Volunteers, the *Aud* did not have any radio equipment.)

Two Limerick car owners who were Irish Volunteers with Limerick's City battalion agreed to offer their vehicles for a planned Kerry run. Tommy McInerney drove his own Maxwell model. Garage owner John J. Quilty was unable to drive his 'new 20 horse-power Briscoe American open touring car'. He selected Sam Windrim to replace him. Windrim was immediately recruited and 'was sworn into the IRB there and then...he was told he was going on a gun-running expedition, and would first have to pick up five Volunteers at Killarney Railway Station.'[9] Some anomalies were to lead to further complications as the number plates were practically identical although the Maxwell was one year older. Worse still, Windrim's driving licence had expired in 1915. Furthermore, the men carried a large supply of petrol in cans for their journey to Caherciveen. The motorists departed the Treaty City early on Friday 21 April 1916 with a cover story that they were to meet the touring party of one Colonel Warrick. The RIC were on alert in west Munster following the report that Casement was in custody in Kerry but the motorists, although armed and with an out-of-date driver's licence, bluffed their way through the Newcastle West and Castleisland RIC checkpoints.

They arrived in good time for the Killarney Railway Station rendezvous on Good Friday. Having 'collected the fistfuls of grass which would be used for identification purposes'[10], they awaited the arrival of the 8 pm train. The agreed passwords were, 'Are you from Michael?'...'Yes, who are you'? The Dublin men's reply to that would be, 'I am from William.'[11] After that exchange and after showing the fistfuls of grass the raiding party headed into Iveragh on a very misty evening. The five-man Dublin party insisted upon a cover story indicating they were delivering a new car to Mr Horton in Waterville. This clashed with the account offered by the Limerick drivers at earlier RIC checkpoints.

Windrim travelled with Colm Ó Lochlainn and Denis Daly, who said that he knew the road. Windrim's car refused to halt for a Killorglin RIC man at 9.15pm. Soon afterwards when the second car – carrying Con Keating, the radio man, Tommy McInerney, Charles Monaghan from Belfast and Donal Sheehan of Rollinson's Bridge, Templeglantine, County Limerick – approached Killorglin, 'a policeman held them up and was proving so inquisitive that Keating finally drew his revolver and ordered him off.'[12] Having lost sight of the Maxwell, the men enquired of a young girl about road directions to Caherciveen. 'One of the cars, with the only wireless operator on board, took two wrong turnings at Killorglin and ran out over Ballykissane Pier into the sea, and three of the four occupants...were drowned...They were the first casualties of the 1916 Rising.'[13] McInerney and Keating got out of the vehicle and tried to swim to safety but Keating was drowned.

When Windrim and his companions reached a Caherciveen under police alert they abandoned their project and returned safely to Killarney via Ballaghasheen, 'the Way of Oisín,' through the centre of the Iveragh Reeks. Denis Daly and Colm

Ó Lochlainn took the train from Killarney to Kingsbridge, Dublin. Explaining the inactivity of Kerry at Easter, 1916, after all the brave preparations that had been made, Desmond Ryan, the historian of the Rising, says, 'The events that paralysed Kerry were: a tragedy at Ballykissane Pier, the sudden arrival of Casement, the arrest of Austin Stack.'[14]

Three Irish Volunteers of this tense and tragic era are commemorated in their native parishes by the fine GAA stadia erected in their memories – Austin Stack Park, Tralee, Dick Fitzgerald Memorial Stadium, Killarney and Con Keating Park, Caherciveen. Three Casement memorials ring the north Kerry shoreline at McKenna's Fort, Banna Strand and Ballyheigue village. A large Celtic Cross stands as memorial at Ballykissane Pier where the Laune River, which drains the Killarney Lakes, meets the Atlantic. The GAA's Casement Park in West Belfast is likewise a memorial stadium.

LONELY BANNA STRAND

> *'Twas on Good Friday morning all in the month of May*
> *A German ship was signalling beyond there in the bay,*
> *'We've twenty thousand rifles here, all ready for to land,'*
> *But no answering signal came from the lonely Banna*
>   *Strand.*
>
> *A motor-car was dashing through the early-morning gloom,*
> *A sudden crash, and in the sea they went to meet their doom,*
> *Two Irish lads lay dying there just like their hopes so grand,*
> *They could not give the signal now from lonely Banna Strand.*

'No signal answers from the shore,' Sir Roger sadly said,
'No comrades here to welcome me, alas! they must be dead;
But I must do my duty and at once I mean to land,'
So in a boat he pulled ashore to lonely Banna Strand.

The German ships were lying there with rifles in galore.
Up came a British ship and spoke, 'No Germans reach the shore;
You are our Empire's enemy, and so we bid you stand.
No German foot shall e'er pollute the lonely Banna Strand.'

They sailed for Queenstown Harbour. Said the Germans:
     'We're undone,
The British are our masters man for man and gun for gun.
We've twenty thousand rifles here, but they never will reach
     land.
We'll sink them all and bid farewell to lonely Banna Strand.'

They took Sir Roger prisoner and sailed for London Town,
And in the Tower they laid him as a traitor to the Crown.
Said he: 'I'm no traitor,' but his trial he had to stand
For bringing German rifles to the lonely Banna Strand.

'Twas in an English prison that they led him to his death.
'I'm dying for my country,' he said with his last breath.
He's buried in a prison yard far from his native land,
The wild waves sing his Requiem on the lonely Banna
     Strand.[15]

Anonymous

16

FRONGOCH
'A VERITABLE UNIVERSITY OF REVOLUTION', 1916

> *And from their cells their voices swell*
> *And loudly call on you*
> *To ask, men, the task, men,*
> *That yet remains to do.*

So goes the street ballad of Dublin children about the Rising, sung by Dick Blake in Frongoch Internment Camp to the delight of Michael Collins and comrades. In *The Invisible Army* Desmond Ryan describes Collins's fellow-inmates 'All Ireland listens, every grade and type of Ireland urban, rural, exiled, home-staying, sane, mad, nondescript, in the diverse garbs of Ireland, with Ireland's many accents...'[1]

This motley group of 2,500 Irish detainees in Frongoch included thirty-seven Kerrymen. Among them were Dick Fitzgerald and four Killarney neighbours, harness-maker Mick Spillane of Bohereencaol, Pat O'Shea, Willie Horgan, and M.J. O'Sullivan a New Street shopkeeper. Maurice Horgan, who later became Commandant of 4th Battalion Kerry No. 2 Brigade IRA, gives a good account of the lead-up to the internment of the Kerry Volunteers after an uncertain and tragic Easter weekend in the county:

> On Holy Thursday evening Captain M. Spillane
> handed me a large envelope to hand to Bishop
> Mangan. I did not then know what the envelope
> contained. The Bishop did not approve of the
> contents and told me I was a foolish young man
> to allow myself to be led into trouble. I told this
> to M. Spillane and he told me that the envelope
> contained the Proclamation...I with Pat O'Shea,
> then Adjutant, Killarney Company, was instructed
> to go to the International Hotel to meet the driver
> of a motor car and to get him oil and petrol. The
> driver's name was McEnerney [*sic*], conveying
> Con Keating and others to Caherciveen. This car
> went over Ballykissane Pier and all the occupants
> except the driver were drowned...On Saturday
> morning I was sent to Tralee to inform the Brigade
> O/C Austin Stack of the mishap to the car...P. J.
> Cahill informed me that Austin Stack had been
> arrested and that he was Acting O/C...He gave
> me verbal orders...that Rathmore Volunteers were
> to proceed to Killarney and join up with Killarney
> Company, but were first to break up railway lines
> and all line of railway communication.
>
> The Killarney Company 'stood to' on Easter
> Sunday. Their orders were to proceed to Killarney
> Post Office and break and disconnect all lines of
> communication, then with Rathmore Company to
> march to Castleisland where other orders would
> await them...I returned to Killarney and 'stood to'

with the Company, fully armed and with rations, on Monday, Tuesday and Wednesday awaiting further orders. None came and the company was dismissed. The British rounded up the officers of the company on the following Monday.'[2]

On Dick Fitzgerald's way to internment in Frongoch in 1916 he spent shorter spells in the local Great Southern Railway Hotel (now the Malton) which was a military HQ, in the military prison in Victoria Barracks, Cork, and in Dublin's Richmond Barracks. Then he was transported via the North Wall to Knutsford Prison in Cheshire where he spent 'three weeks'.[3]

In March 2007, on the very day I first visited Lincoln and its famous jail from which Éamon De Valera escaped on the night of 3 February 1919, I received a gift of *A Family Memoir of Tomás Mac Curtáin* from his granddaughter Sheila Ward. It contains the following manuscript entry in Mac Curtáin's Irish prison diary: '*Leigeadh amach mé chun mé féin do nighe annsan chonnach go raibh ana chuid eile de's na buachaillí sa charcar im' theannta. Bhí in aice liom Dickeen Fitz – (Captaon lucht imireatha líathroide Ciarraidhe) – ó Chill Áirne.*'[4] 'I was allowed out to wash myself and then I saw that there was a great number of the boys in jail with me. Near me was Dickeen Fitz (captain of the Kerry football team) from Killarney.' He names fifteen fellow inmates in Victoria Barracks, and according to an accompanying note there is a blank space to include further names as they occurred to him.

After the execution of the leaders of the Rising in Dublin, British military commander Sir John Maxwell turned his attention to Volunteers and sympathisers nationwide. In all 2,519 Irish people were arrested and deported to ten British jails during 1916. On 11 May 1916 Tomás Mac Curtáin was arrested in his own home and placed in Victoria Barracks in Cork:

> On Wednesday 31 May 1916 we got orders to prepare ourselves to cross the Irish Sea to England…headed to Kingsbridge Station (Dublin)…The people gathered and followed, and by the time we reached O'Connell Bridge thousands gathered around us and they shouted, roared and cursed the soldiers – they were vicious against the soldiers…we noticed the results of the 1916 Rising, houses were in ruins around Sackville [now O'Connell] Street and the Bridge…We went on board ship at the North Wall and were put in amongst the cattle.[5]

Mac Curtáin was first sent to Wakefield Prison and 'on Saturday morning, 10 June 1916 at 10 am went by train to Frongoch in North Wales…and it was there that they took from me my note book that I had from the beginning and they would not return it.'[6] German prisoners of war were moved to make way for the Irish detainees in a former distillery set high in bleak North Wales near Barra. Tomás and Michael Collins 'were allowed to mix and the leaders set about keeping the men busy. Classes were set up – Irish and history lessons – and an air of self-imposed discipline descended on the prison. Tomás and Michael put the time to good use and began to plan for the future…two weeks later he (Tomás) was sent to Reading Jail, and found Terry Mac (Swiney) in the adjoining cell.'[7]

> On 11 July, a group of 30 men, including most of the leadership were transferred to Reading Jail…

Terence MacSwiney...Tomás Mac Curtáin, Seán T. O'Kelly [later President of Ireland 1945-59]... the prisoners decided to hold an impromptu banquet. Invitations to the banquet were issued styled 'Farewell banquet to the Irish Huns on their departure from Frongoch, North Wales'. Continuing in this humorous vein the invitation was extended by the Ministry of the Interior and the banquet was timed to begin at 6pm on 10 July. Music was to be provided by Kilmartin's Orchestra under the baton of Richard Fitzgerald. A meal with meat was prepared, tea was served and cigars and cigarettes distributed...

The camp authorities continued to remove prisoners who they deemed gave leadership to the others, or, as the British put it, 'in the interest of the discipline of the camp'. Notwithstanding the removal to Reading Jail of the prisoners' leaders on at least three occasions, a new crop of quality leaders came forward each time. This was indicative of the depth of talent among the men in Frongoch'.[8]

Seán O'Mahony from Castleisland, whose comments on the Frongoch leadership is given above, is one of the few students of Irish history to concentrate on this north Wales internment camp. The blurb of his 1987 book, *Frongoch – University of Revolution*, indicates how Sinn Féin took full advantage of this opportunity to both 'develop the philosophy of revolution' and make ready for the War of Independence. During 2005 the North Wales Stage/Project Arts 6 Production presented the drama *Frongoch* at various Irish theatres including Siamsa

Tíre, Tralee and Limerick's Belltable Arts Centre. This focused particular attention on the camp's Welsh-born medical officer Dr Peters MD who took his own life in the Tryween River. A novel feature of the production was the screening of the name of every single Irish inmate of Frongoch. O'Mahony states: 'The men felt a general regret at the death of Dr Peters…(who) was intimidated from discharging his professional duties many times by the camp authorities.'[9] A newspaper reported: 'A verdict of suicide while of unsound mind was returned at the coroner's inquest. It was stated he was worried by statements concerning the treatment of prisoners.'[10]

In *Dublin's Fighting Story* John Brennan analyses 'Frongoch University and after, 1916-1919'. Seán O'Mahony relates that Tim Healy MP visited Frongoch during August 1916.[11] The origin of the camp's alleged university status springs from the way in which it was described by Tim Healy in the British House of Commons as 'a Sinn Féin University'. 'It became almost the equivalent of a military academy in which insurrectionary forces enlisted new recruits, and planned to re-arm, re-organise and resume the war against England as early as possible'.[12] According to Brennan: 'There were moments of relaxation even in Frongoch. For instance there was 'Croke Park', in which many an exciting football match was played, and where Dick Fitzgerald, captain of the Kerry team, could be seen in action'[13]:

> The pitch in Frongoch was called Croke Park after the GAA stadium in Dublin. Major fixtures were advertised throughout the camp by means of posters. The admission to games was said to be five shillings and the internees were advised to leave their wives and sweethearts at home! Dick

Fitzgerald from Killarney, who captained Kerry to All-Ireland victories in 1913 and 1914, was a key organiser of Gaelic football in the camp. Among the prisoners there were two others who captained their counties to All-Ireland successes prior to their internment and shared this rare distinction with Fitzgerald. Among the fine crop of footballers and hurlers were Frank Burke, Bill Flaherty, Frank Shouldice, Brian Joyce, Paddy Cahill, Seamus Dobbin, Stephen Jordan, Michael Collins, Billy Mullins, M.J. Moriarty, Sean O'Duffy and Benny McAllister.

Two matches were played daily and the men were keen to be exercising and stretching themselves after jail confinement. The games were physical and tough, and the rough behaviour led one guard to comment to another, 'If that's what they're like at play, they must be bloody awful in a fight.'

A league competition was organised among four teams and each team had to compete in six games. The teams were called in honour of the leaders executed after the Rising and Frank Burke recalled that South Camp teams played with a blue stripe running from the right shoulder to left waist, while North Camp sported red stripes. Three teams were fielded by South Camp, which housed a good sprinkling of fine footballers.

The fourth team was nicknamed 'the Leprecauns' because it included many players of small stature. They were coached by Dick Fitzgerald, who knew all the tricks and skills of the game. To everybody's surprise the Leprecauns won the competition in

South Camp and afterwards won a competition organised in North Camp when South Camp was closed. Dick Fitzgerald may have peaked as a footballer a few years earlier, but Séamus Ó Maoileoin, a County Westmeath volunteer who write a book about the troubles called *B'fhiú an Braon Fola* ('It Was Worth the Drop of Blood Spilled'), thought Dickeen was better in Frongoch than he ever was in Croke Park in his heyday.

In July a token final of the Wolfe Tone Tournament (a football tournament played every year in Croke Park) took place in Frongoch between Kerry and Louth. Billy Mullins of Kerry recalled that it was the most important game played in the camp and also a repeat of the 1913 Railway Shield Final between these two counties. We can assume there was plenty of 'needle' in the game. W.J. Brennan-Whitmore of Ferns, County Wexford, who was Camp Adjutant, recalled that a veterans' match was also played and that both players and spectators enjoyed it thoroughly. As well as inter-county games, matches were played by teams chosen from the four provinces.

The Frongoch sportsday took place on 8 August and there were competitions in the main track and field events. Michael Collins won the 100 yards race from M. W. O'Reilly, Commandant No. 2 Camp. O'Reilly quotes Collins as saying when overtaking him 'Ah, you whore, you can't run.' Sean Hales of Bandon, who had been Munster Champion in this event, won the 56lb throw by a few yards. His fellow Corkman Michael Collins was runner-up. In a debate in the House of Commons, reference was made to these sports: a suave cabinet minister, Major Newman, held that the food in the camp couldn't have been too bad as the prisoners 'had a concourse over which they did 100-yard sprints…they had hop, step and jump and other sports…'[14]

Dreaming In Frongoch.

Listen! I hear it! No! I cried,
She is not sitting by my side,
  I sit and muse till dreams efface
  The consciousness of time and space;
  And then the rustle of the wind
  Brings her sweet treble to my mind:
Words, once, like low-breathed prayers, whose tone
was prayer and answer both in one —
Words, now, like farewells wafted o'er
  The waves to a receding shore —

Frongoch,
Camp Adjt.   23
                      Oct.
                      1916.

W. J. Brennan Whitmore
                    Comdt.
          Field Intelligence Officer
          Chief of General Staff, I.R.A.

Clonee Ferns,
Co. Wexford

G.P.O
North Earl St.,
Imperial Hotel.

"Educate that you may be free".
          — Davis.

Poem by W.J. Brennan-Whitmore in
Frongoch Autograph Album (Courtesy of Maura Allman [Ring])

Dick Fitzgerald and his three Killarney neighbours, Sullivan, Horgan and O'Shea, were released on 1 August, just in time for the All-Ireland Semi-Final against Mayo. Ennis hosted this match five days later. The *Killarney Echo* reported: 'It was worth being in Frongoch and other parts to come out and be welcomed as Dick was…At the entrance of the teams, the Kerry captain received a great ovation…Our senior team, or what could be collected together of it, had to meet Mayo'.[15] Historian T. Ryle Dwyer recounts that six of the winning Kerry Juniors 'were drafted into the senior team which proceeded to lose by just two points.'[16]

Signature of Austin Stack in
Frongoch Autograph Album (Courtesy of Maura Allman [Ring])

Dickeen's freedom was short-lived because 'on 22 September M. J. Moriarty of Dingle, Dick Fitzgerald of Killarney, Timothy Ring of Caherciveen and John Francis O'Shea of Portmagee arrived back at the Camp. They had been arrested under the Defence of the Realm Act. No charges were brought against them…' It doesn't look as if we're going home when they send back Fitzgerald and Moriarty,' was a common refrain among the inmates. Others claimed that the Kerry crowd had sent Fitzgerald and Moriarty back so that Kerry could win the football in the camp.'[17] This was Dick Fitzgerald's sixth spell in jail since Easter 1916; eventually he was released at Christmas of that year.

In his memoirs Billy Mullins recalls: 'The Kerry contingent, comprising fourteen men, travelled home on one voucher, held by Henry Spring of Firies. Going through England he spied 'bar and restaurant' on a railway platform so he offered to buy all the lads a drink. The drinks were served but the lady behind the counter refused to accept one payment as there was an anti-treating law in force. Between her English and his Kerry brogue, impasse was reached and a police inspector was summoned. He too failed to resolve the problems as he faced similar difficulties. The exasperated officer, who wanted these people out of his jurisdiction, bundled them on the next train. So the fourteen Kerrymen 'enjoyed a Christmas drink at the expense of John Bull'.

And so the men returned home for Christmas. They came back as heroes to a land that earlier in the year had spurned them. In the struggle for national liberation, 1916 was a momentous year – the Easter Rising had sparked the flame of freedom. The men who had organised the Rebellion were clear of mind and firm of purpose; but they were dead. Those who ended up in Frongoch may have been uncertain and hesitant but in the camp a new certainty and a new purpose evolved. In the shared experiences of the men, a consensus about what lay ahead, was formed. From disparate elements a national amalgam was forged.

The men returned to a country that had changed utterly since they had left it a short time before. The Home Rule Party was doomed to extinction; the middle classes were nervous and insecure; the government was watchful and suspicious; and the Church, as always, was determined to be on the winning side. But the most important transformation had taken place among the ordinary people. For a while at least they were determined to have done with an empire that had trod on them for centuries. The spirit of freedom was blowing across the land. The men of Frongoch had indeed returned home for Christmas, but soon they would be ready to strike another blow against the ancient enemy. The next time they would not be beaten.[18]

In his biography of Michael Collins his fellow-revolutionary Leon Ó Broin called Frongoch 'a veritable University of Revolution'.[19]

Paddy Foley (the Dingle-born writer and journalist known as 'P.F.') prefaced his comments on the scene in his native Kerry in 1916 by acknowledging that 'an unofficial All-Ireland was played at Frongoch between Kerry, captained by Dick Fitzgerald, and Louth under the captaining of Old Tom Burke. Kerry won by a point. At home it was no time for football.'[20] The *Kerryman*, for which P.F. later worked as sports journalist, relates how its plant was dismantled and the paper suppressed by the military for a six-week period. This is not surprising, given that both its co-founders were avowed nationalists. Managing Director Maurice Griffin was detained in Wakefield Prison in England while Tom Nolan constantly promoted the fund-raising activities of the Irish Volunteers Dependants' Fund of which he was President. A group of North Kerry nationalist sympathisers were fined under the Defence of the Realm regulations for singing a rebel song: 'Activities on the Kerry playing fields came to a standstill, as other events of historic significance succeeded each other in rapid succession…Many years were to elapse before sporting conditions in the Kingdom again became normal.'[21]

Dickeen Brings Clare Footballers
to All-Ireland Final, 1917

Clare, who were All-Ireland Senior Hurling champions for the first time in 1914, contested the Senior Football Final in Croke Park under trainer Dick Fitzgerald three years later. Kerry did not contest the 1917 championship. Clare's spirit was epitomised by their unusual sporting slogan and distinctive banner: 'Up de Valera'. This was the first time Éamon de Valera was elected Westminster MP for East Clare. He was one of four Sinn Féin candidates successful on an abstentionist ticket during 1917. He went on to hold this seat until he retired from the Dáil to become President of Ireland in 1959.

Much had ensued during the post-Frongoch year. According to historian T. Ryle Dwyer: 'Having been deported in disgrace little over a year earlier, the men returned to Ireland to a great welcome. De Valera was undoubtedly the hero of the hour: he was now the widely accepted leader of the men of Easter week.'[1] Once de Valera was released from prison he added Presidency of the Irish Volunteers and Sinn Féin to his roles during 1917.

The GAA had a £2,000 credit balance and 'unanimously decided not to pay the entertainment tax and to reconvene if the government tried to enforce its collection'.[2] As the year advanced, cases were brought against the Association by the government. Limerick became a test case when the County Secretary, James Ryan, was summoned for refusing to allow RIC members to enter a game to investigate if the statutory entertainment tax was being paid. GAA Congress reconvened when Dublin County Board lost its tax case and issued a defiant resolution: 'That no club, county or province pay the tax.'[3] This brought the whole saga to an end. 'So far as can now be ascertained the British government made no further effort to collect the tax from the GAA.'[4]

To help the dependants of those who took part in the 1916 Rising two aid funds were established. Aid came from many sources, including the USA, but the GAA became the principal fund-raiser with hurling and football games organised right across the country. The 1917 Committee was the result of the amalgamation of the Irish Volunteers Dependants' Fund founded by the widow of executed leader Tom Clarke and Dublin Corporation's Irish National Aid Association. Joe McGrath, later to be a Free State government minister, become first secretary of the Irish National Aid Volunteer Dependants Fund and was soon replaced by Michael Collins. A three-man executive steered this very influential movement, which became popularly know as 'National Aid'. 'The GAA became the principal source of National Aid funds...served to restore morale after the failure of the Rising and to involve in the political aims of the executed leaders many who had hitherto held aloof from the separatist movement.'[5] Although the government maintained its ban on the use of trains to bring supporters to GAA matches, increasing the number of trains to race meetings, the GAA flourished during 1917: '7,000 attended the Wolfe Tone Memorial Final in late August and by now £400 had been collected for National Aid.'[6]

Harry Boland had emerged as an enthusiastic GAA activist and mentor. He was re-elected Chairman of Dublin County Board in 1916, and Austin Stack was re-elected Chairman of Kerry County Board. In late November 1917 the Volunteers choose to hold their third annual convention in Croke Park.

The *Saturday Record* of 1 December 1917 celebrates the exceptional and unexpected success of the local Banner County's senior footballers. 'As 1916 was an eventful year for Ireland, 1917 has been, and we hope will be, an eventful one for Clare. This year the Clare football team has proved to be a "dark horse". Clare was supposed to be rather backward in football, but all doubts have been rudely dispelled by Clare's sudden jump from practical oblivion into prominence of first magnitude.'[7] Thus the Clare journalist pens his tribute to the reigning Munster champions, who qualified to meet a fine Wexford team seeking three All-Ireland titles in a row.

The story began in Waterford on 15 July 1917, when 'Clare entered the arena this year with a new untried team against Waterford of whom they disposed by a comfortable margin.'[89] The first round score line was 2-6 to 0-3. 'The next battle, against Tipperary, was much stiffer, but they won after a hard struggle.'[9] This second round championship match refereed by T. Irwin of Limerick was played in the Market's Field, Limerick on Sunday 26 August, resulting in a one-point victory for the men from Clare, 0-5 to 0-4. The 1917 Munster Senior Final was a repeat of the previous year: 'Then followed the game with Cork, and after a brilliant and scientific encounter, Clare emerged victorious.'[10] The final against Cork, hosted in Tipperary town on Sunday 15 October, was refereed by Waterford's Willie Walsh, who had been interned after the 1916 Rising. 'After an evenly-contested first half the Banner took control of the exchanges to win by

5-4 to 0-1.'[11] The defending champions were dealt an eighteen-point defeat by an ever-improving Clare side.

It is difficult to ascertain at what point Dick Fitzgerald entered the Banner County's winning odyssey as trainer. As Munster Council delegate Dick Fitzgerald would have been well known to the Clare delegates, especially James 'Sham' Spellissey, a fellow Provincial delegate who was a playing member of the successful 1914 hurling team. 'Kilkeeman and Kildare native Jim Foran, all 6'3' of him organised the training for the side with 1914 hurler Sham Spellissey.'[12] The publication of Fitzgerald's ground-breaking instructional book *How to Play Gaelic Football* in 1914 and his acknowledged All-Ireland experience – in particular against Wexford – no doubt encouraged the Clare mentors to seek Dick Fitzgerald's help. 'Tull' Considine and Liam Stack, both IRA officers, may have personally known Dick.

'Finally came the game at Athlone with Galway, on Sunday 18 November It is no secret that Galway previously trained for the game, and the fact that Clare not only won but won well proves Clare, with a reasonable amount of training should secure premier honours. Everyone expected that Galway would "wipe of" Clare, and it must be something of a surprise when the result proved entirely the other way. The best team had certainly won, and the victors thus qualified for All-Ireland competition.'[13] 'Clare were best against Galway 2-1 to 0-4. Martin McNamara and Eddie Carroll got the Clare goals and 'Tull' Considine the point. Clare were into their first All-Ireland Final against Wexford who were going for their third successive title.'[14]

The appeal for the Clare team's training fund was widely publicised, with three Miltown-Malbay men in charge of all subscriptions – Chairman J. Fitzpatrick assisted by Treasurer P. Killeen and H. Roche, Honorary Secretary. The advertisement in the *Clare Champion* said they 'expect generous subscriptions from all true Gaels in the Banner County. All subscriptions only acknowledged in Clare papers.'[15] 'Miltown-Malbay Club (County Clare champions) have been entrusted with the selection… and to Miltown the credit is due for having brought them so far.'[16]

'Will Clare win?…Clare represents a historic county…The present Clare team is certainly a good one. The team enters training for a fortnight, and by strict hard gruelling should be in a fit condition to uphold successfully the honour of the old county. The team is undergoing a very hard course of training in Kilkee and will strip very fit. It is the first time the Clare Football Team has trained for a match.'[17]

Tipperary journalist and author Raymond Smith ranks some of these Bannermen among the 'Football Immortals':

> Wexford had two titles in the bag and in their bid for the three-timer in 1917 were opposed by Clare.
>
> President de Valera had been elected Sinn Féin candidate for Clare. There was a surge of nationalistic feeling and Aidan Doyle recalled that neutral spectators were behind Clare to a man. Harry Boland carried the Sinn Féin flag at the head of the parade – and to the crowd the Claremen were patriots all and they wanted it very much to be the Banner County's day.
>
> Clare had done two weeks collective training in Kilkee under Sham Spellissey, a member of the victorious hurling team in 1914. The emphasis was on route marching to build up stamina rather than on football practice.
>
> It was not lack of stamina or football ability

that proved Clare's undoing but rather lack of experience of playing the parallelogram on the big occasion. They had a goal and a point disallowed for 'square' infringements – and they were only beaten in the end by four points. Jim Foran generously acknowledged that Ned Wheeler at full-back was the match-winner for Wexford.

'Big Jim' Foran from Kildare stood 6 ft. 3 ins., was captain of Clare and The Blues (Kilkee). A fine figure of a man, quiet but commanding, his word was law. No one dared break the training schedules for club or county – and no man could think that he was indispensable, no matter how great his ability. Jim Foran's courage was a byword on and off the field. They talk to this day in Kilkee of the time when two girls were drowned in the summer season and Jim Foran led a few fishermen colleagues out in a boat against the mountainous seas to search for the bodies.

He had fine footballers under him steeled in memorable club games between Kilkee, Kilrush and Miltown Malbay – Tull Considine of Ennis at midfield, star of the 1932 hurling semi-final against Galway (with eight goals to his credit) and brother of Brendan; Pa O'Brien of Cooraclare at centre back; Martin McNamara of Ballykett on the '40'; Ned Carroll of Miltown on the wing; Mick Conole of Kilfenora in goal…also Paddy O'Donoghue of Ballyvaughan, Ned Roche, Michael Malone and Jim Fitzgerald of Miltown and Michael McMahon, Kilrush Shamrocks…[18]

In *All Ireland Glory*, Frank Burke hails the new force in the Munster and national sporting arenas.

> In the final Wexford were warm favourites to make it three in a row but Clare made them fight every inch of the way. Clare were trained by Dick Fitzgerald (Kerry) and they tore into the champions as if their lives depended on it. The robust tactics upset Wexford who found scores hard to come by. Wexford had enough class and experience to ride out the storm and led at half-time 0-6 to 0-4. In the second-half Wexford maintained the distance between the teams and won by 0-9 to 0-5.[19]

IN PRAISE OF HEROES: WEXFORD 1915–18

> *Hurrah for Gorey and New Ross*
> *And bold Bunclody too,*
> *And 'Tearin' Tom' from Ballyhogue,*
> *So quick to dare and do!*
> *And Wexford town of old renown –*
> *We'll cheer them on the breeze,*
> *And one cheer more will give a score*
> *For the dauntless Rapparees.*
>
> *Now, God be praised for men like these –*
> *The thoughts our proud souls fill.*
> *They're worthy sons of those who died*
> *For freedom on our hills.*
> *God bless the men of Wexford,*
> *God bless the women too,*
> *And keep to their motherland*
> *In joy and sorrow through![20]*

Anti-Conscription, 1918

Austin Stack and Dick Fitzgerald represented Kerry at the All-Ireland GAA Congress held in the Mansion House in Dublin on 31 March 1918. Kerry announced that they were back in business now that the GAA players imprisoned over the previous few months had been released. The Central Council, which enjoyed a credit balance of £2,071/2s/3d, granted a subvention to the Kerry County Board. 'Congress responded to an appeal from Austin Stack with an immediate grant of £100; later an inter-county football tournament (Kerry versus Wexford) was successfully organised by the Council to raise more money for the county, the final attracting 12,000 to Croke Park in June.'[1]

Jack Mahon, in his *History of Gaelic Football* reports 'a low scoring game, with Wexford leading 0-1 to nil at half-time. In the second half Wexford proved to be worthy champions but the wonderful Gus Kennedy picked up a knee injury, the beginning of the end of a great career.'[2] Profits from the gate amounted to £277 and went towards revitalising Kerry GAA. This attendance is all the more striking because the government's ban on trains to GAA games was still in operation.

The month of April 1918 was a time of acute anxiety for the British government. For three weeks the British Army in France had been sustaining a terrific attack on a front of fifty miles…

The government decided that conscription of Irishmen was to begin as soon as the necessary preparations were completed.'³ Lloyd George's government's ploy to offer a measure of Home Rule while enforcing conscription was strongly rejected. A broadly-based conference convened in the Mansion House, Dublin, on 18 April 1918 rejected conscription and proposed that every parish should sign the Anti-Conscription Pledge drafted by Éamon de Valera: 'Denying the right of the British Government to enforce compulsory service in this country we pledge ourselves solemnly to one another to resist conscription by the most effective means at our disposal.'⁴

The war on the Conscription Bill intensified the same day as conference members sent a delegation to the Irish bishops' meeting in Maynooth. The hierarchy met Lord Mayor O'Neill of Dublin, Éamon de Valera, John Dillon, T. M. Healy and Labour's William O'Brien, and issued the following manifesto: 'We consider that the conscription forced in this way upon Ireland is an oppressive and inhuman law which the Irish people have a right to resist by every means that are consonant with the law of God'.⁵

The following Sunday, 21 April, the Anti-Conscription Pledge was signed at Catholic church doors 'by nearly all Nationalist Ireland'.⁶ Two days later a general strike was organised nationally, affecting transport, businesses and shops everywhere except Belfast. In a wide-ranging swoop on the night of 17 May police arrested seventy-three Sinn Féin leaders including de Valera, Arthur Griffith, William Cosgrave, Count Plunkett and three leading women, Countess Markievicz, Maud Gonne McBride and Kathleen Clarke. All were transported to British jails without trial and for unlimited detention. Michael Collins succeeded in eluding the authorities.

There was a big anti-conscription meeting in Killarney and all sides turned out for it. John Murphy, ex-MP, took the chair (self-constituted) and suddenly said 'Mick Spillane will now address you.' Though not much given to public speaking, [Spillane] did address the crowd and told them what they should do in no uncertain manner. The RIC, of course, were taking notes but stayed outside the crowd. The Volunteers organised collections for the anti-conscription fund… The first job Mick Spillane did after his release (from Durham Prison) was to return the Anti-Conscription money to the subscribers. There were only three who took it back. The remainder asked that it be given to GHQ There must have been about £1,000 in all, and it was accordingly done.[7]

The rallying cry of the volunteers in Killarney:

A NATION ONCE AGAIN

When boyhood's fire was in my blood,
I read of ancient freemen,
For Greece and Rome who bravely stood,
Three hundred men and three men,
And then I prayed I yet might see
Our fetters rent in twain,
And Ireland, long a province,
Be a nation once again.

Chorus
A nation once again,
A nation once again

And Ireland long a province,
Be a nation once again.

And, from that time through wildest woe,
That hope has shone, a far light;
Nor could love's brightest summer glow
Outshine that stolen starlight;
It seemed to watch above my head
In forum, field and fane;
Its angel voice sang round my bed,
'A nation once again'.
Chorus

It whispered, too, that freedom's ark
And service high and holy,
Would be profaned by feelings dark
And passions vain and lowly;
For freedom comes from God's right hand,
And needs a godly train;
And righteous men must make our land
A nation once again.
Chorus

So, as I grew from boy to man,
I bent me to that bidding –
My spirit of each selfish plan
And cruel passion ridding;
For, thus I hoped some day to aid –
Oh, can such hope be vain?
When my dear country shall be made
A nation once again.
Chorus[8]

SINN FÉIN LANDSLIDE
AND GAELIC SUNDAY, 1918

In early July 1918 the government proscribed Sinn Féin, the Volunteers and Cumann na mBan. Furthermore, Dublin Castle issued an order banning all public meetings held without an official permit. As this edict effectively ended all GAA meetings and games the Association met it head-on by organising what became known as 'Gaelic Sunday'. Central Council met on 20 July and passed two resolutions. It resolved never to seek an official permit and called on every County Board to organise football and hurling games at 3 pm on Sunday 4 August. The GAA was clearly in a defiant mood.

Dublin's Luke O'Toole placed advertisements in the press on Saturday 3 August reiterating Central Council's command and predicting: '54,000 Gaels will actively participate in national pastimes all over Ireland.' In Dublin alone twenty-four matches were held despite RIC interference. Since the armed forces prevented entry to Croke Park the ladies held their camogie challenge on the road outside the stadium. Games were held nationwide – 'fifteen hundred hurling matches were played in Ireland'.[1] In his book *A History of the Gaelic Athletic Association*, Marcus de Búrca maintains that 'much closer to 100,000' togged out in what 'became notable as the greatest single act of defiance outside the purely political sphere between 1916 and 1922.'[2] Former Kerry player Donie O'Sullivan notes: 'Gaelic Sunday was a huge success. Crowds, some of whom were attending GAA activities for the first time, were present at games all over the country…After "Gaelic Sunday" the police ceased to interfere with the games. The *Kerryman* of August 10 announced: Gaelic Games all over Ireland – No Police Interference.'[3]

The 22nd Oireachtas planned for Belfast was proscribed by the authorities. As the Killarney branch of the Gaelic League, Craobh na nÁirne, had successfully hosted the 1914 festival, Killarney was chosen as a last-minute venue.

'The attendance on opening day was very good…a number of Anzac soldiers and some Australian, New Zealand and American officers'[4] on furlough from the World War I trenches enjoyed the cultural activities. Lusk Pipers, founded by Lispole's Thomas Ashe, won the Pipe Band competition.

Oireachtas 1918 coincided with Gaelic Sunday (4 August) but the Killarney weather forced the organisers to abandon two planned challenge matches. However, the men of Kenmare lined out to face their Kilgarvan hurling neighbours in a friendly match with Dick Fitzgerald acting as referee. Eoin Mac Néill and Seán T. O'Kelly issued a joint statement in Irish lamenting the fact that many colleagues were imprisoned both at home and in England and called upon all Gaels to support the cause of language and liberation.[5]

Dick Fitzgerald, who was a member of the Kerry selectors for 1918, does not figure on the Kingdom line-out for the first time since 1903. Kerry's first team since 1915 defeated the 1917 All-Ireland runners-up Clare at the Market's Field, Limerick by 5-3 to 1-3. Tipperary were none too confident facing the Kerrymen in the Athletic Grounds, Cork on Sunday 22 September 1918 with Cork's P.D. Mehigan or 'Carbery' as referee. 'In the final Kerry were hot favourites but Tipperary got a great start with a great goal by Billie Grant. Kerry replied with a point by Con Clifford just before half-time. The only score in the second-half was a point by David Tobin for Tipperary. The full time score was Tipperary 1-1; Kerry 0-1.'[6]

World War I ended on 11 November 1918 with the loss of 8.4 million lives. '49,000 Irishmen, citizens of Ireland and thousands of the Irish race from America and Australia and other countries had fallen in the war.'[7] It is estimated that the Spanish flu, which spread across Europe, resulted in the deaths of almost as many at this very time. Lloyd George called a general election and on 25 November the British parliament was dissolved. Sinn Féin were ready to contest the election and female supporters were pleased that for the first time women over thirty years of age could vote and stand for parliament:

> Sinn Féin now stood for sovereign independence and an Irish Republic…[it] was working under great disabilities; more than a hundred of its responsible leaders, men and women, were in jail; a great part of the country was under military rule; Sinn Féin itself and every other national organisation was banned; all Republican papers had been suppressed and every newspaper in the country was under censorship; the whole election machinery and the Post Office were under British control; experienced Republican speakers and organisers of nearly every town and village in Ireland were in prison and their places had to be

filled by novices. It was in these circumstances that Sinn Féin nominated candidates and appointed Robert Brennan to direct its election campaign.

The drafting of the election manifesto was a matter of deep deliberation: 'Sinn Féin aims at securing the establishment of that Republic.

By withdrawing the Irish Representation from the British Parliament, and by denying the right and opposing the will of the British Government, or any other foreign Government to legislate for Ireland.

By making use of any and every means available to render impotent the power of England to hold Ireland in subjection by military force or otherwise.'[8]

Commandant Maurice Horgan submitted his memoirs to the Bureau of Military History on 3 June 1954. 'I was recruited into the Killarney Company by the late Dick Fitzgerald.' Below is his account of the 1918 general election:

The Volunteers were ordered to take control and we were asked to proceed to Dublin to help in the election campaign of the late Seán McGarry. I was accompanied by Dick Fitzgerald, T. O'Shea (now D.J., Kilkenny), P. S. Devane and Seán Kerins. When we reached Dublin we found this campaign was overcrowded with helpers and we were ordered to Donegal with Seán Ó Muirthuile in charge of our party to help in the election of J. Sweeney. We worked there and returned to Dublin after polling day.

The German plot came about this time and Michael Spillane was arrested. I took over duty and was subsequently elected O/C, 4th Battalion, by the Battalion officers.

The British Military were stationed at the Great Southern Railway Hotel, Killarney, about 800 strong. An aeríocht [rally] billed for Killarney was proclaimed by the military. Large contingents of Volunteers came into the town, as also did RIC from Cork and Limerick. A football match was also proclaimed, the teams taking part in the match being John Mitchels, Tralee, versus Dr Crokes, Killarney. The members of the teams on their way to the playing field were attacked and batoned by the RIC, who were supported by the military with fixed bayonets. The aeríocht could not be held in the advertised place but was held at Allen's farm, Madam's Height. An Oireachtas was held the same year in Killarney and was managed by the Volunteers. Special services were organised in the Volunteers – signalling, first-aid and intelligence. Special units comprising these were formed in each Company area and functioned. The Volunteers' activities became more intense and, as a result, Volunteers were being arrested and held in RIC and military barracks. Killarney Cumann na mBan supplied all their meals, which were prepared and provided by the late Mrs B. Twomey, Glebe Place, Killarney. All outside RIC barracks had been burned and main Headquarters for RIC and Military was Killarney, all their activities branching out from here. The Volunteers took over the Rural District Council and control of all monies used by them, directing the Manager of the National Bank that we wanted account changed to the names of Pat Mahony, Tim O'Sullivan and Dick Fitzgerald.'[9]

Polling day was 14 December and the election results were declared on 28 December 1918. The election resulted in the annihilation of the Irish Parliamentary Party, which lost seventy-three of its 80 Westminster seats. Sinn Féin won seventy-three seats and polled a 70 per cent total in favour of the Republic, while the Unionists secured twenty-six seats. The revolutionary role of east Kerry women during this period has not been well documented. Kate Breen, who later became active in local politics as a Sinn Féin member of Killarney UDC, was a sister of the parish priest commemorated at Kenmare's Canon Breen Memorial Park. She was one of the five Cumann na mBan members from Killarney who were detained in Cork Jail in 1919. Killarney author and master printer Paddy MacMonagle recognised the active involvement of local women in his 1979 publication, *Echoes From Killarney*, celebrating the tenth annual reunion of exiles in London. His book includes a historical photograph from the Daniel MacMonagle archive which shows the rousing reception at Killarney Railway Station that marked the homecoming of imprisoned Cumann na mBan members. The jarvey driving the waggonette was Billy Lynch, a member of the Kingdom's 1903 All-Ireland winning side. He and his brother Jack played on the Dr Crokes first County-Championship-winning team of 1901. Jack married Ann Dillon, sister of goalie Pat, and all of them lived in Brewery Lane.

Cumann na mBan members are welcomed home to Killarney Railway Station, 1919. Left to right jarvey William Lynch and son Billy, Peg Cahill, Lottie Foley, Brigid Gleeson, Kate Breen and Etta Woods with Tricolour. Facing camera on left is Maurice Horgan (Kerry No. 2 Brigade) who later married Etta Woods. (Picture courtesy Paddy MacMonagle.)

Munster Champions Tipperary defeated Mayo in Croke Park on 12 January 1919 on a score 2-2 to 1-4. Dick Fitzgerald refereed both semi-finals of the 1918 campaign. Johnny Skinner, the All-Ireland winning Kerry panellist and protégé of Dick Fitzgerald, had found employment in Clonmel and declared for Tipperary. The final had been seriously delayed by the devastation caused by the Spanish flu pandemic of 1918–19 and by the Soloheadbeg incident of 21 January 1919 when members of the Third Tipperary Brigade ambushed a RIC party carrying

gelignite and killed two policemen. This incident coincided with
the day of the first meeting of the new Dáil, the forum for the
seventy-three Sinn Féin TDs in December's landslide victory.
The action of Dan Breen, Seán Treacy, Seamus Robinson, Seán
Hogan and their companions at Soloheadbeg is recognised
as the critical opening salvo of what is known as the War of
Independence. Austin Stack TD, who was appointed substitute
Minister for Home Affairs in the First Dáil, would soon be
turning his energies to the next phase of the revolutionary
campaign in Kerry: to rid Ireland of British rule. Dick Fitzgerald
and his east Kerry Volunteer comrades were soon engaged in
this struggle and would be taking to the Reeks.

My late father recalled how his uncle Pat Dillon used to row
across Loch Léin to O'Sullivan's Cascade to bring supplies and
messages to Dick Fitz and his column. The suspicions of the
authorities were not raised as Dillon, the former Kerry goalie
who had lost an arm in a railway accident, did not appear to
pose a security threat. In fact, Dick Fitzgerald spearheaded a
successful benefit match in Croke Park in 1919 in aid of his
former team colleague and later brother-in-law. The testimony
of Spillane and O'Sullivan to the Bureau of Military History,
recorded on 8 June 1953, gives the following account of the
manoeuvres of the Kerry No 2 column in the Black Valley:

> Kerry II Brigade Active Service Unit was started
> on 5 March 1921. It was to consist of twenty-
> six men, five from each battalion. Mick Spillane
> volunteered and was refused on the grounds of
> being an indispensable senior officer.
>
> The brigade ASU took up quarters in the Gap
> of Dunloe on 5 March. The twenty-eight men of

the Black Valley Company had to act as armed sentries during day and night while the ASU were being trained. They had also to provide food and carry despatches – these had to be brought on foot for eighteen miles between Brigade HQ in the Gap and Kilgarvan, where they were conveyed further by others to reach Division HQ.

It is hard to imagine the work involved for this small Company in affording security, rations and means of communication for three important units, i.e., brigade headquarters, battalion headquarters and the brigade ASU. Admittedly, they were mountainy men and were born to toughness and endurance, but the long hours of duty, arduous travelling and responsibility for the safety of those entrusted to them must have told on them. Theirs is a story not known to many and they have never received the recognition and credit due to them for duty well done. Forgotten, too, are the families of those men, their parents who gave shelter and rest, their sisters who cooked for the men whom they guarded, and even the children, born scouts, who were quick to tell of any suspicious signs they observed in the locality. And all of them, if questioned, knew nothing and saw nothing.

Later in March the ASU left the Gap of Dunloe and took up a position at Laune Bridge. While there, they were observed by a retired British Army doctor named Digby. He saw the column in position from his own house and set off along the high road to warn the military in Killarney.

However, he himself was observed by a friendly watcher who notified the ASU, which moved off before a big contingent of British arrived to try and take them by surprise.

It was on 24 March that the ASU moved to Headford Junction and there took part in the celebrated attack on the troop train, where British casualties were twenty-five killed and four wounded. Irish casualties were 2 killed, Dan Allman, i/c of the column, and Jimmy Bailey. On Allman's death in action, Tom McEllistrim took over command while the fight continued and was Q/C Column thereafter.

The ASU returned direct to the Gap after the Headford Junction fight. Ammunition was short now. Mick Spillane got twenty-six dozen of ball cartridges filled with an extra charge of powder and the ball instead of small shot. The ball shot was locally made and used for shooting deer. He also provided a couple of hundred rounds of.303 ammunition.

Mick Spillane, Pádraig Devane, Eugene Tangney and Dick Fitzgerald had a narrow escape one day on their way from the Gap of Dunloe to Coolick School, Kilcummin, across the lake, where a Brigade meeting was to be held. Getting behind a hedge to satisfy a natural need they were just hidden in time from three lorries of military passing by. As they continued on their way across the fields Mick Spillane looked back and saw a man stretched across the ditch and looking after them with a scowl on his face. Shortly afterwards Dick Carey, the Battalion SS man in the Post Office in Killarney, produced for them a letter posted locally and going through to 'British Officer i/c Railway Hotel, Killarney'. The letter ran, 'IRA Officers Spillane, Devane, Tangney and Fitzgerald are in this district for days past. XXX.' The writing, which was very good, was closely scrutinised to see if the writer could be identified, but without success. Another letter in the same handwriting and addressed in the same way was also intercepted by Dick Carey. This letter said: 'There is a hard lot in the Gap of Dunloe. They are billeted at John O'Sullivans, Derrycama, entrance to the Black Valley. They have armed sentries day and night. They left for the Headford ambush and returned after it. Cremin, of Dunloe, is their commissariat officer. XXX.' This was obviously written by a man familiar with military terms, as the word 'commissariat' was not one in general use. Furthermore, the phrase 'a hard lot' was not a Kerry expression. Nevertheless, the writer was never tracked down. Mick Spillane has his suspicions of the observer on the day he and his comrades were bound for the brigade meeting but there were no definite grounds upon which to proceed against him, and it would just not do to carry out any hasty action where there was a doubt.[10]

HEADFORD AMBUSH (AS SUNG BY JIMÍN CONNOR)

Now comrades pay attention and listen to me a while
The story I will tell to you will cause your blood to boil
It's all about one of our captains who lately was laid low
Striking a blow for freedom's cause against the mighty foe.

Dan Allman was the young man's name from well known
*   Beauty's Home*
And men should never forget him no matter where they
*   roam*
He's a credit to his column and to his little town
His one idea while in command was to shoot the red flag
*   down.*

It was at Headford ambush poor Allman met his doom
For he found his little country was daily going to ruin
He called up his volunteers, he found he had work to do
To strike a blow for Ireland's rights and the rights of Róisín
*   Dubh.*
Allman stood on the platform as the train came up the line
His little band outside the wall with bayonets they did shine
And as the train came nearer the crowd they grew small
In that townland where the tyranny was caused by you,
*   Lloyd George.*

Allman fired the pistol shot just as the train had stopped
And out of it the Tommies stepped and one by one they
*   dropped.*
And when the fight was in full bloom poor Allman also fell
His bravery while in that fight sure God could only tell.

Likewise brave young Bailey by Allman's side did fall
He shed the last drop of his blood down by that old stone
     wall.
He did not dread cold steel or lead nor British tyranny
To see him laid in his grave 'twas a shocking sight to see.

To his broken-hearted mother the story then was told
About her brave and gallant son who was fearless to behold
Who fought the English to the last as Irish men should do
Who fought and died for Ireland's rights and the rights of
     Róisín Dubh.

Now, my song is ended and I must leave down my pen
Revenge we had and revenge we want for those two gallant
     men
Captain and young Bailey who showed us the road to take
Who fought for Ireland's glory and died for freedom's sake.[11]

20

'The Line Between the Garrison and the Gael'

Dr Crokes nominated Dick Fitzgerald as their delegate to Kerry's GAA convention, hosted in Tralee in March 1919. He played a central role in discussion of the two main topics on the convention's agenda: the Association's amateur status and the Oath of Allegiance to the King. 'Dick Fitzgerald strongly objected to money being played for in Gaelic football. He said that football should be played for the honour and glory of the game and nothing else.'[1] In all this he was merely reiterating the forthright conviction about amateur sport that he had stated in his *How to Play Gaelic Football* manual of five years earlier.

The major issue that emerged at convention was the controversial Oath of Allegiance. Austin Stack TD, Chairman of the County Board and himself a civil servant, indicated that circumstances existed that compelled civil servants and others to take this oath. Dick Fitzgerald sought the decision of the Kerry convention before showing his hand. Both men attended the annual GAA congress in Dublin on Easter Sunday 1919 when the decision of the Kerry delegates with regard to the oath was defeated by fifty votes to thirty-one. The discussion preceding the vote was often tense and emotional and Harry

Boland's contribution was probably the deciding factor. In a moving speech, he said, 'The GAA owed its position to the fact that it had always drawn the line between the Garrison and the Gael.'[2] Congress voted: 'that GAA members taking the Oath of Allegiance would be expelled from the Association.'[3]

Central Council entrusted the two Kerry delegates with £277 that had been raised from the benefit matches organised to help the Kerry County Board.

Fitzgerald was selector for club and county and the teams advanced in the 1919 County and Munster Championship respectively. In the first round the Kingdom defeated Tipperary by one point in Cork's Athletic Grounds on 25 May 1919. The score was 2-4 to 2-3 with T. Irwin of the host county as referee. The one-sided Munster Semi-Final against Waterford was played in Tralee on July 7 with Limerick's A. Quillinan officiating. The outcome was 3-5 to no score. Clare enjoyed home advantage, having comfortably accounted for Limerick. W. Benn of Tipperary refereed the Munster final in Ennis on Sunday 3 August and Kerry ran out victors 6-11 to Clare's 2 goals.

Later in the championship, Galway proved too strong for the rebuilding Kerry squad. Their first semi-final meeting resulted in a draw, Kerry 2-6 to Galway's 3-3. In the replay the Tribesmen's star Michael 'Knacker' Walsh proved a match winner by scoring two goals more than Kerry's 2-2. Galway's next opponents, Kildare, proved much stronger with the introduction of Olympian Larry Stanley, Paul Doyle and the goal-scoring experience of the 1905 veteran Frank 'Joyce' Conlon.

The Kerry County Board was in the red. It had losses amounting to £115 – costs involved in training the county team. Dick Fitzgerald was appointed to raise funds by appeal.

On the County Championship scene Dick Fitzgerald and his fellow selectors successfully guided their black-and-amber brigade to another county semi-final, defeating Ballymacelligott, the County Champions en route. Dr Crokes defeated Firies by one point on 13 July 1919, then accounted for neighbours Kilcummin on 5 October. The football standards in town and country appeared to be equalising, according to the *Kerryman*'s puzzled sports reporter of 19 July: 'I wonder is it that football in country districts has improved or that the town team has deteriorated'?[4]

Ballymacelligott, the defending County Champions, were clear favourites to retain their crown but Dickeen's men had other plans. 'Killarney's defeat of Ballymacelligott came as a surprise to many who looked on the Crokes as a dead letter. There is one thing anyway that can be said in favour of Killarney Gaels; they act silently and thoroughly and when they make up their minds to do something they do it and no more about it.'[5] This All Souls' Day quarter-final clash ended on the score of 3-2 to 2-1 in favour of Dr Crokes.

The 1919 county semi-final against Tralee Mitchels took place in Tralee on leap-year Sunday, 29 February 1920. Crokes were returning to their winning ways: 'and their recent defeat of Ballymacelligott – the champions – makes it appear as if 'Richard' (Fitzgerald) once more holds the goods with the material at his disposal, there are few men in Ireland, if any, capable of moulding them into first class footballers as the said 'Richard' and when he does make up his mind to win a championship, it takes some stopping to keep him from getting there.'[6] Crokes dominated the early stages but succumbed to Tralee 2-1 to 0-2. Crokes successfully objected to earn a replay but again Tralee Mitchels proved too strong and went on to conquer Dingle in the county final on 25 April 1920.

This proved to be the last Kerry County Football Final until 24 April 1927, which concluded the 1925 campaign! War, revolution, imprisonment and civil strife together with 'men on the run' intervened. This turbulent period devastated the local club scene. Despite all this, Kerry harvested nine Munster senior football crowns – 1923, 1924, 1925, 1926, 1927, 1929–31 – and six All Irelands – 1924, 1926 and their first four-in-a-row, 1929–32. They were beaten by Dublin in the 1923 final (played 25 September 1924).

Kerry lost the 1925 series although they defeated Cavan in an All-Ireland semi-final encounter in Tralee. The Breffni men deemed the 1924 Kerry captain, Phil 'the Master' O'Sullivan, illegal. They claimed he had played football for UCD and hurling for Dublin club Faugh a' Bealach (Faughs) that same year. The dispute became such a cause célèbre that a terrier coursing enthusiast from Rock Street, Tralee, named his all-star Kerry Blue 'Cavan Objection'! As Cavan objected and Kerry counter-objected both counties were disqualified.

Dick Fitzgerald was prominent during this period as trainer for Dr Crokes, selector for his county, delegate on the County Board and sometimes acting County Board chairman, representative on the Provincial Council and Central Council officer. He also served as referee for club and inter-county games, including the two All-Ireland semi-finals of 1918. During this time he earned his livelihood from the family business: the Fitzgeralds were butter, poultry and egg exporters.

21

'March Over the Dead Bodies
of Their Own Brothers, 1922–3'

The local election results for Killarney Urban District Council in 1920, 1925 and 1928 indicate Dick Fitzgerald's political leanings, changing allegiance and community activism. It was a period of huge change and political divisions as brother faced brother and GAA team members faced down former colleagues after the Treaty and the outbreak of the Civil War.

On 15 January 1920 Dick Fitzgerald exceeded the quota by eight votes and was declared elected to the UDC together with his flying column leader Michael Spillane. Both were representing Sinn Féin. Four years later Fitzgerald was one of three Cumann na nGaedheal councillors returned for the East Ward in the uncontested election of 23 June 1925. Two Labour and one Independent councillor completed this ward. The West Ward electorate with 912 voters returned two Sinn Féin, two Cumann na nGaedheal, one Labour and one Independent Councillor. Interestingly, Sinn Féin polled 246 first-preference votes as against Cumann na nGaedheal's 131 in this Ward. Fitzgerald's third term as local councillor representing the East Ward saw him polling in fourth place on the Cumann na nGaedheal ticket. He had sixty-five first preferences. As the 1928 quota stood at ninety-seven he was clearly elected on the PR system, benefiting from the transfers of party colleagues Denis Counihan and consistent poll-topper Eugene O'Sullivan, the former MP, County Board Chairman and footballing colleague of Dick Fitzgerald.

Councillor Fitzgerald's first contribution is recorded in the minute book of Killarney's UDC meeting of 2 February 1920. He moved that the council strongly back the Irish hierarchy's 'opposition to the proposed Education Bill'. Sinn Féin colleague, Kate Breen, seconded the motion, which was passed unanimously. It is noteworthy that throughout all his UDC days Fitzgerald was prominent in support of the developing technical education programmes in Kerry. He was appointed to serve on the County Technical Committee at the Town Council meeting of 12 March 1920, a role he fulfilled for the next ten years. His pioneering contribution to the development of technical education in Kerry as Ireland gained political and economic independence merits further study.

Council minutes report on the everyday affairs of Killarney town life – roads, water and sewage services, health, quality of milk, housing and regular funding of various tourism promotion initiatives in Ireland and England. His early days on the council show Dick Fitzgerald opposing British rule, moving a motion to recognise Dáil Éireann on 9 April 1920 and supporting the release from US prison of Jim Larkin 'so that he may stand in the midst of the workers encouraging and supporting them in their fight for existence.'[1] The question of prisoners' welfare and release was a constant preoccupation of the council throughout this decade of successive British, Civil War and Free State jurisdictions. Fitzgerald moved a motion 'to present an address of welcome to Mr John McCormack on his (concert) visit to

Killarney'.[2] As the minute books recording UDC business during the Civil War period of 1922-3 are lost, we are unable to review council debates and decisions during that disturbed period.

The Anglo-Irish Treaty of 1921 came about when the five representatives accredited by Éamon de Valera, President of the Irish Republic, opened negotiations with Britain in London on 11 October 1921. Despite strong reservations surrounding the questions of dominion status, the Oath of Allegiance and the six counties of Northern Ireland remaining under British rule, the delegates signed a treaty with Britain on 6 December 1921, under threat of an immediate resumption of war. Two days later four Irish Ministers accepted the Treaty but De Valera, Cathal Brugha and Austin Stack voted against. A month later, on 7 January 1922, the Dáil voted by sixty-four votes to fifty-seven to accept the Treaty. The debate on the Treaty raged nationally through the following months while divisions widened.

Killarney commanded national headlines in mid-spring 1923, when de Valera and Collins addressed large gatherings. The former's five-day Munster tour 'were five days that shook the nation'.[3] Opposing the Treaty, de Valera addressed a large Killarney gathering with these complex and controversial words on 19 March 1922:

> In future, in order to achieve freedom if our Volunteers continue…and we suppose that this Treaty is ratified by your votes, then these men, in order to achieve freedom, would have to, as I said yesterday, march over the dead bodies of their own brothers. They will have to wade through Irish blood….Therefore, they will oppose even the troops of the Irish government

set up in accordance with that, because it will be felt that, even if the Treaty were ratified, it would not be ratified with your free will, but under the threat of War.'[4]

Reportage focusing on the image of having to 'wade through Irish blood' as an incitement to civil war was roundly condemned by De Valera next day in Tralee before an audience of 7,000. Historian T. Ryle Dwyer comments: 'From a careful reading of his actual words in Killarney, it is clear de Valera was not personally threatening civil war. He was saying that such a conflict would almost inevitably ensue if the Treaty was ratified.'[5]

The next month Michael Collins visited Killarney and Tralee and faced major hostilities and opposition. On Saturday 22 April Collins and his party were informed by an Anti-Treaty officer that the Killarney meeting had been proscribed. In fact the reception platform had been burned but after the intervention of a local Franciscan friar 'Collins was allowed to hold his rally in front of the Franciscan church, where the sloping ground formed a natural platform.'[6] 'The Big Fellow' emphasised the powerlessness of the republic existing under British powers, urging his audience to endorse the Treaty. He made a similar plea at another acrimonious rally of 4,000 people in Tralee.

The Collins party posed with local sympathisers in Killarney for a group photograph but, curiously, sitting UDC Councillor Dick Fitzgerald does not feature in it. But as Civil War approached Councillor Fitzgerald was about to side with his former Frongoch companion Michael Collins.

Two months into the Civil War, after what Liam Deasy termed 'the Great Split'[7] Michael Collins was killed during an ambush in Béal na mBláth ambush on 22 August 1922. Deasy's autobiographical account, *Brother Against Brother* records that De Valera – who was in Béal na mBláth earlier the same day, 'remarked that it would be a pity if Collins were killed because he might be succeeded by a weaker man. De Valera then left us to rejoin (Liam) Lynch in North Cork...'[8] Deasy recalled that upon receiving the news of the death of Collins they had 'heavy hearts...our sorrow was deep and lasting...I considered him to be the greatest leader of our generation and I have not changed that opinion...His death...brought about in us a real desire for the end of the war.'[9]

Former Crokes and Kerry footballer Eamonn Fitzgerald interviewed local historian Margaret O'Leary, daughter of Dick Fitzgerald's friend 'Small' Jer O'Leary, in his Dr Crokes 1996 publication, *Decade of Glory*. She reflected:

> Neil Jordan's film *Michael Collins* is highly acclaimed, and justifiably so. Pity his researchers didn't get the Frongoch story. Dick Fitzgerald and Michael Collins were interned there together. Dickeen organised an inter-county football competition among the prisoners, which Kerry won. What few people knew is that Dickeen organised safe houses for Michael Collins all over the country. Dickeen was a national hero in GAA circles and he had a network of people in every county. He often came to our house here in Main Street and that continued after the Treaty.[10]

Margaret O'Leary shared this family memory with me when I visited her in her antique shop in Main Street Killarney on 8 March 2008:

> Dick Fitzgerald brought Michael Collins to this house. My father and Dickeen had made friends with an older Collins brother during their student days in Cork. Jer asked Collins about the Treaty in this shop as the children were playing. He replied, 'Your children will have a great life but I won't live to see it.' 'Are you serious?' asked Jer. 'I will be got rid of,' was the reply.

It is important to note Dick Fitzgerald's move from Sinn Féin to Cumann na nGaedheal. The great silence surrounding the Treaty and succeeding Civil War politics in East Kerry makes it difficult to understand the mentality and response of the participants leading up to, during and following that tragic ten-month period.

Between 28 June 1922 and 20 April 1923 Ireland was in turmoil and Kerry was not spared. Dorothy Macardle's subjective study, *Tragedies of Kerry*, published during May 1924, clearly takes the side of the Anti-Treaty or Irregulars in recording the multiple deaths, executions and personal injuries in the Kingdom. My late father recalled going to the local Monastery school on the morning of 15 March 1923 and seeing the body of Captain John Kevins of Beaufort being brought in a donkey and cart to the morgue at St Columbanus's Home. My late mother often recounted how as a child she played in the Radrinagh dug-out with her father's first cousin, Stephen Buckley and some of his four Republican colleagues before their capture and execution at Countess Bridge, Killarney on 7 March 1923. Volunteer Tadhg Coffey had a lucky escape on that occasion, as did Stephen Fuller, who lived to tell the tale when eight of his Anti-Treaty companions were massacred at Ballyseedy near Tralee, during the same week in March 1923. 'There were nineteen prisoners put to death that week, in Kerry within six days.'[11] With hindsight it is impossible to evaluate or imagine the mindset of Irish people living through this hell of violence and uncertainty.

Many participants and survivors were loth to set down their Civil War thoughts and experiences. In cases where they did we often encounter a very subjective account. However, as the time gap has widened, further reminiscences and documentation have come on stream for historians to study.

Cumann na nGaedheal, led by William T. Cosgrave, was founded in April 1923. The party enjoyed strong support in the east and midlands of the country and took sixty-three Dáil seats in the general election of August 1923, polling 39 per cent of national vote. (In 1933 Cumann na nGaedheal combined with the National Centre Party to form Fine Gael.)

Fianna Fáil was founded on 16 May 1926 but followed an abstentionist line until 1 August 1927. Then the party broke with Sinn Féin's policy and gained 35.2 per cent of the national vote in the 1927 election, winning fifty-seven seats. Fianna Fáil won 44.5 per cent of the vote (seventy-two seats) in March 1932. The party held power for the next decade.

THE HEALING FORCE OF KERRY GAA

The *Kerryman* of 10 February 1924 reported:

> Whatever may be the result of the match between the ex-internees and the Munster champions, it must be admitted that the former are making a decent effort to give a creditable display. Every day during the past week the thud of a football can be heard in the Sportsfield, and the early morning hours are

devoted to walking exercises; so that, all things taken into consideration, it will be admitted that the ex-internees are fully determined to pull the laurels from the brows of the Kerry team.

The *Kerryman* reported on 23 March 1924: 'Sunday's return match between the ex-internees and the Kerry team resulted in an overwhelming victory for the former, and placed them as undoubtedly the better team. With the exception of Con Brosnan and Phil Sullivan the majority of the county team seemed to be in a parlous condition. In connection with the match it was fought out in a fine sporting spirit which reflected the utmost credit on both combinations.'

GAA historian Donie O'Sullivan addresses this question of reconciliation in his article in *Dr Crokes Gaelic Century*:

The parish rule served the GAA well at this juncture; it was strictly enforced and this ensured that GAA members, who were bitter opponents in the Civil War, played together on the same team and served on the same administrative committees...Most of the Republican prisoners were released by early 1924 and only then did Kerry begin to resume its full role in GAA competitions. In June of that year Kerry refused to play Dublin in the 1923 All-Ireland Final because Austin Stack, Chairman of the County Board, was still in prison. In late July the remaining prisoners, including Stack and de Valera were released...No part of Ireland had been more divided by the Civil War than Kerry. Yet, men who had been prominent on opposing sides in that tragic conflict lined out together in Croke Park on the last Sunday of September, 1924. This game has been described as one of the best finals seen. Dublin won narrowly by two points...It is certain that the challenge games earlier in the year between the official Kerry team and the ex-internees were a major factor.[12]

The following year a Kerry side trained by Dr Eamonn O'Sullivan reversed the 1923 result. It was the beginning of a golden era in Kerry football.

Jo Jo Barrett's important work *In the Name of the Game* (1997) treats of this turbulent and divisive decade that culminated in Kerry's first four-in-a-row. He portrays his late father, Joe Barrett, at the very heart of Kerry's success, playing a central role in both football and reconciliation. Joe Barrett is one of six Kerry football stars profiled in the book, which is described in the blurb as 'A Book of Reconciliation'. In the blurb Tim Pat Coogan comments: 'J.J. Barrett has told a splendid tale of how the horror and the high heroic of the Civil War entwined, and how the game became a healing force.' Paddy Downey of *The Irish Times* also writes: 'Not until now, however, has the story of that healing been told in detailed length, and with deep insight and an intimate knowledge of the subject.'[13]

Jo Jo Barrett considers the footballing lives and political outlooks of three Tralee men – John Joe Sheehy of John Mitchels (Boherbee) GAA club, Joe Barrett and John Joe ('Purty') Landers of Rock Street and (since 1929) Austin Stacks GAA club. All three were Republican and Anti-Treaty sympathisers. The other three were Con Brosnan from Moyvane, a freedom fighter who became a captain in the Free State Army, his younger Ballylongford neighbour Johnny Walsh, who became a Fine

Gael activist, and Tim O'Donnell of Annascaul who became a member of An Garda Síochána in 1931.

These county players, who between them won a total of twenty-nine All-Ireland Senior Football medals, qualify for the title 'bridge builders'. They helped to 'set a foundation stone so that in the following two decades from 1923–41 Kerry would win eleven All-Ireland titles….John Joe Sheehy and Con Brosnan captained one each, and Joe Barrett captained two…giving his third captaincy to his friend and one time political foe, Con Brosnan.'[14] Joe Barrett took a brave and controversial stance by insisting on passing his own right to be Kerry senior captain to Con Brosnan from Moyvane, who 'accepted the captaincy and brought the Sam Maguire to Kerry for the third successive year. This fairy tale ending to the 1931 captaincy issue saw Brosnan captain Kerry to beat Kildare by 1-11 to 0-8 in a hectic final.'[15]

This 1931 final was the first Kerry football victory since the death of Dick Fitzgerald the previous year but he would have endorsed the ongoing work of healing and rebuilding unity through the GAA. Although Jo Jo Barrett later opposed GAA Central Council's 2006 decision to amend Rule 42 and permit the playing of international rugby and soccer matches in Croke Park, he hoped that the Kerry GAA's post-Civil War contribution to the healing process might be a template for the peace process in Northern Ireland.

Con Houlihan of Castleisland contributed an insightful foreword in Brendan Fulham's *The Throw-In – The GAA and the Men Who Made It*. (I recall Con playing many a rugby game against Killarney the late 1950s and early 1960s in the same Cricket Field where Dick Fitzgerald played his Gaelic football):

The Gaelic Athletic Association is often credited with healing the wounds inflicted by the Civil War. This would have been a miracle. But it helped to lessen the bitterness, in varying degrees in different counties. The conflict had been especially obscene in Kerry; the GAA played a big part there in restoring a degree of sanity. John Joe Sheehy was head of the Anti-Treaty forces in west Munster; Con Brosnan was a captain in the National Army – they played together in the great Kerry team of the late 20s and early 30s.[16]

22

Title Regained after Ten-year Lapse, 1924

When Kerry and Dublin lined out to contest the 1924 All-Ireland Final at Croke Park on 26 April 1925, the atmosphere was fraught with tension and feelings of resentment were running high. For it was really something in the nature of a grudge contest between two teams who had already clashed in the previous year's final in September, 1924, when the Metropolitans took the laurels by a two-point margin (1-5 to 1-3).

As a matter of fact that 1923 final was very nearly not played at all. At first Kerry had refused to play. Their stance was endorsed in a letter from the Erskine Childers Cumann of Sinn Féin in Dublin which appeared in the *Kerryman* on 5 July 1924:

> A chara
>
> At a meeting of the above Cumann, held on 17 June, the following resolution was passed unanimously: 'That we the members of the E. Childers' Cumann Sinn Fein appreciate the splendid action of the Kerry team in refusing to play the Dublin team until the prisoners are all released.'

The committee of the Cumann would be very much obliged for the publication of above resolution. The letter was signed by Tomás Ó Boirne, Runaidhe.

But after a general amnesty for the majority of the approximately 2000 interned Republicans prisoners was declared in August, the game went ahead after all and it was rescheduled by the Central Council for 28 September 1924. Kerry County Board gave its approval for the game at a meeting in Tralee Courthouse on 23 August.

But the war-flames had already been fanned by previous events. Dublin objected earlier to Kerry's then erstwhile star Dick Fitzgerald refereeing the Dublin-Cavan semi-final. The matter came to a head at a meeting of the Central Council in Dublin at which a letter was read from the O'Tooles Football Club and the Dublin County Board objecting to Mr Fitzgerald's appointment as referee of the game and calling for the appointment of 'a neutral referee'.

Dublin team member Paddy Carey told the meeting that the reason they were objecting to Mr Fitzgerald was because of an incident in the 1923 semi-final between Dublin and Mayo when Mr Fitzgerald was an umpire. He said the ball went over the Dublin end line, struck the netting and rebounded into play and was finally sent into the net. Mr Fay of Cavan, the other umpire, said it was no score but Mr Fitzgerald allowed a goal.

Mr Fitzgerald, who happened to be Kerry's representative on the Central Council, stood up to reply to the allegation. He said he was glad this statement had been made. Mayo had scored a goal above board and Mr Fay did not say it was not a score. It was a fair goal and he Mr Fitzgerald would not be intimidated by Dublin.

Continuing, he said that when he was leaving the field, Mr McDonnell of Dublin, who had been playing in the match, said to him, 'You wanted a soft thing for Kerry,' and some of the Dublin followers called him names.

The matter was finally resolved when the Central Council chairman Mr P.D. Breen of Wexford, said that the Council had already given its decision and the appointment of Dick Fitzgerald would stand.'[1]

'Kingdom Rethroned' is the chapter title under which Eoghan Corry described Kerry's 1924 victory over Dublin. In his *Catch and Kick: Great Moments of Gaelic Football 1880-1990* he relates that:

A year in internment camps had sharpened up the Kerrymen. They halted Dublin's bid for four-in-a-row at the last hurdle in the 1924 All-Ireland Final, not played until April 1925...a rejuvenated Kerry defeated them 0-4 to 0-3 in a fabulous game, watched by 28,844 spectators...gate receipts of £2,564...Kerry's man of the match was Con Brosnan who scored the winning point. Spectators paid five shillings to sit in the newly erected wooden Hogan stand, named after the Tipperary footballer who died

on Bloody Sunday (one of ten killed in the Black and
Tans' reprisal in Croke Park during a Tipperary versus
Dublin football challenge on 21 November 1921). A
new scoreboard on the railway wall was in use for
the first time. It was a tremendous game which was
probably the best in Gaelic football history to date.[2]

Two O'Sullivans played a major role in this Kingdom replay
victory. The captain, Phil O'Sullivan, 'the Master', is credited
with engaging the services of his friend Dr Eamonn O'Sullivan
to train Kerry for the replay. The doctor son of J. P. 'Champion'
O'Sullivan, captain of the losing 1892 Kerry team, Dr Eamonn
is credited with introducing the idea of the scoreboard for the
first time in Gaelic sport. Dr Eamonn occasionally played for
Kerry and was to make a major sporting contribution to football
in the county over the succeeding five decades.

The very first transmission of a live sporting event in Europe
took place on Sunday 29 August 1926 on Ireland's recently
established 2RN. Cork's P.D. Mehigan was the broadcaster on
this historic occasion. He also acted as commentator for the
Kerry versus Kildare All-Ireland Final replay in Croke Park on
17 October 1926. Thirty-four trains transported the eager fans
but across the land people were seeking out the few homes that
could afford the new 'listening in' with the legendary wet and
dry batteries.

Mehigan announced half-time and introduced an accordionist
to play a medley of traditional airs while he took a health break.
John Dillon from Abbeydorney, who had been a confidant of
Dick Fitz since the previous decade, had travelled from Tubrid
Station, Ardfert. Anticipating a Kerry victory, he reputedly sent
the following message to the broadcasting box: 'Will somebody

listening in please call to tell them in Abbeydorney that Jack Dillon will be late coming home to milk the cows.'

The message went on air through the Marconi transmitter, which was housed in a wooden hut in McKee Barracks, close to Phoenix Park and reached the ears of some responsive North Kerry listeners. After the final whistle, when victory had been secured, the emergency message was personally delivered to the Dillon household but they had already heard it on their own 'listening in'!

KERRY VERSUS KILDARE, ALL-IRELAND 1926

There's joy tonight in Kerry hearts
From Doon to Farranfore,
From Scartaglin to Beauty's Home,
From Dingle to Rathmore.
From sweet Listowel to dear Tralee,
From Headford to Kenmare,
The very hills ring out with glee
Since Kerry beat Kildare.

The coin was spun, the Kingdom won,
The ball was set to roll —
Jack Riordan grand took up his stand
To guard the Clonliffe goal.
And when Kildare came dashing down
In fierce but fair attack,
With lightning like velocity
Joe Barrett drove them back.

The Leinster hopes soared mountain high
When Stanley got the ball,
For many thought that from his try
The Kingdom's fort would fall.
But Riordan's catch and mighty kick
Deprived them of a score –
More worthy shoulders have not yet
Pat Dillon's mantle wore.

Like greyhounds racing from their slips
Came Captain Con and Stack,
And burst right through Kildare's defence
For who could hold them back?
'Twas glorious down the Kingdom's right
To see the battles royal
Between the Guard Paul Russell
And their peerless winger Doyle.

Hats off to John Joe Sheehy's men –
They are Ireland's champions still.
Let bonfires bright blaze through the night
Along each Kerry hill.
And when the Roll of Fame is called –
In football feats I mean –
May every player be shining there
In Kerry's gold and green.[3]

Patrick C. O'Connors

23

'The World's Championship': the US Tour 1927

The Kerry County Board's deliberations regarding a Kingdom tour to Australia were abandoned in favour of their very first USA tour in 1927. The Tipperary hurlers had had a very successful coast-to-coast tour in 1926, with games enjoyed by huge attendances. The Board was greatly encouraged by the Tipperary tour and the stated aim of the football tour the following year was that: 'from any profits arising out of the event it was agreed that the Tralee Sportsfield would be bought out by the County Board, and that other Kerry grounds would benefit also.'[1]

Kerry appointed Dick Fitzgerald as team manager and famed octogenarian Ted Sullivan as American tour promoter. Baseball was his forte and field of speciality interest. He had written books on the subject and organised tours. The US-based manager of the tour was Muiris Kavanagh from Dunquin, better known as 'Kruger'. Dick Fitzgerald's brother Fr Edmond, who was a curate in Kinsale, went ahead of the main party in early May 1927 to copper fasten all arrangements for the touring party. Unknown to them Kerry were sailing into a major financial swindle.

On the eve of the feast day of St Brendan the Navigator, 15 May 1927, the HMS *Baltic* sailed from Queenstown in the Cobh of Cork. The deck proved a suitable training ground for the All-Ireland champions under the vigilant eye of team manager

Dick Fitzgerald. The Kerry footballers were not only All-Ireland champions but 1926 Railway Cup champions. They had defeated Kildare 1-4 to 0-4 in the All-Ireland and both Ulster and Connacht in the provinces' final, which had been revived after a twenty-year lapse. The men from the Kingdom were clear favourites to capture what was widely advertised in America as 'the World's Championship' although Central Council of the GAA was none too pleased with this label, coined by the Irish of the diaspora.

Renowned journalist Paddy Foley, better known as P.F., accompanied the touring party and gave a comprehensive account of the matches hosted in American cities and townships. The first encounter was held in the Polo Grounds, home pitch of the famed New York Giants. Kerry were scarcely acclimatised when they met the well-prepared New York team four days after docking, on Sunday 29 May. The visiting All-Ireland champions were no match for their super-fit hosts, who led by two points at half time and by 2-4 on a score of 3-11 to 1-7 at the final whistle. The 30,000 fans were surprised by Kerry's ineptitude and the Kerry exiles felt let down. The 1903 Kerry veteran Dan McCarthy 'commentated of the poor quality of Kerry fielding... Not one of them would catch a ball with the players of his day.'[2] Excuses were made and blame was apportioned but P.F. himself admitted that Kerry 'were soundly beaten at all points of the game by a much superior side'.[3] Two decades later in the Famine Commemoration All-Ireland of 1947 Kerry were defeated by Cavan in the same Polo Grounds venue.

After this weak start, things did not get better. The eleven-week tour was marred by the disappearance of the designated promoter Ted Sullivan and all the gates. Many of the fixtures attracted smaller numbers of spectators than anticipated, notably Boston (6,000), Chicago (8,000), and Springfield, Massachusetts, (4,000).

Some San Francisco-based Kerry exiles had invited the team to travel west from Chicago with all expenses guaranteed. Sullivan sought monies in advance but as the Californians declined to advance anything this leg did not materialise and the team returned to the East Coast. The side was left high and dry in New York by the promoter but treated generously by various Kerry associations in the city.

P.F. notes: 'A Kenmare man, resident in New York, approached John Joe Sheehy in that city and offered him a bank deposit receipt. "These," said our New York friend, "are my life earnings. The boys can have them." There was no need to accept the very generous offer.'[4] I have identified that generous man as John Quinn. His daughter, Mary Ellen, who now lives in Kenmare, provided the proof. She was married in New York to Templenoe's Donal ('Dode') Spillane, late uncle of the famed footballing trio, Pat, Mick and Tom.

The altruism of this exile was surpassed by the intervention of the local Kerryman's Patriotic and Benevolent Association (founded 1881) which decided to make a grant of $500 to the abandoned visitors and initiated further benefit activities, including banquets. Local knowledge and advice from Mayo exile, attorney William O'Dwyer, dissuaded Fitzgerald and his party from seeking redress by legal means. But the New York exiles supported their own.

After the first defeat Kerry played and defeated a divisional side in Liberty Park, Springfield, Mass. The third challenge was played in Braves' Field, Boston where 6,000 fans saw Kerry win. Next stop was Hartford, Connecticut, where Kerry again defeated a local team. After travelling the 900 miles to the midwest Kerry defeated a Chicago selection at Comiskey Park, another baseball stadium. From Chicago they headed eastwards to New Haven. It was here, close to Yale University, that the Kerry players embarked on a stiff programme of training for their return match with New York.

Once again the Polo Grounds hosted the encounter on Independence Day: 'in sweltering conditions. New York repeated their superiority in most convincing fashion and won by twelve points to three. This was the last game of the World's Championship'. 'A friendly match was finally played at Celtic Park between Kerry and New York. This was the most interesting of the series...ended in favour of the homesters 2-5 to 2-1.'[5]

Kerry were happy to return home after their eleven-week sojourn. They retained their Munster title at the expense of Tipperary and Clare but found it hard to account for Leitrim, that season's championship surprise, in the All-Ireland Semi-Final. The Central Council's ban on any grant aid towards collective training thwarted Kerry's hopes of back-to-back success. The travel-weary Kingdom side failed to reach full fitness for their championship defence in Croke Park on Sunday 24 September 1927, when 'the Lily-Whites' of Kildare took full honours in a low-scoring final (0-5 to 0-3) before a crowd of 36,529. The following year, 1928, proved no better for Kerry's footballing fortunes, as lowly Tipperary ousted Kerry in the Munster semi-final. In the final, Kildare captured the Sam Maguire trophy, newly created to honour the Cork patriot and London's footballing captain of 1903.

Kerry had time to reflect on the mistakes they had made in the course of the 1927 US venture. The lessons they learned for the future were to make shorter trips with very much stronger panels for the field of play and of course to pay closer attention to financial matters. Subsequent tours helped to realise fundraising goals:

> The Kerry tours were much more successful…on one…a profit of £20,000 was realised…At one of the Kerry-New York matches the attendance was 60,000. This was a record for a Gaelic game until surpassed by the 1938 All-Ireland Final (Kerry versus Galway). Kerry benefited by these tours financially and as a result the County Board was enabled to buy out and improve the Tralee Sportsfield which was renamed the 'Austin Stack Memorial Park'[6] in 1929.

There is no report of a homecoming pipe-band reception when the vanquished 1927 team arrived back in Cobh with manager Dick Fitzgerald. Nevertheless the group must have felt immense satisfaction at having moved, socialised and played among many thousands of their own exiles during their three-month tour.

'Peerless' Phil O'Sullivan of Tuosist would soon return to New York to marry Kathleen O'Mahony, a Tipperary exile. He met her at a reception for the visiting team where she was a pianist. There he would spend the rest of his life. Phil 'the Master' is the first All-Ireland-winning Kerry captain to be buried overseas, in Calvary Cemetery, Woodside, Queens. The memorial raised by his Tuosist neighbours and fellow exiles reads:

> In Memory of
> Philip J. O'Sullivan
> Native of
> County Kerry, Ireland
> 1894–1952

THE ALL IRELAND FINAL 1924

The twenty-sixth we shall long remember
As the sun's bright rays down the hilltop rolled
And shone in beauty where the teams did duty,
The boys in blue and in green and gold.

The brilliant bands in that grand arena,
Announced the coming of a struggle rare,
Whilst seas of faces filled all the spaces
And for once old Ireland seemed free from care.

Full 30,000 were anxious waiting
The Triple Champions again to see
The coin was spun, the Kingdom won
And the teams were slipped by the referee.

For a rock he is famed Joe Barrett,
With Phil the peerless the true and tried,
And Johnnie Murphy in the ruck shone brightly
Those three defenders all foes denied.

'Twas a free to Kerry,
Con Brosnan took it,
With steady nerve and unerring aim,
He scored a point and again we led them
'Twas the final flag in a hard fought game.[7]

24

Shocking Death and All-Ireland Requiem, 1930

The Kerryman report filed on Friday 26 September 1930 reads:

MR DICK FITZGERALD DEAD
WELL-KNOWN GAELIC PLAYER
PASSES AWAY
Killarney, Friday

Mr Dick Fitzgerald, for many years a member of the Killarney Urban Council, and formerly captain of the Kerry football team, died here to-day.

About 2 pm he fell off the Courthouse and sustained serious internal injuries, to which he succumbed about an hour after.

The news of Mr Fitzgerald's death, coming as it does on the eve of an All-Ireland Final, in which Kerry is engaged, is all the more poignant. It will cause a deep shock all over the country, for few followers of the Gaelic code did not know Dick Fitzgerald. *Go ndeine Dia trócaire air.*

Our Killarney correspondent writes: 'The news of the death of Mr Richard Fitzgerald, which took place to-day was learned throughout Killarney and district with profound regret.

The late Mr Fitzgerald, or Dick, as he was popularly known, was a familiar and prominent figure not only in Killarney and Kerry, but in Gaelic circles throughout the country for years past. He was a great Gael and will long be remembered as a man who in his time helped to bring Gaelic football to the position of pre-eminence which it now enjoys in the country.

It is a tragic coincidence that his funeral which will take place on Sunday will synchronise with the playing of the All-Ireland Final in which the team that he captained with distinction and success for many years is taking part. Everybody who knew Dick will deplore his passing for he was not only a great footballer but in social life he was a most companionable, genial and loyal friend.[1]

The Kerry County Board organised a special meeting on Friday night 'to consider the situation'[2]. Killarney delegates favoured postponing the fixture. The County Board reconvened in Tralee Courthouse the next morning. Dr Eamonn O'Sullivan and Eugene O'Sullivan, Chairman of Killarney UDC urged deferral. The County Board, cognisant of the huge number of fans who had already left for Dublin, (the return rail fare was fifteen shillings) eventually decided to fulfil the fixture and voted to pass 'a vote of condolence…It was also decided to ask the relatives of the late Mr Fitzgerald to postpone the funeral till Monday next, so as to give the Gaels of Kerry and of Ireland an opportunity of attending same.'[3]

The family concurred and arranged the funeral for Monday

29 September in St Mary's Cathedral, Killarney. Dick's older brother, Fr Edmond, was celebrant.

It is remarkable that the inquest into this sudden death was held on the very evening of Dick's passing. A report was published in the national daily, the *Irish Independent* the following Monday, along with a full match report of Kerry's ninth senior All-Ireland victory. That edition carried five match photographs, one of which showed the Croke Park Tricolour at half-mast and another showing Monaghan captain P. Kilroy sporting a black armband as a mark of respect. The page 7 caption reads 'Prominent Gael's Death – Story at the Inquest...A verdict of death due to shock and haemorrhage was returned at the inquest on Mr Richard Fitzgerald, who fell from the roof of a house in the market.'[4] The report lists the multiple tributes of colleagues and provincial councils including that of 'the special GAA Convention on the motion of the Chairman, Mr Seán Ryan...The resolution was passed in silence'.[5]

The *Kerryman* of Saturday 27 September published a more complete account of Coroner Dr William O'Sullivan's findings.

THE INQUEST

Mr Coroner Wm. O'Sullivan and a Jury of which Mr Eugene O'Sullivan was Foreman held an inquest into the death of Mr Richard Fitzgerald, Killarney, on Friday evening.

Supt. Gantly and Sergt. Lande represented the authorities.

Patk. Kenny, brother-in-law of deceased, said he saw him about two o'clock sitting on the roof of a house in the Market. He said he was coming down.

The Foreman asked whether from the position he was in he was likely to slip off.

Witness said yes.

Patrick Cronin said he saw him on the roof and when asked to come down said he would. He turned over on the roof and next he saw him falling down, his hips striking the ground.

Guard Grimes corroborated, and said that in his opinion when he was about to come down he over-balanced and fell off.

Dr Moriarty, Killarney, said he arrived an hour before he died. He was quite conscious and spoke to him in a normal way. Death was due to shock and haemorrhage due to internal injuries to abdominal and chest by a fall from some height.

The Jury found that Richard Fitzgerald came by his death on the 26 Sept., from shock and haemorrhage due to internal injuries to abdomen and chest as a result of falling off the roof of a house in the Fair Green, Killarney.

The Coroner said: This evening we assemble here to hold an inquisition into the death of Dick Fitzgerald. It is a mournful – a sad business. We all knew Dick and he had endeared himself to everybody by his kindness and manliness. As a footballer he was best known. Who can forget Dick as he led famous Kerry teams to victory against Wexford, Kildare and Louth to mention only a few. Dick was not only a county hero, he was a national one. Everywhere in whatever part of this globe a football was kicked his name was honoured. He was probably the greatest exponent of Gaelic football that ever lived. In other Irish activities Dick was in the forefront. He had the knack of imbuing others with his own enthusiasm. We now mourn him and we sincerely regret his departure. It is particularly sad that we are here inquiring into the death of an old Kerry footballer like Dick Fitzgerald. This court is presided over by an old Kerry footballer – the Foreman, a former captain of the Killarney team. He and several members of the Jury were members of the famous Kerry team in the past. We are all very sorry that we are here assembled this evening for this sad purpose and we all deeply regret his death, and sympathise with his relatives.

The Foreman, (Mr E. O'Sullivan), said the Jury and himself desired to be associated with what the Coroner had said. He found it difficult to express his sorrow at the death of poor Dick. He had been an intimate friend and colleague of his both in the football field and socially for a considerable number of years and no friend had ever gone whose passing he regretted so much or whose place it would be so difficult to fill. He had in common with all his colleagues throughout the country to deplore his death and their sympathy went out to his relatives.

Supt. Gantly on his own behalf and on behalf of the Guards associated himself with the Coroner's and Foreman's expression of sorrow. Since he came to Kerry he got in touch with the late Mr

Fitzgerald in connection with Gaelic matters and he and the Guards in general deeply regretted his death.

Mr John Clifford as an old Gael and pal desired to be associated with what the Coroner and Foreman had said.[6]

Margaret O'Leary recounted her father's personal memory of that black Friday in Killarney to me on 8 March 2008:

Dickeen and my father were due to travel together to the All-Ireland that afternoon. Dick was ready early and dressed for Dublin. He went drinking. Jer was here at home getting ready when someone burst in to the shop shouting, 'Come on quick!' Jer, with unmade collar and untied bootlaces, rushed up College Street to the Courthouse where he witnessed Dick sitting on the roof and the crowd urging him to come down. Dick was wearing new shoes. He turned to come down but the leather soles got no grip and he slipped on the mossy slates and fell.

Monday's *Irish Independent* reported:

A special Mass for the late Mr Fitzgerald was offered at St Francis Xavier's Church, (Gardiner Street, Dublin) yesterday, and was attended by the teams playing at Croke Park in the evening, by members of the Central Council and other councils and County Boards…Mr Fitzgerald was author of an interesting book *How to Play Gaelic Football* which met with a

ready sale when published in 1914. He was a member
of Killarney UDC. He suffered a heavy bereavement
by the death of his wife a few years back.[7]

His wife Catherine (Kitty) Dillon who died on 10 April 1927
is buried in the Dillon and Looney family plot in Aghadoe, across
the path from the eastern gable of the Hiberno-Romanesque
Church looking out on Loch Léin and the McGillycuddy
Reeks.

All-Ireland Sunday was fine as Tipperary took the minor
title and Kilkenny took junior honours. It was not a day for the
men from Ulster: even though Monaghan got away to a winning
start their challenge petered out against a Kerry side en route to
their first four-in-a-row. The Farney men, who scored two first-
half points to the Kingdom's 1-4, failed to score in the second
period, while Kerry's tally came to 3-11. The Kingdom won the
new Sam Maguire trophy for the first time. Captain John Joe
Sheehy received the Sam Maguire, a feat to be repeated by his
son Seán Óg in 1962.

The analysis of the unsigned *Irish Independent* sportswriter
was captioned: 'Cheerless Final at Croke Park' and 'Poorest Final
on Record'. He acknowledged:

> The recent death of Mr R. Fitzgerald, the famous
> mentor of Kerry footballers, cast a gloom over the final,
> and had a restraining influence on the enthusiasm of
> the champions' followers, who were present in large
> numbers...Attendance 33,280; Receipts £3,038...
> included the largest crowd that has ever followed a
> Northern county.'[8]

Monaghan, the Ulster champions, had beaten Kildare – the 1928 All-Ireland winners – by two points but they failed to repeat their semi-final form in their first ever All-Ireland appearance.

The Kerry fans headed south to bury Dickeen.

'There was no big welcome home for the champions. Instead, the crowds gathered in huge numbers in Killarney on the Monday after the game to pay their final respects to a man who had become a legend in his lifetime.'⁹ St Mary's Cathedral was the scene of an immense gathering for the Requiem Mass on Monday 29 September. The detailed report of the *Kerryman* of Saturday 4 October lists the attending clergy led by Dick's brother Edmond Fitzgerald CC, together with relatives and friends and a great array of national and local personalities, representing many organisations and committees. Foremost were many former adversaries from the political and the football field, now united in grief and solidarity.

IMPOSING FUNERAL CORTÈGE
PUBLIC MAINIFESTATION OF SORROW
The funeral of the late Mr 'Dick' Fitzgerald, which took place on Monday, was of immense proportion, and rarely, if ever, has there been such a signal mark of public esteem witnessed as that shown to the deceased by the attendance at his funeral. Members of the Central and Provincial Councils of the GAA, in addition to the County Board and Gaels of Kerry, were present. Indeed, so great was the esteem in which he was held that there was scarcely a Gaelic body in Munster which was not represented in the cortège.

The remains were removed from the Cathedral

to the bier, accompanied by a guard of honour from his own Club, the Dr Crokes, which Club had also charge of the arrangements and acted as marshals. Headed by the Killarney Pipers' Band playing the Dead March, the funeral procession was as follows. Clergy; members of Central Council, Munster Council and Kerry County Board; past and present members of the Kerry team; Killarney Urban District Council; Garda Síochána; Central Club; Killarney Gaelic League; Killarney Dr Croke Club and Killarney Legion Club; Killarney Camogie Club; public bodies; general public.

Kerry: All members of the Kerry County Board GAA, together with the Kerry team (All-Ireland Champions) marched in the procession.

As the mournful procession passed through the streets all business establishments were closely shuttered, business was suspended, and blinds were drawn in private houses as a mark of respect to the deceased.[10]

The New Cemetery lies a mile to the north of Killarney town off the main road to Tralee and a hundred yards past the railway bridge. Lord Kenmare granted this site overlooking the town and the lakes to the people of the town. Here Dick Fitzgerald was laid to rest with this parents and brother Patrick, who predeceased him in 1915. The high Celtic Cross crafted by the noted stone mason O'Connell of Cork has the names of the interred Fitzgeralds engraved on the plinth facing the McGillycuddy Reeks. To the south is Tahilla, Sneem, which was the Fitzgeralds' ancestral Kerry home. The north-facing panel reads: '*Thugadar a saol ag obair ar son teanga, ceol, cluichí agus saoirse na hÉireann*' – 'They gave their lives working for the language, music, games and freedom of Ireland'.

Forty-seven paces south-west lies the grave of A. George of the Royal Fusiliers, one of the British soldiers shot dead in the Headford ambush of 21 March 1921. The other British troops killed at Headford Junction were transferred to their home cemeteries. The tombstone of Private Arthur George 6446510 shows a Christian cross to the front and the Jewish Star of David symbol on the northern face. There is a crown atop the engraved belt surrounding his regimental rose with the legend '*Honi Soit Qui Mal y Pense*'.

The Headford Junction action had been carried out by colleagues of Dick Fitzgerald's No. 2 Brigade. Close by is the grave of his College Street neighbour, Chief Engineer Patrick McCarthy, 'accidentally killed while on active service' on 29 June 1921. In the south-eastern corner of the graveyard is the Republican Plot. The tribute on the fifteen-foot cross reads:

In proud and loving memory of
Sec. Com. Seamus Daly
Adj. Stiophán Buckley
Vol. Tadhg Murphy
Vol. Diarmuid O'Donoghue
Captain Seán Kevins
who were cruelly done to death while prisoners of war
in the hands of the Free State Forces.
'*A Íosa chéasta, is Tú ár ndóchas*'

This monument was created by Killarney stone-mason O'Sullivan of High Street.

The *Irish Independent* of the Thursday after Dick's funeral carried a photograph of a dramatic accident at Drumlusk Bridge on the Killarney-Sneem road. Dick's relatives survived a serious accident when returning to Tahilla after the funeral. The Daniel MacMonagle photograph shows four men standing near the overturned Tudor Ford saloon car belonging to Mr Edward Fitzgerald. The owner was brought to a Cork hospital. His wife, along with two ladies and one gentleman, escaped with facial injuries following 'the accident…at midnight in a wild mountainous part of Kerry. The driver mistook the opening at the side of the bridge for the public road.'[11]

The following poem appeared on the programme for the official opening of Fitzgerald Stadium on 31 May 1936. The author Phil O'Neill ('Sliabh Ruadh') was Dick's friend at Mungret College in Limerick.

IN MEMORIAM
Dick Fitzgerald, of Killarney, who died 26 September 1930.

Over Loch Léin, where the sad moon pales,
Rises a caoine for a chief of the Gaels,
A leader gone from the fighting line –
A scion true of the Geraldine!

Through the mist of years his name will gleam,
When he blazed the trail with his Kerry team,
And brought to the Kingdom name and fame
In the greatest tests of the Gaelic game;

Kildare and Wexford and Louth can tell
Of his deeds, and now his requiem swell,

And tribute pay to a gallant foe,
Who played the game as we Gaels know.

And when Ireland called when the fight was thick,
She called not in vain to our old friend Dick;
For he came with the boys who were never slack,
Who were led by Ashe and Austin Stack,

And he did his time on the cold plank bed,
When all thought Ireland's cause was dead.
And now he's gone from the field of fame,
But thousands still shall speak his name,

And tell of his deeds on the Gaelic field,
For the Irish crown and the Railway Shield.
And whilst the Gaels the old games play,
And Kerry still may hold the sway,

We'll speak of him as a pioneer
Of the cause and the games we all hold dear,
And many a prayer will arise, I ween,
From the Gaels who knew and loved 'Dickeen'.[12]

'The Finest Playing Field in Ireland'

Tralee fares better than Killarney when it come to honouring its famous footballers. As you enter Tralee from Ballymacelligott to the east you meet the imposing 2007 monument featuring Kerry's high-fielding heroes. The traveller may circle the Paddy Paul Fitzgerald or Joe Keohane roundabouts and travel along John Joe Sheehy Road, the Dan Spring or 'Bracker' Regan ring roads or pass Stack's Villas before reaching Kerins's Park and Cahill's Park. The lone terrace in Killarney named after Dick Fitzgerald does not have his name on a plaque to honour the decision taken in the UDC chambers on 6 March 1931. The minutes of the meeting read: 'Mr Ahern moved that in memory of the late Mr Richard Fitzgerald the Moyeightragh houses in course of construction be named Fitzgerald Terrace. Mr Hansard recorded the motion which was unanimously agreed to.'[1]

Dr Crokes convened a meeting to consider establishing a monument to Dick Fitzgerald some ten weeks after his death, on 14 November 1930. The last survivor of the thirty-six Dr Crokes members who attended this meeting was Jacko Keeffe, a player on the 1931 All-Ireland-winning Kerry minor side. He died the day the Sam Maguire was brought home to Kerry in 2006. Despite the Depression of the 1930s and the Economic War with England, these men realised their dream with the

Undated portrait of Dick Fitzgerald, late 1920s
(Picture courtesy of Looney family)

The College Street team, Killarney Street League champions, 1925.
Dick Fitzgerald is sitting on the right.
(Picture courtesy Edmund Eagar)

Dick Fitzgerald (on the far left wearing white shirt), team manager, with the Kerry team
en route to New York on the Baltic, 1927
(Picture courtesy Edmund Eagar)

The Kerry team training en route to New York on the Baltic, *1927.*
Dick Fitzgerald is on the left in the foreground.
(Picture from John Barry and Eamon Horan, Years of Glory, *1977)*

A composition photograph
of Dick Fitzgerald with
Jack Walsh during the Kerry
team's New York trip, 1927.
(Picture courtesy
Edmund Eagar)

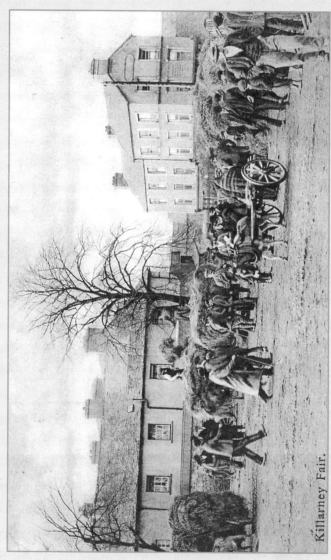

Killarney Fair.

The Fair Field, Killarney, scene of the untimely death of Dick Fitzgerald in 1930 as the result of a fall from the Courthouse. The Criterion (now the Royal) Hotel can be seen on the right.

The official opening of Fitzgerald Stadium, Whit Sunday, 31 May 1936.
Kerry goalkeeper, Pat Dillon, brother-in-law of Dick Fitzgerald, leads the 1903–9 victors' section
in the parade. Defeated All-Ireland finalists, Laune Rangers (1892), can be seen on the left.
(Picture courtesy Edmund Eagar)

Jerry O'Leary, Dinso Hurley, stadium architect Mícheál Ó Riada and Eugene O'Sullivan survey the
grounds at Fitzgerald Stadium before the 1937 All-Ireland.

Dick Fitzgeralds, Senior County Champions, 1951
Back row from left: Andrew Larkin; Billy Fleming; Dan Kavanagh; Donie Murphy; Denis Fleming;
Pa Joe Teahan, Michael Leary; Gerald Teahan
Front row from left: Connie Riordan; Paddy Tangney; Teddy O'Connor; Dan O'Neill; Miah Larkin;
Tadhgie Lyne; Donal Prendiville
(Picture from Eamonn Fitzgerald (ed), Dr Crokes Gaelic Century, 1986)

Dick Fitzgeralds Kerry Minor County Champions 1951

Liam Brosnan	Gene Moriarity	Sean O'Shea	Liam Murphy	Sean Myers	Michael Looney
Johnny Teahan	Pa Joe Cronin	Michael O'Callaghan	Connie Riordan	John Cahill	M Williams
Michael O'Connor	John O'Leary	Mick Bartlett	Michael Fleming	Con Sullivan	Patrick O'Donoghue
		Pa O'Brien	Paddy O'Shea	G O'Donoghue	

(Courtesy Brian O'Callaghan)

Killarney reunion of All-Ireland Champions: photograph taken in Charlie Foley's pub, New Street, in the early 1960s, including Mike Murphy, brother of 'Con of the Hundred Battles 'Murphy; 'Small' Jer Leary; Maurice McCarthy; Jack Myers, Dinny Curran, Dinny Breen. Charlie Foley is on the extreme right. Standing behind is Dan Kavanagh, son-in-law of Jack Myers.

(Picture courtesy Denis Moriarty)

The Kerry and Cork teams parade in Fitzgerald Stadium before the Munster Final, 1 July 2007.
St Finan's Hospital can be seen on the right.
(Picture Valerie O'Sullivan)

Kerry captain Declan O'Sullivan celebrates victory in the Munster Championship
with young supporters, 1 July 2007
(Picture Valerie O'Sullivan)

blessing and opening of the Fitzgerald Stadium six years after Dick Fitzgerald's death.

By spring of 1931, Dr Crokes had set up two committees to spearhead the stadium project. Local solicitor Conno Healy was appointed chairman of the finance group, which sought to raise funds at home and abroad. John Clifford and the O'Sullivan cousins, Eugene and Dr Eamonn, were entrusted with the task of acquiring a site.

A meeting at the Gresham Hotel on 6 September 1931 established a strong Dublin-based group. Next the club involved exiles in the US. While touring with Kerry in 1931, Dee O'Connor and Paul Russell helped set up fund-raising committees in Chicago, Philadelphia, San Francisco and other cities. Dickeen's former playing colleague Johnnie Mahony headed a strong New York committee to provide a support network for the efforts of the club at home. This is a solid example of the generosity of countless generations of Irish exiles who have traditionally dug deep to help families and communities at home. The 1947 Polo Grounds final in New York, the Whit Wembley Games and the ongoing touring of clubs, county teams and All-Stars in the US and Britain have been gestures in recognition of this generosity, initiated by Michael Cusack himself when he sent Ireland's elite fifty-four hurlers, footballer and athletes to the US in 1888. The return has proved of immense value to projects like the development of the Fitzgerald Memorial Stadium and purchase of the Tralee Sportsfield.

At a Dr Crokes club EGM in March 1932 a three-man sub-committee – Eugene O'Sullivan, John Clifford and Dr Eamonn O'Sullivan – recommended that the club purchase Dan Courtney's land at Kilcoolaght for £750. Dick Fitzgerald's former flying column comrade Tim O'Mara from High Street moved that the proposal be accepted. The famous referee and local barber Charlie Fleming seconded Tim's proposal, which was carried.

The club appointed a delegation to approach the Munster Council of the GAA, of which the sub-committee's Dr Eamonn O'Sullivan was an elected member. Club chairman and former Kerry football star Eugene O'Sullivan addressed the provincial gathering, indicating that their project had received Kerry County Board's tacit approval. He outlined Dick Fitzgerald's lifelong GAA involvement, which merited a Gaelic stadium as a fitting memorial. Dick's classmate and close friend, Jer O'Leary of Main Street, Killarney, and his flying column companion, crack marksman, Neilus McCarthy, supported their chairman's plea. The Munster Council, which had 463 affiliated clubs in 1932, allotted '£756 to new grounds[2]'. On the proposal of Dr Eamonn O'Sullivan, seconded by T. Considine of County Clare, it was decided to allocate £400 to the Dick Fitzgerald memorial park.[3]

Next stop was GAA Central Council, which Eugene and Dr Eamonn approached in October 1932. Dr Eamonn, himself a famed coach, 'referred to Dick Fitzgerald's work for the GAA and said that the Central Council should do its part in perpetuating his memory. The Council postponed its decision until the next finance meeting, at which they decided to give £300.'[4] The club's hope had been that the respective councils would offer their £400 and £300 grant aid as subscriptions rather than as investments. This was to prove a sticking point in later debates concerning rights, control and ownership of the park. By March 1933 challenges were already arising about control of the uncompleted park.

At that month's County Board meeting Eugene O'Sullivan

defended his Dr Crokes position: 'I regret to say that we asked for the cooperation of the clubs in Kerry and so far we have not got one solitary contribution'.[5] It was pointed out that a Kerry team had travelled to play Waterford as a fund-raiser on behalf of the project but Eugene maintained his criticism of the clubs.

In 2001 Jacko Keeffe, the last surviving founder member and Patron of Dr Crokes recalled:

> Eamonn's position as RMS [director] of the Mental Hospital played a huge part in the development of the stadium. Occupational Therapy in those hospitals had been unheard of up until then. He sought and gained permission at a meeting of the Killarney Mental Hospital committee in March 1933 to allow the patients to work on developing a field which was not the property of the committee. There was some condemnation of Eamonn's project in the local press; nevertheless he was in no doubt that the work was of great therapeutic value to the patients. He added, 'It was the very first undertaking of the subsequently developed Occupational Therapy Department of the hospital and could be described as its magnum opus.' In a letter to the hospital, the Minister for Local Government said he was pleased to learn the work had beneficial effects on the health of the patients and a number of cures had resulted from it.
>
> It was only fitting that the pavilion and stand erected in the 1970s should be named in honour of Dr Eamonn. This development was officially opened by Eamonn's son Anthony in 1977...All

involved in the development of the stadium were in agreement that his contribution was massive. [Eamonn] always told us of the great help that came from the staff of the Mental Hospital, in particular – Denso Hurley, Myo Murphy, and Tim O'Donoghue – and of course the patients, without whom nothing could have been achieved. Remember it was nearly all manual work at that period of our history.

Many thought at the time that he was too ambitious, but as we look back from today we now appreciate that he could see way further into the future than any of us.[6]

On Sunday 21 October 2001 that unique volunteer contribution by the workforce of Kerry patients was publicly commemorated when a plaque was unveiled by Dr Brendan Lynch on the face of the imposing press box on the Michael O'Connor Terrace. The inscription, carved in stone, reads:

Erected in Appreciation of the Contribution of Staff and Patients of St Finan's Hospital to the Development of Fitzgerald Stadium 1930–1936.

Stadium Chairman Pádraig O'Sullivan said:

We assemble to unveil a plaque to the memory of the staff and patients of St Finan's Hospital, whose contribution in the initial stages of the development of the Fitzgerald Stadium laid the foundation for the magnificent sports facility which we enjoy today.

Though belated in proposed execution it will in time for future generations commemorate the labours of the hospital patients and staff who built the original earthen terrace...At that time to allow the patients to work on a voluntary basis on this development was the brainchild of the late Dr Eamonn O'Sullivan who was a man before his time to introduce this type of occupational therapy which hastened the entry of the patients back into normal life style... Another milestone...the recent plaque unveiled by the Munster Council of the GAA to commemorate famous events in the illustrious history of the Stadium – and in particular the hosting of the 1937 All-Ireland Hurling Final between Tipperary and Kilkenny.[7]

Donal Hickey reported the occasion in the *Kingdom* of 23 October 2001:

STADIUM A MONUMENT TO FORMER ST FINAN'S PATIENTS

In the warm sunshine on last Sunday morning Fitzgerald Stadium Killarney looked its exquisite best. It was entirely appropriate that a special event at the arena should be staged under blues skies. Sixty-five years after the opening of the grounds many of those who shed honest sweat in doing the hard graft with wheelbarrow, pick and shovel were belatedly honoured.

A plaque was unveiled by Dr Brendan Lynch in acknowledgement of the contribution of the patients and staff of St Finan's Hospital to the stadium. Stories of long-forgotten days in the 1930s were recalled. Up to sixty patients were involved in what was seen in those days as a pioneering project in occupational therapy. Only a few words are carved on the simple limestone plaque on the front wall of the press box. The workers don't need many words – the stadium is their monument. But the achievements of those now nameless people have at last been publicly recognised lest we forget.'[8]

When he officially opened the stadium on 31 May 1936 GAA Patron and Archbishop of Cashel and Emly Dr Harty said: 'This park is the finest playing field in Ireland and can compare with any stadium in the whole world'. The ideal weather and local scenery added to a memorable sporting occasion for the more than 20,000 patrons who attended the occasion. They witnessed the footballers of Mayo having the better of their Kerry hosts and Cork defeating their traditional hurling rivals Tipperary. The gala opening included a parade of all surviving members of All-Ireland Kerry teams, led by the hurling heroes of 1891 who brought home national honours. In their footsteps followed fourteen veterans proudly bearing their banner reading 'Ciarraí 1892 Laune Rangers'. It would be impossible to exaggerate the deep sense of pride in the minds of all the volunteers who had a hand in transforming a rolling hill into an exceptional sporting arena. There is no better example of the volunteerism at the very heart of the GAA's ethos than the genesis and creation of Fitzgerald Memorial Park.

Margaret O'Leary, whose father Jer played a key organisational role in the project, recalls how the children of the town loaded scraws (grass sods) on to drays on Sunday mornings from a site where houses were being built – to be called O'Sullivan Place after Dick's friend Eugene O'Sullivan. They would follow the horses along Lewis Road and place the scraws by hand on the new terrace in the making. Margaret's relative, Timothy J. O'Leary, uncle of 'Small' Jer O'Leary, who was a member of staff of the Crawford College of Art in Cork, designed the poster used to publicise the opening of the stadium, on Whit Sunday 1936. The Blessing was imparted by Bishop of Kerry Michael O'Brien. Mícheál Ó Riada (Michael Reidy), Principal of Killarney Technical School, designed the Celtic-style concrete façade now surmounted by the limestone relief of Dick Fitzgerald. Further examples of Reidy's outstanding work can be seen in the façade and interior of the Arbutus Hotel, on the street where Dick Fitzgerald was born, and the 1928 monument to poet Tomás Rua Ó Súilleabháin in Derrynane Abbey, Caherdaniel.

The original cinder athletic track surrounding the field was later converted into concrete sideline seating, in turn incorporated into the present development which maximises space for fans. In 1985 the Prunty pitch was laid at a cost of £70,000, giving a better all-weather sod in a region accustomed to frequent rain. The hand-crafted terrace with sight of the McGillycuddy Reeks has since been replaced by a state-of-the-art concrete one dedicated to the memory of the late Michael O'Connor NT. He was a former Dr Crokes player and administrator who, having been Secretary of the Stadium Committee, served as Chairman of the Munster Council 1986-9. The Dr Eamonn O'Sullivan Stadium Pavilion, which cost £100,000, was opened by Seán Ó Síocháin, Director General of the GAA and Dr Eamonn's son, Anthony, in June 1977. It was extended in 1986 to celebrate the stadium's golden jubilee. The dressing rooms commemorate another celebrated footballer, Paddy Moynihan of Glenflesk and Killarney.

While Dr Crokes, the founding club, failed to secure control of the stadium, it retains the right to nominate one trustee out of four. Jackie Looney, cousin of the author, reflects on this impasse:

> The Dr Croke Club…did not get the control exercised by clubs who purchase and develop at the present day and have three trustees out of a total of five, the other two going to the Kerry County Board and Munster Council…the club did not want to get involved in a disagreement over a project which was perpetuating the memory of a former chairman and which was a labour of love. They were conscious that irrespective of who controlled the field it was going to be a boon to the town of Killarney…The stadium remains as a permanent memorial, not only to the great footballer it commemorates but also to the gigantic work put into it over four years of development.[9]

The club has developed two other grounds: Deerpark purchased at the cost of £72,000 in 1982, and Páirc na gCrócach at the old CIE Ballast Pit, Lewis Road, which was acquired from its trustees, the Fitzgerald Stadium Committee, on 2 March 1993. It has also developed three pitches, a clubhouse, a stand and a night lighting system on this 'fourth green field'. The story is well told by Dan Kelliher and Niall Keogh in their book *Decade of Glory*, published in 1996.[10]

THE DICK FITZGERALDS CAMOGIE TEAM

Some ladies of Dr Crokes camogie team took the decision to change their club allegiance on the death of their long-time hero and club trainer Dick Fitzgerald. Thus they became the Dick Fitzgeralds. This was at a time when the county camogie team enjoyed considerable success, even defeating Cork.[11]

This move coincided with the foundation of the East Kerry Camogie Board in June 1933. The split in the Croke camp led to a civil war of words centred on the right of the Dick Fitzgeralds to wear the traditional black and amber of their mother club. As the newly formed team had registered their club and colours prior to Dr Crokes, the board chairman ruled that they would wear the black and amber. Following a year of controversy Killorglin were crowned 1933 league champions after defeating the Dick Fitzgeralds in April 1934. 'On 7 November 1933 an excursion train ran from Killarney to Cork to accommodate the large crowd who wished to see Lee Hosiery, Cork, challenge Kerry for the Kingdom Cup. The fixture created great interest and an attendance of six to seven thousand was present.'[12] Cork won easily, 5-2 to nil. Killarney provided eight players on the day with seven Dick Fitzgeralds including county captain Teresa O'Connor lining out in the green and gold. The long-serving GAA administrator Dick Fitzgerald would have been well pleased with the news that: 'Miss O'Connor, Killarney, was elected treasurer of the new Munster Council in 1934.'[13]

The East Kerry Board was founded 'on 17 May 1925 – at a meeting in Central Club, Killarney – The following officers were elected: Chairman R. Fitzgerald; Vice-do Humphrey Murphy; Hon. Secs. Paul Russell and Michael O'Leary; Joint Treasurer Conno Healy and T. Mahony.'[14] Delegates from nine neighbouring clubs followed new County Board directives and set in motion a District Board that was to serve the Association and its members splendidly. Dick Fitzgerald and his fellow officers established a sound 'administrative structure...and the foundation for the growth of the GAA in the area had been laid'.[15]

THE DICK FITZS

As Dr Crokes had failed to win the County Championship since 1914 the Club took a decision on 10 February 1944 to try to organise a divisional team. They wrote to East Kerry Board Secretary, Danny O'Sullivan of Listry, who promptly convened a meeting in the Central Club, College Square, Killarney. This property was owned by the family of Brian Ó Ceallaigh, relatives of Seán Kelly who served as GAA President (2003–6).

When I spoke to him on 14 January 2008 in his home in Drombrick, Listry, Danny O'Sullivan, by then ninety-two years of age, described the meeting chaired by Tom Lynch, father of Kerry stars Brendan and Paudie Lynch of Beaufort. As delegates from Listry, Kilcummin, Rathmore, Headford, Beaufort and Dr Crokes agreed to form a championship panel they struggled 'to arrive at an appropriate name. Many saints and patrons were suggested. Danny O'Sullivan's gaze fell on the portrait of Dick Fitzgerald on the wall of the room and he exclaimed, 'Isn't that man fine?' No worthier man was the consensus and the Dick Fitzgeralds was launched. The Crokes colours of black and amber were equally acceptable.'[16] Sixty-three years later Danny O'Sullivan clearly recalled that portrait on the wall of the Central Club's meeting room and confirmed his own inspirational suggestion as 'perfect'.

The first year, 1944, saw three epic encounters between Dr Crokes and Killarney Legion, which had been founded in

1929. Legion progressed to the semi-final. 1945 was a better championship year for the Dick Fitzs – or Dicks as they became popularly known – when they contested the County Semi-Final with Shannon Rangers in a three-game saga. Rangers won in the end and became County Champions, defeating Killarney Legion in the final replay. P.F. paid tribute to the 1945 semi-finalists: 'Two teams...have won the hearts and captured the imagination of thousands of football fans...their names will blazon forth like first-class thrill-makers and fine, sporting, manly players.'[17]

The Dicks easily accounted for both Castleisland and John Mitchels in the early rounds in 1946. Their quarter-final victory over neighbouring rivals Legion on the score 1-5 to 0-4 has entered local folklore because of a the Rule 27 objection lodged against Jimmy Joy, a Dublin-based Killorglin man, who had allegedly played rugby in the capital. 'Legion duly objected within the specified seven days. Fitzgeralds counter-objected to Fr Mickey Lyne who, they alleged, was a member of Glasgow Celtic soccer club. And there the saga began.'[18] When one considers that 20,000 people had witnessed the quarter-final in Fitzgerald Park on 14 July it is easy to imagine the keen interest shown in the subsequent County Board deliberations and decisions. Twenty-two of the players involved were county minor and senior stars, six of whom were panellists on the Kerry team that defeated Roscommon in the replayed All-Ireland final later that summer. Both objections were withdrawn following negotiations but the Dicks refused to abide by County Chairman D.J. Baily's command to replay the match. 'One of the Fitzgerald delegates said that both objections were withdrawn and that if that was so why should his club after winning the match be ordered to replay.'[19]

The chairman refixed the game for 14 November despite Fitzgeralds' assurances that they would not line out. Legion went on to win the final against John Mitchels 0-7 to 0-5.

The Dicks succumbed to Dingle in the 1947 semi-fnal and astounded the GAA public by amalgamating with the Legion under the name 'Killarney' for the 1948 Championship. 'Perfect agreement and unanimity has been reached by all parties and the new 'coalition' has but one objective and that is to place on the field a team that will bring back to Killarney the county honours.'[20] The new green-and-amber team was defeated by eventual champions Dingle in the semi-final but achieved their objective by defeating John Mitchels 2-7 to 2-3 in the 1949 County Final. They won their first four games the following year and having drawn with Castleisland in the 1950 County Final lost their county crown in the replay 1-7 to 1-4. The Killarney minors lost their final to North Kerry 5-4 to 2-5. Record gate receipts came to £583/8s on that Sunday, 13 November 1950.

Dick Fitzgeralds re-emerged the following year in a campaign which was to prove their most successful. 'The Legion formed the nucleus of the Killarney team…Clubs to the east wished the team to be called after the famous poet of that district Eoghan Ruadh (Ó Súilleabháin), while the Croke Club wanted their immortal Dick Fitzgerald honoured.'[21] Honour him they did by winning the Kerry double in Tralee on Sunday 30 September 1951.

Their six-game campaign was a roller-coaster one. 'Shannon Rangers held Dick Fitzgeralds to a draw in the semi-final, but they were no match for the Killarney men in the replay. The final was played on 30 September and Dick Fitzgeralds won – fittingly on the twenty-first anniversary of the death of the man after whom the team was named. It was a keenly contested game, at times over vigorous…and at the finish they were seven points ahead and deserving winners.'[22] The minors completed a glorious double by turning the tables on their North Kerry conquerors of the previous year 3-3 to 1-5. Many of those were members of the Killarney sides, led by the charismatic Laoisman, Den Campion, who won three-in-a row Minor County Championship hurling titles 1950, 1951 and 1952, and were runners-up to Kilmoyley in 1953.

The Dicks remained together for four seasons – until 1955 – but never again reached the heights of their 1950 and 1951 campaigns. The vision of the men who forged the Dicks from the Killarney, Lauragh, Sliabh Luachra and mid-Kerry districts added greatly to the mystique surrounding the legendary Dickeen Fitzgerald.

JUDGING DICK

Danny 'Colonel' O'Sullivan places Dick Fitzgerald as left-corner forward in his best East Kerry team of all time.[23] In a special feature based on their 2007 publication, *Princes of Pigskin: A Century of Kerry Footballers*, authors and journalists T.J. Flynn and Joe Ó Muircheartaigh select their first choice thirty-man panel, placing Dick Fitzgerald at No. 9.[24] 'Kings for a Lifetime – Mad about Sport' counts down its top 30 Kerry footballers of all time, spanning the century between Dick Fitzgerald and Colm Cooper'.[25] Both 'Dickeen' and Colm Cooper of Dr Crokes made the first XV, along with fellow Crokes Tadhgie Lyne (at No. 13), Ventry's Tom Long (No. 27) and Paul Russell (No. 28).

In its special supplement of 12 September 2007, in advance of that year's All-Ireland Senior Football Final, the *Kerryman* commissioned Ballyduff statistician Sylvester Hennessy to highlight the Kerry top championship appearances. His study 'records...footballers who have shown remarkable longevity and others who have made it to the 50-match barrier.' Dick Fitzgerald stands at No. 4 at the beginning of the 2008 championship season. This is noteworthy considering that the Kerry County Board was defunct in 1907 and 1917 and in dispute with Central Council in 1910. Furthermore, due to Fitzgerald's imprisonment in Frongoch during 1916 he managed to play only one championship game. Therefore, his tally of fifty-eight games merits fourth place behind Darragh Ó Sé's (An Ghaeltacht) 67, goalie Dan O'Keeffe's (Kerins O'Rahilly's) 66 and Glenflesk's Seamus Moynihan's 61 senior appearances. It must be recognised that the qualifier (or 'back-door') system introduced in 2001 involves more games for players of modern times.

Respected sports journalist P.F. posed this question in his 1945 classic *Kerry's Football Story*: 'What was the greatest side Kerry ever fielded? In my opinion it was the team that beat Louth in the Croke Memorial Final replay in 1913. The match is regarded by many as the greatest ever played.'[26] Dick Fitzgerald lined out 'on the forty' or at centre half-forward. 'Many Kerry poets composed songs to celebrate the county's great victory in the Croke Memorial Final. Kerry people saw motion pictures of the match at the Theatre Royal, Tralee, a few days after the event.'[27] The days of sending match reports by carrier-pigeon were coming to an end as ciné introduced a new era of communications and promotion. The six Croke Cup games netted £2,734 enabling the GAA to purchase Jones's Road 'from their secretary Frank Dineen for £3,641/8s/5d and rename it Croke Memorial Park'[28]. East Kerry folklore credits captain Dick Fitzgerald's classmate and friend Jer O'Leary with helping to seal the deal in Wynn's Hotel, Dublin. His wise and timely interjection of 'Split the difference' influenced the sale and purchase of the national stadium on 22 December 1913. According to Galway football star Jack Mahon, 'The game of Gaelic Football has never looked back.'[29]

P.F. scanned the GAA's first six decades when making his selection. Eoghan Corry comments on those who bravely selected the Teams of the Millennium in 1999 – 'No one on either the football or hurling teams predates the 1940s'.[30] Celebrated sportswriter P.D. Mehigan ('Carbery') chose Dick Fitzgerald as his all-time full forward, flanked by his former Nils' colleague Bill Mackessy at right-corner forward and Kerry's John Joe Sheehy.[31] Mackessy, who attended Fitzgerald's funeral, is listed in *How to Play Gaelic Football* as one of some 'forty-two best players of his era in his instructional manual'.[32]

HOW TO PLAY GAELIC FOOTBALL

Dick Fitz's own publication enjoys the distinction of being the first ever GAA manual. With Guy's of Cork he designed a user-friendly work that came to be a treasured volume in many homes. It is surprising that this delightful work was never reprinted until now. It is remarkable that while captaining his county team and seeking back-to-back All-Ireland titles Dickeen found the motivation and time to produce this work.

Graphic artist Thomas Barker of Cork depicts the author on the front cover receiving the 'pigskin' with two hands. His alert stance is true to Dr Eamonn O'Sullivan's mantra of later training sessions: 'eye on the ball'. Barker's design, art and lettering typify the Celtic revival of the early decades of the twentieth century. Dick includes team photographs of the All-Ireland winning sides of 1903-04 and 1913 together with seven pictures outlining technical skills of what be terms 'a scientific game'[33].

Two portraits are printed in the early pages – Dr Croke, patron of the GAA, and Dick's own. The portrait of Dick Fitzgerald was most likely photographed at his College Street home. Set against a background of ivy, on an ornate Victorian stand, is the Croke Memorial Cup. Engraved on this trophy, now in possession of Dick's own club, is the legend: 'The Property of the Killarney Dr Crokes'[34]. Dick Fitzgerald's work of innovation and reflection on football and – to a lesser degree – hurling is another lasting memorial.

'The Most Colourful Personality'

In *Kerry's Football Story*, Paddy Foley (P.F.) devoted many pages to Dick Fitzgerald's playing career. As a journalist he accompanied Kerry on their disappointing 1927 US tour with Dickeen as team manager. It was P.F. who wrote in 1945: 'He was the most colourful personality the game has ever known.'[1] All accounts describe Dickeen as an even-tempered and affable man. He evidently enjoyed good company and the cut and thrust of debate and banter.

In his self-published memoir *Killarney – Top of Towns*, published in 1996, Killarney octogenarian Tim McCarthy devotes one section to 'Brewery Lane and Football':

> The next four houses belonged to the Dillon family. There were four sisters and one brother, Pat. Dick Fitzgerald, the famous Kerry footballer found a wife here – Miss (Kitty) Dillon. At one time all the Dillon sisters made lace, which was exhibited and sold in the last house near Kenmare Place. At one time, lace was very fashionable with all local ladies. Tourists were the best customers. We were constantly meeting these famous Kerry footballers. Dick Fitzgerald often had heated arguments (about

football) with Katie O'Shea (Mackey's sister) who left nothing go with him.

Dick was always a very affable character around the streets. Well dressed – three piece suit, and, of course, hat. He would don the black and amber (Dr Crokes colour) sometimes, but was slowing down very much. Brother La Salle got him to train us in the Monastery team once or maybe twice. He showed us some of his tricks, but he preferred to play, laugh, and gazzay with us.

In his time there were no radios, TV or phones in the country districts…Country teachers came to town on Saturdays in a pony and trap, or bicycle. Naturally, they would not be as well versed in current events as Dickeen. On one occasion, Dick had a very heated argument in a public house with another townsman. Finally, Dickeen shouted at him: 'You are as ignorant as a country school master.'[2]

(Tim's own late wife Margaret (nee O'Donoghue) was an esteemed school principal at Tiernaboul NS in the rural heartland of Spa, Killarney, where she taught Kerry's first ever footballing All-Star, Donie O'Sullivan.)

The marriage register of St Patrick's Church, Cork, records that on 17 October 1925 Richard Fitzgerald of College Street, Killarney, married Catherine (Kitty) Dillon, Kenmare Place, Killarney. Her sister Bridget (popularly known as Bee) was bridesmaid, and the College Street, solicitor Cornelius (Conno) Healy (a member of the 1923 Kingdom side) was best man. Fr Edmond Fitzgerald CC was the officiating minister. Kitty had worked as a hotel receptionist in Cobh, County Cork. Eighteen months later Kitty Fitzgerald was dead and the unsigned *Irish Independent* journalist reported to the nation on All-Ireland Monday 1930, two days after Dick Fitzgerald's own tragic death: 'He suffered a heavy bereavement by the death of his wife a few years back.'[3]

Dr Eamonn O'Sullivan knew Dick Fitzgerald personally. Both were involved in Dr Crokes club, athletics and Kerry football at all levels. Reflecting on their alma mater, St Brendan's Seminary, Killarney, Dr Eamonn reminisced: 'It produced many famous footballers among its sixty-one All-Ireland Senior medallists, the most notable being that wizard of Gaelic forwards – the late 'Dickeen' Fitzgerald of Killarney, who was on Kerry winning teams from 1905 to 1914. I have a vivid recollection of a single coaching lesson he gave the footballers in my last year in St Brendan's in 1914. I recall distinctly that equipped with only ordinary street boots, he said to me, "I will show you how to curve a ball from near the end line." With consummate ease he screwed a free kick about five yards from the end line, it curved over the bar. I have yet to see a Gaelic footballer repeat this performance.'[4] This is high praise from the mentor who trained eight Kingdom teams to Senior All-Ireland victories – 1924, 1926, 1937, 1946, 1953, 1955, 1959 and 1962.

Dick Fitzgerald's book of 1914 proposed that Gaelic Football was 'a scientific game'[5]. A similar vision was promoted by Dr Eamonn forty-four years later when he published *The Art and Science of Gaelic Football* in 1958.

Danny O'Sullivan, the East Kerry Board secretary who coined the name 'Dick Fitzgeralds' for their newly-formed divisional team, has vivid memories of Dick Fitzgerald at the Cricket Field. 'He would welcome all the young lads at the entrance gate with the greeting '*Dia bhur mbeatha-sa, a bhuachaillí, agus fáilte,*' proffering his hand in an encouraging welcome. He always used the Irish.' The enduring memory of Killarney's Fr Seán Quinlan also featured Dickeen at the Cricket Field:

> I have spent about forty years living away from Killarney. In those years I had twin preoccupations: the Kerry team and Killarney's Dr Crokes. Once in Denver, Colorado, since Reuters sent sports results worldwide, irrespective of code or country, I called a local TV station for an All-Ireland result. The man was most obliging, and said, 'I can't figure this goals and points stuff.' But I did and made the translation as he read to me. It was Kerry's All-Ireland! Another memory is of a kind of fun game run by the Crokes in the old Cricket Field. I have often wondered what happened the gate crowned with iron pine cones, where you entered the field.
>
> The game was a minor carnival. A diminutive jarvey from the laneway between the Handy Stores and the Ross Hotel, who had the nickname Mickey Lump, was on the field. So was Jack Sewell, the chemist, who had his togs in a splendid Gladstone bag. (He was a former Irish rugby international).
>
> Walking up and down near the forty, joking and laughing, was Dick Fitzgerald. He wore his hat, a long trousers, but the Crokes jersey. And once in the game, if it was a game, he scored a point, his one and only for me.
>
> It was not much later when the Kerry team, back from beating Monaghan, the Crokes, and a

raggle-taggle of small boys marched all the way to the New Cemetery with the body of Fitzy. The one face I still remembered in the guard of honour is that of Purty Landers.[6]

Cork-based missionary, Fr Michael Carrick MSC, clearly recalls a sideline comment of the legendary Dickeen Fitz. The Boherbee native attended an inter-county game across the road from his Tralee home in 1918. Kerry were playing poorly when selector Dick moved from the sideline on to the pitch, loudly remonstrating, 'This is not Kerry football.'

The respected Gaeltacht *scéalaí* and *seanchaí* Jack Kevane reminisced that Dick Fitz was *'laoch mór caide'* – 'a mighty football hero'. This centenarian, resident in Dingle Hospital, is a respected student of Kerry football.

The nickname 'Springheel' or 'Aeroplane' denotes the high-fielding supremacy of a man who played senior football for Kerry over six seasons and who saw active service as a War of Independence Volunteer. We are indebted to Raymond Smith for recording Pat 'Aeroplane' O'Shea's assessment of his colleague and county captain, Dick Fitzgerald;

> It is generally acknowledged that dark-haired Pat O'Shea was one of the greatest fielders to have come out of the Kingdom. It was not surprising then that he got the middle name 'Aeroplane'. He came from the little village of Castlegregory, lying on the Dingle Peninsula, sixteen miles from Tralee. Pat O'Shea's midfield partner was Con Murphy, champion ploughman of Listry. Pivot of the attack was, of course, Dick Fitzgerald at centre-forward.

'I first saw him in action,' said Pat O'Shea, 'in a club match in Tralee in 1905. A mere stripling then, he yet displayed all the coolness and skill which made score-getting look easy. These qualities he retained during his entire playing career, even when he became a much heavier man and less speedy. He was the most unselfish forward I ever saw, always parting with the ball to any of his forwards better placed. He dropped the ball in front of the man's position, using a ground pass or fast, low punt. The forward started running as Dick kicked the ball and so caught it on the run. Many was the occasion that he pulled a game out of the fire with seconds to go.

Above all Dick was a great captain – a captain who knew his responsibilities. Normally jovial and witty, he became serious and responsible when a big match was in the offing, our champion and guardian, looking after our comfort with fatherly care and making sure that if we worked hard, we also relaxed. On the field he was always the captain. If an order or advice was needed, he delivered it gently but firmly, for he was at heart a kind and good man. On public occasions, when speeches had to be made, Dick was equal to every demand. And yet oratory was not an exercise he greatly favoured. He was modest in victory, he was cheerful in defeat – in a word a man whose name will never be forgotten in the Kingdom.[7]

Aran Islander Breandán Ó hEithir struck up a friendship with Dr Jim O'Brien, a local publican, bibliophile and medical man while attending Coláiste Einde, Galway, as a boarder. Ó hEithir, nephew of Liam O'Flaherty, likewise had the gift of ink. Among his best books is *Over the Bar*, first published by Ward River Press during the GAA Centenary Year of 1984. Ó hEithir tells how Jim O'Brien mentioned:

> ...a book he had picked up from a barrow on the Dublin quays...and produced a little green-covered book which he told me I could keep. This rare offer startled me more than the sight of *How to Play Gaelic Football* by Dick Fitzgerald, the first book on Gaelic games I ever possessed.
>
> Dick Fitzgerald played for Kerry in the All-Irelands of 1903, '04, '05, '08 and '09 and captained the team in the All-Irelands of 1913, '14 and '15, as well as captaining teams in various jails during the War of Independence. He is regarded by those who saw him play, or played against him, as one of the greatest of all time.[8]

Ó hEithir, who played a key role in the making of Gael Linn's celebrated 1964 film about Christy Ring, devotes four pages to Dick Fitzgerald's 1914 presentation of 'the scientific game...and accordingly we trust that, while it will ever be developing on the scientific side, it may never become the possession of the professional player.'[9]

> A lot of what Fitzgerald wrote went over my head and the only practical knowledge I gained from

reading his book was the importance he placed on ball control on the ground: dribbling the ball and playing it off the ground with the foot, in defence and in attack. But at last I had something Irish to add to the pile of books and magazines on sports of all kinds I had accumulated since inheriting Roger Hammond's collection.

About the author I knew little, except that his life ended tragically in 1930 and that the fine stadium in Killarney is named in his honour. Later I learned that in Kerry, during his lifetime, he was known simply as 'Dickeen'.[10]

Peil was a Louis Marcus film on Gaelic football commissioned by Gael Linn in 1960, drawing on Dr Eamonn O'Sullivan's 1957 book, *The Art and Science of Gaelic Football*. Ó hEithir's role as commentator immersed him in a Kerry footballing controversy surrounding the failure to appoint legendary Dr Eamonn O'Sullivan to train the Kerry side of that year. The players favoured Dr Eamonn but the Gael Linn film crew retreated from Killarney as the County Board refused to change their decision. The Sam Maguire crossed the Border for the very first time as Down took centre-stage in Marcus's *Peil*.

An *Irish Press* journalist for many years, Ó hEithir was friendly with 'Séamus de Faoite, the short story writer from Killlarney…Séamus, who worked as a sub-editor, was probably the most dedicated Kerry supporter that I ever met…deadly serious and partisan.'[11] Con Houlihan's foreword to de Faoite's *Death of a King and Other Stories* analyses the literary insight of the man who abandoned a good job in Killarney's Hilliard and Palmer Shoe Factory for the Abbey Theatre and the *Irish Press*.

'Killarney is a town almost as famous for its lanes as for its lakes. It fosters intimacy; its people do not look outwards for their values. A provincial is someone who believes that the capital of the world is elsewhere. For de Faoite, the capital was located somewhere between the Cathedral and the Friary.

'I have long envied the citizens of that laked-blessed town: when they came to Castleisland to a game of Gaelic football or perhaps rugby, they speak as if they are on an expedition to a foreign country…It is marvellous innocence. And if asked to apply one word to Séamus de Faoite's stories I wouldn't go beyond 'innocence'. It is, however an innocence that goes hand in hand with wisdom – like that of Charles Kickham's in *Knocknagow*… Some of de Faoite's stories are like the photograph – simple things expressed because he saw their significance.

'My favourite of his stories is "Pictures in a Pawnshop"– a tale of two men who set out from Killarney to a county final in Tralee. It embodies two of his passions – his belief that ordinary life is fraught with possibilities and his love of Gaelic football.'[12]

'Two foot-weary travellers took a late decision to attend a war-time County Football Final in Tralee. The pair of "Boys from Below the Bridge" stopped off at Firies Well where Champion J. P. O'Sullivan and his son Dr Eamonn had been born. Old Jack and young Joe Jack's animated conversation centred on the merits of the 1903 Kerry team on display on the pub wall.

> Joe Jack began to look round the place to avoid looking at the old man. A picture of the 1903 Kerry team caught his eye,
> 'The 1903 team.'
> 'Oh, clear I see them,' said Jack from under the

cap.

'There they all are now taking the pitch in their prime. Dickeen, Paddy Dillon, Austin Stack, Champion Sullivan, Dinny Kissane, Big Jack Myers. Fine, I can see them now skying balls to the sun and rising halfway to meet them coming back.'

Joe was stung into shouting: 'There was good men since.'

'Good men, Joe Jack, but never as good as the men I'm with now. Rocks to play for gallant men to break on, and men to laugh with and drink with when the waves were spent. Oh, God be with ye, the men I'm with now.'

'Was Paul Russell as good as any of them?' said Joe Jack.

'Was any son as good as his father?'

'Was any wan of them as good as Joe Barrett, or Con Brosnan, or John Joe Sheehy, or Miko Doyle, or Purty Landers, or Timmie Leary, or Jackie Lyne?'

'Good men all, but never as good as the men I'm with now. Fit to carry the game you shaped for them, Dickeen boy, but no more than that, Dickeen, you king in a Kingdom of kings.'

'O God be good to you, Dickeen Fitz,
You king in a Kingdom of kings.'[13]

NOTES

CHAPTER 1
1. Fitzgerald 1986: 13
2. Larner 2005: 197
3. Hickey and Leen 1986: 26
4. Hickey and Leen 1986: 26
5. Cronin 2005: 327
6. O'Muircheartaigh and Flynn 2007: 16
7. Cronin 2005: 330

CHAPTER 2
1. Woulfe 1923: 365
2. Farrell 2000: 8
3. Larner 2005: 231
4. Fitzgerald 1986: 12-13
5. Fitzgerald 1986: 22
6. Larner 2005: 249
7. O'Shea 1998: 30
8. Fitzgerald 1986: 31
9. O'Shea 1998: 30
10. O'Shea 1998: 31
11. De Faoite 1980: 66

CHAPTER 3
1. Fitzgerald 1986: 34
2. O'Shea 1998: 32
3. O'Shea 1998: 32
4. Corry 1989: 67
5. Foley 1945: 31
6. Foley 1945: 31
7. Barry and Horan 1977: 12
8. Foley 1945: 31
9. Foley 1945: 32

10.   Foley 1945: 33
11.   Barry and Horan 1977: 14
12.   Foley 1945: 35
13.   Puirséal 1984: 134
14.   Puirséal 1984: 134
15.   Barry and Horan 1977: 14
16.   Foley 1945: 35-36
17.   Fitzgerald 1986: 20
18.   Foley 1945: 57
19.   Foley 1945: 37
20.   'Comóradh an Chéid Bhlian' 1988: 4
21.   Fitzgerald 1986: 36
22.   Coiste Staire and Munster Council 1986: 83
23.   Foley 1945: 37
24.   Smyth 2007: 354

CHAPTER 4

1.   Barry and Horan 1977: 17
2.   Barry and Horan 1977: 17
3.   O'Súilleabháin 1990: 52
4.   Barry and Horan 1977: 19
5.   Foley 1945: 40
6.   Barry and Horan 1977: 19
7.   Fitzgerald 1986: 90

CHAPTER 5

1.   Fitzgerald 1986: 35
2.   Fitzgerald 1986: 38-39
3.   Fitzgerald 1986: 39
4.   Fitzgerald 1986: 39
5.   Fitzgerald 1986: 39
6.   Coiste Staire and Munster Council 1986: 71
7.   Foley 1945: 42
8.   The *Kerryman:* 21/6/1907
9.   Foley 1945: 42
10.   Foley 1945: 40
11.   James Lyman Molloy

CHAPTER 6

1.   de Búrca, 1980: 93

2.   Fitzgerald 1914: 40
3.   O'Shea 1998: 44
4.   O'Shea 1998: 45
5.   Fitzgerald 1986: 41
6.   Fitzgerald 1986: 41
7.   O'Shea 1998: 48
8.   Foley 1945: 43
9.   Foley 1945: 43

CHAPTER 7
1.   Foley 1945: 43-44
2.   Foley 1945: 44
3.   Foley 1945: 45
4.   Barry and Horan 1977: 23

CHAPTER 8
1.   The *Kerryman* 5/11/1910 and Foley 1945: 47
2.   Foley 1945: 47
3.   Foley 1945: 48
4.   Foley 1945: 48
5.   Coiste Staire and Munster Council 1986: 86
6.   Foley 1945: 49
7.   Foley 1945: 49
8.   Foley 1945: 50
9.   Trustees of Muckross House 1984: 7
10.   Mahon 2001: 17
11.   Puirséal 1982: 150

CHAPTER 9
1.   Fitzgerald 1986: 45
2.   O'Shea 1998: 52
3.   Fitzgerald 1986: 45
4.   Fitzgerald 1986: 46
5.   Fitzgerald 1986: 45
6.   Foley 1945: 53
7.   Burke 2005: 71
8.   Foley 1945: 53

CHAPTER 10

1.   O'Shea 1998: 60
2.   Fitzgerald 1986: 47
3.   The *Kerryman* 18/10/1912
4.   Ó Súilleabháin 1990: 70
5.   The *Kerryman* 20/12/1912
6.   *Kerry Evening Star* 23/12/1912
7.   O'Shea 1998: 60
8.   Martin, 2006: 10
9.   Fitzgerald 1986: 51
10.   Ó Súilleabháin 1990: 71
11.   Ó Súilleabháin 1990: 71
12.   The *Kerryman* 28/9/1913
13.   Fitzgerald 1986: 49
14.   Fitzgerald 1986: 49
15.   Fitzgerald 1986: 49
16.   O'Shea 1998: 64
17.   O'Shea 1998: 64
18.   The *Kerryman* 24/1/1914

CHAPTER 11

1.   Burke 2005: 5
2.   Fitzgerald 1986:69
3.   The *Kerryman* 17/4/1915
4.   The *Kerryman* 17/4/1915
5.   Ó Súilleabháin 1990:81
6.   Ó Súilleabháin 1990:81
7.   Corry 96: 1989
8.   Ó Súilleabháin 1990: 82
9.   Ó Súilleabháin 1990:82
10.   Ó Súilleabháin, 1990: 82, 84

CHAPTER 12

1.   Fitzgerald 1914:2
2.   O'Sullivan 1916: 190
3.   O'Sullivan 1916: 192
4.   Kerry GAA Centenary 1988: 11
5.   Foley 1945: 58
6.   Fitzgerald 1986: 52
7.   Fitzgerald 1986: 52
8.   Smyth 2007: 357

CHAPTER 13

1. Coiste Staire and Munster Council 1986: 95
2. Barry and Horan 27: 1977
3. Coiste Staire and Munster Council 1986: 95
4. Foley 1945: 64
5. Foley 1945: 65
6. Muckross 1984: 24
7. Barry and Horan 1977: 28
8. Foley 1945: 65
9. Smyth 2007: 359
10. Foley 1945: 67
11. Foley 1945: 67
12. Corry 1989: 97
13. Corry 1989: 97
14. Foley 1945: 68
15. Burke 2005: 75
16. Foley 1945: 69-70
17. Smith 1968: 53
18. Smith 1968: 55
19. Foley 1945: 70
20. Coiste Staire and Munster Council 1986: 97
21. Foley 1945: 71
22. Smyth 2007: 359

CHAPTER 14

1. Deasy 1973: 3
2. Barrett 1997: 48
3. Joyce 1966: 336
4. Spillane and O'Sullivan WS132: 3
5. Joyce 1966: 336
6. The *Freeman's Journal* 2/7/1918
7. The *Freeman's Journal* 30/7/1914
8. Hickey and Doherty 2005: 414
9. Hickey and Doherty 2005: 414
10. Joyce 1966: 337
11. T. Ryle Dwyer 2001: 56
12. Joyce 1966: 337-8
13. Fitzgerald 1986: 63
14. *Kerry's Eye* 28/2/2008
15. Fitzgerald 1986: 63

16. Fitzgerald. 1986: 21
17. Puirséal 1984: 162
18. Corry 2006: 49
19. T. Ryle Dwyer 2001: 157
20. Mullins 1983: 16
21. Mullins 1983: 38
22. Gaughan 1977: 39
23. NL1 MS12168 *History of Irish Volunteers* and Gaughan 1977: 31
24. Gaughan 1977: 39
25. Smyth 2007: 359 – 362

CHAPTER 15
1. Coiste Staire and Munster Council 1986: 101
2. Fitzhenry 1935: 61
3. Spillane and O'Sullivan W.S. 132 File No. 786
4. Joyce 1966: 341
5. Joyce 1966: 341
6. Hickey and Doherty 2005:22
7. Ryan 2007: 90
8. Joyce 1966: 345
9. Joyce 1966: 348
10. Joyce 1966: 350
11. Joyce 1966: 349
12. Joyce 1966: 351
13. Barrington 1976: 124,228
14. Joyce 1966: 351
15. Fitzmaurice 2000: 209-1

CHAPTER 16
1. Ryan 1968: 52
2. Horgan, M., No. W.S. 952, File No. S. 2261: 2-3
3. Ryan 2007: 18
4. Mac Curtain 2006: 239
5. Mac Curtain 2006: 85
6. Mac Curtain 2006: 88-89
7. Mac Curtain 2006: 90-91
8. O'Mahony 1987: 62-3
9. O'Mahony 1987: 127
10. O'Mahony 1987: 128
11. O'Mahony 1987: 121
12. *Dublin's Fighting Story*, Undated: 115

13.   *Dublin's Fighting Story*, Undated: 118
14.   O'Mahony 1987: 99-101
15.   Killarney Echo 14/8/1916
16.   T. Ryle Dwyer 2001: 108
17.   T. Ryle Dwyer 2001: 109
18.   O'Mahony 1987: 167-8
19.   O'Broin 1980: 25
20.   Foley 1945: 77
21.   Foley 1945: 77

CHAPTER 17

1.   T. Ryle Dwyer 1991: 30
2.   Coiste Staire and Munster Council 1986: 105
3.   Coiste Staire and Munster Council 1986: 106
4.   de Búrca 1980: 138
5.   de Búrca 1980: 136-7
6.   de Búrca 1980: 138
7.   *Saturday Record* 1/12/1917
8.   *Saturday Record* 1/12/1917
9.   *Saturday Record* 1/12/1917
10.   *Saturday Record* 1/12/1917
11.   Coiste Staire and Munster Council 1986: 106
12.   Corry 1989: 107
13.   Saturday Record 1/12/1917
14.   Burke 2005: 78
15.   *Clare Champion* 24/11/1917
16.   *Saturday Record* 1/12/1917
17.   *Saturday Record* 1/12/1917
18.   Smith 1968: 58-59
19.   Burke 2005: 78
20.   Smyth 2007: 360

CHAPTER 18

1.   de Búrca 1980: 140
2.   Mahon 2001: 24
3.   Macardle 1938: 260
4.   Macardle 1938: 261
5.   Macardle 1938: 262
6.   Macardle 1938: 263
7.   Spillane and O'Sullivan, No. 862, File No (ii) S.787: Pages 6, 10-11
8.   Thomas Davis

CHAPTER 19

1. Macardle: 1938: 269
2. De Búrca 1980: 142
3. Fitzgerald 1986: 63-64
4. *The Freeman's Journal* 5/8/1918
5. *Fáinne an Lae* 31/8/1918
6. Burke 2005: 80
7. Macardle 1938: 273
8. Macardle 1938: 274-275
9. Horgan W.S. 952 File No. S. 2261
10. W.S. 862 File No. (i)S. 786; (ii) 5787 Pages 21-24
11. Song recorded by Dan Greany and transcribed by Siobhán and Aoife McSweeney, Kilcummin, Killarney

CHAPTER 20

1. Fitzgerald 1986: 64
2. Fitzgerald 1986: 64
3. Fitzgerald 1986: 64
4. The *Kerryman* 19/7/1919
5. The *Kerryman* 8/11/1919
6. The *Kerryman* 18/2/1920

CHAPTER 21

1. UDC Minutes 2/7/1920
2. UDC Minutes 11/7/1920
3. T. Ryle Dwyer 2001: 344
4. T. Ryle Dwyer 2001: 345
5. T. Ryle Dwyer 2001: 346
6. T. Ryle Dwyer 2001: 347
7. Deasy 1998: 32
8. Deasy 1998: 77-78
9. Deasy 1998: 80-81
10. Fitzgerald 1996: 77
11. Macardle 1998: 25
12. Fitzgerald 1986: 66-68
13. Barrett 1997: blurb
14. Barrett 1997: 110-111
15. Barrett 1997: 170
16. Fulham 2004: Vi

CHAPTER 22

1. Barry and Horan 1977: 19
2. Corry 1989: 125-7
3. Smyth 2007: 369-74

CHAPTER 23

1. Foley 1945: 89
2. Foley 1945: 91
3. Foley 1945: 91
4. Foley 1945: 94
5. Foley 1945: 92
6. Foley 1945: 95
7. Barrett 1997: 153-4

CHAPTER 24

1. The *Kerryman* 4/10/1930
2. 'P.F.' 1945: 104
3. The *Kerryman* 4/10/1930
4. The *Irish Independent* 29/9/1930
5. The *Irish Independent* 29/9/1930
6. The *Kerryman* 4/10/1930
7. The *Irish Independent* 29/9/1930
8. The *Irish Independent* 29/9/1930
9. Barry & Horan 1977: 56
10. The *Kerryman* 4/10/1930
11. The *Irish Independent* 2/10/1930
12. 'Sliabh Ruadh' or Phil O'Neill, who was a colleague of Dick's in Mungret College, Limerick 1901-02.

CHAPTER 25

1. Killarney UDC Minutes 1931
2. Coiste Staire and Munster Council 1986: 153
3. Fitzgerald 1986: 113
4. Fitzgerald 1986: 153
5. Fitzgerald 1986: 113
6. Fogarty 2007: 63
7. Copy of original manuscript in the possession of the author
8. The *Kingdom* 23/10/2001
9. Fitzgerald 1986: 115
10. Fitzgerald 1996: 64-70

11.   Ó Súilleabháin 1990: 128
12.   Fitzgerald 1986: 97
13.   Fitzgerald 1986: 98
14.   Hickey and Leen 1986: 42
15.   Hickey and Leen 1986: 43
16.   Fitzgerald 1986: 123
17.   The *Kerryman14*/9/1945
18.   Slattery 1979: 41
19.   Slattery 1979: 41
20.   Slattery 1979: 49
21.   Fitzgerald 1986: 134
22.   O'Shea 1998: 173
23.   Hickey Leen 1986: 46
24.   'Game On-Keys to a Kingdom', *Sunday Tribune*, Sports Monthly
      25/11/2007: 35
25.   *Sunday Tribune*, Sports Monthly 25/11/2007
26.   Foley 1945: 155-157
27.   Foley 1945: 62
28.   Corry 1989: 92
29.   Mahon 2001: 18
30.   Corry 2005: 234
31.   Corry 2005: 253
32.   Corry 2005: 242-3
33.   Fitzgerald 1914: 13
34.   Fitzgerald 1986: 53

CHAPTER 26
1.   Foley 1945: 159
2.   McCarthy 1996: 59
3.   The *Irish Independent* 29/9/1930
4.   Fogarty 2007: 221
5.   Fitzgerald 1914: 13
6.   Fitzgerald 1996: 11
7.   Smith 1968: 48-49
8.   Ó hEithir 1991: 69
9.   Fitzgerald 1914: 15
10.   Ó hEithir 1991:72
11.   Ó hEithir 1991: 171-2
12.   de Faoite 2005: vii-ix
13.   de Faoite 1980: 66

BIBLIOGRAPHY

Barrett, J.J. (1997) *In the Name of the Game*, Bray: The Dub Press.

Barrington, T. J. (1976); *Discovering Kerry – Its History, Heritage and Topography*. Dublin: The Blackwater Press.

Barry, J. and E. Horan. (1977) *Years of Glory*. Tralee: The Authors.

Burke, F. (2005) *All Ireland Glory – A Pictorial History of the Senior Football Championship 1887–2005*. Galway: Frank Burke.

Coiste Staire and Munster Council GAA (1986) *Munster GAA Story*. Munster: Comhairle na Mumhan CLG.

Corry, E. (2006) *An Illustrated History of the GAA*. Dublin: Gill and Macmillan.

Corry, E. (1989) *Catch and Kick – Great Moments of Kerry Football 1880-1990*. Dublin: Poolbeg Press.

Corry, E. (1989) *Kingdom Come – A Biography of the Kerry Football Team 1975–1988*. Dublin: Poolbeg Press.

Corry, E. (2005) *The GAA Book of Lists*. Dublin: Hodder Headline Ireland.

Cronin, J. (2005) *Making Connections – A Cork GAA Miscellany*. Cork: Cork County Board of the GAA.

Deasy, L. (1998) *Brother Against Brother*. Cork: Mercier Press.

De Búrca, M. (1980) *The GAA – A History of the Gaelic Athletic Association*. Dublin: Cumann Lúthchleas Gael.

De Faoite, S. (2005) *Death of a King and Other Stories*. Dublin: The Lilliput Press.

De Faoite, S. (1980) *The More We Are Together*. Dublin: Poolbeg Press.

Donegan, D. (2005) *The Complete Handbook of Gaelic Games – A Comprehensive Record of Results and Teams (1887–2005)*. Dublin: DBA Publications.

Dublin's Fighting Story 1916–21, Told By The Men Who Made It (undated). Tralee: The Kerryman.

Dwyer, D. (2002) *St Finan's Hospital, Killarney – A Medical, Social and Sporting History* (1852-2002). Killarney: St. Finan's Hospital Historical Society.

Farrell, N. (2000) *Exploring Family Roots in Killarney*. Longford: Noel Farrell.

230

Fitzgerald, D. (1914) *How To Play Gaelic Football*, Cork: Guy and Co.

Fitzgerald, E. (1986) *Dr Crokes Gaelic Century*, Killarney: Dr Crokes GAA Club.

Fitzgerald, E. (1996) Dr. Chrócaigh *GAA – Decade of Glory 1986-1996*. Killarney: Dr Crokes GAA Club.

Fogarty, W. (2007) *Dr. Eamonn O'Sullivan – A Man Before His Time*. Dublin: Wolfhound Press/Merlin Publishing.

Fitzmaurice, G. (2000) *The Kerry Anthology*. Dublin: Marino Books.

Foley, P.F. (1945) *Kerry's Football Story*. Tralee: The Kerryman.

Fulham, B. (2004) *The Throw-In – The GAA and The Men Who Made It*. Dublin: Wolfhound Press/Merlin Publishing.

Gaughan, J. A. (1977) *Austin Stack: Portrait of A Separatist*. Dublin: Kingdom Books.

Hickey, D.J. and J.E. Doherty. (2005) *A New Dictionary of Irish History from 1800*. Dublin: Gill and Macmillan.

Hickey, D. and T. Leen. (1986) *The Clear Air Boys – An East Kerry GAA History*. Ciarraí Thoir: The East Kerry GAA Board.

Joyce, M. (1966) *The Capuchin Annual*. Dublin: OFM Capuchin.

Kerry County Council .(1999) *Comhairle Baile-Cheantair Chill Áirne, Killarney UDC Local Election Results* 1899-1994. Killarney: Killarney UDC.

Larner, J. (2005) *Killarney History and Heritage*. Cork: The Collins Press.

Macardle, D. (1938) *The Irish Republic – A Documented Chronicle of the Anglo-Irish Conflict and the Partitioning of Ireland, with a Detailed Account of the Period 1916-1973*. London: Victor Gollancz.

Macardle, D. (1924) *Tragedies of Kerry 1922-1923*. Dublin: Irish Book Bureau.

McCarthy, T. (1966) *Killarney – Top of Towns, Recollections of a Lifetime*. Killarney: The Author.

MacCurtain, F. (2006) *Remember...It's for Ireland – A Family Memoir of Tomás McCurtáin*. Cork: Mercier Press.

Mahon, J. (2001) *A History of Gaelic Football*. Dublin: Gill and Macmillan.

Martin, T. F. (2006) *The Kingdom in The Empire – A Portrait of Kerry During World War One*. Dublin: Nonsuch Publishing.

Mullins, B. (1983) *Billy Mullins Remembers*. Tralee: Kenno (*Kerry's Eye*).

Murphy, J. (1998) *When Youth Was Mine – A Memoir of Kerry 1902–1925*. Dublin: Mentor Press.

O'Broin, L. (1980) *Michael Collins*. Dublin: Gill and Macmillan.

Ó hEithir, B. (1991) *Over the Bar*. Dublin: Poolbeg Press.

O'Leary, J. (2003) *The Story of the O'Donoghue Cup 1954-2003*. Ciarraí

Thoir: The East Kerry GAA Board.

O'Mahony, S. (1987) *Frongoch: University of Revolution*. Killiney, County Dublin: FDR Teoranta.

Ó Muircheartaigh, J. and T.J. Flynn. (2007) *Princes of Pigskin – A Century of Kerry Footballers*. Cork: the Collins Press.

O'Shea, P. (1993) *Face the Ball – Records of the Kerry County Championships 1889-1998*. Tralee: Kerry County Board.

Ó Súilleabháin, S.S. (1990) *Aililiú Rathmore – A History of Gaelic Activities in the Parish*. Rathmore: Rathmore GAA Club.

O'Sullivan, T. F. (1916) *Story of the GAA*. Dublin.

Puirséal, P. (1984) *The GAA In Its Time*. Dublin: The Ward River Press Ryan, A. (2007) *Comrades – Inside The War of Independence*. Dublin: Liberties Press.

Ryan, D. (1960) *Michael Collins and The Invisible Army*. Tralee: Anvil Books.

Ryle Dwyer, T. (2006) *Big Fellow, Long Fellow – A Joint Biography of Collins and De Valera*. Dublin: Gill and Macmillan.

Ryle Dwyer, T. (2001) *Tans, Terror and Troubles – Kerry's Real Fighting Story* 1913-1923, Cork: Mercier Press.

Ryle Dwyer, T. (1991) *Éamon De Valera – The Man and The Myths*. Dublin: Poolbeg Press and the *Irish Independent* (Great Biographies Series 14, 2006).

Slattery, F. (1979) *A Legion of Memories*. Killarney: Legion GAA Club.

Smith, R. (1968) *The Football Immortals – A Comprehensive History of Gaelic Football*. Dublin: Bruce Spicer.

Smyth, J. (2007) *In Praise of Heroes – Ballads and Poems of the GAA*. Dublin: Geography Publications.

Spindler, K. (1965) *The Mystery of The Casement Ship*. Tralee: Anvil Books.

Trustees of Muckross House (1984) *The GAA in Kerry, Taispeántas Comóradh an Chéid, Cumann Luthchleas i gCiarraí 1884-1984*. Killarney: Trustees of Muckross House (Killarney).

Woulfe, P. (1923) *Sloinnte Gaedheal is Gall – Irish Names and Surnames*. Dublin: M.H. Gill & Son.

NEWSPAPERS

The *Clare Champion*, Ennis, Countynty Clare.

The *Clare People*, Ennis, Countynty Clare.

Kerry's Eye, Tralee, County Kerry.

The *Cork Examiner/The Examiner*, Cork.

The *Freeman's Journal*, Dublin.

The *Irish Independent*, Dublin.
The *Kerry Evening Star*, Tralee, County Kerry.
The *Kerryman*, Tralee, County Kerry.
The *Kerry Sentinal*, Tralee, County Kerry.
The *Killarney Echo*, Killarney, County Kerry.
The *Kingdom*, Killarney, County Kerry.
The *Meath Chronicle*, Navan, County Meath.
The *Saturday Record*, Ennis, County Clare.
The *Sunday Tribune*, Dublin.

OTHER SOURCES

An Claidheamh Soluis, Monthly Journal of Conradh na Gaeilge/The Gaelic
    League, Dublin.
An Ríocht, Yearbook of The Kerry Association, Dublin.
Bureau of Military History: Interviews with Maurice Horgan, Michael
    Spillane, M. J. O'Sullivan and Tim O'Mara: National Archives, Bishop
    St., Dublin 8. (W.S. 132, W.S. 862, W.S. 952, W.S. 953).
Fáinne an Lae, Irish Language Journal, Dublin.
Killarney Urban District Council, Minutes and Records of Killarney
    UDC meetings 1920–30 (excepting Civil War period), Urban Council
    Offices, Town Hall, Main St., Killarney, County Kerry.
Local Election Results 1899-1994, Comhairle Baile Cheantair Chill
    Áirne, Killarney UDC; Centenary of Irish Local Government
    1899-1999 (1999), Killarney UDC
St. Brendan's College, Killarney, County Kerry, College Archive c/o Denis
    O'Donoghue, Killarney.
The Capuchin Annual, Dublin, OF.M Capuchin Fathers.
The Gaelic Athlete, (P.D. Mehigan), Dublin.
The *Sunburst Magazine*, Dublin.

MISCELLANEOUS SUPPLEMENTS:
'Comóradh an Chéid Bhlian 1888 -1988', GAA in Kerry (1988),
    The *Kerryman*, Tralee.
'All-Ireland SFC Final 2007', The *Kerryman*, Tralee.
'All-Ireland Senior Club Final', March 2007, *The Kingdom*, Killarney.
'Mad About Sports – Kings for a Lifetime' (Sports Monthly 25/11/2007),
    The *Sunday Tribune*, Dublin.

INDEX OF NAMES

how to play Gaelic football

By dick Fitzgerald.

ONE SHILLING

HOW TO PLAY
GAELIC FOOTBALL.

To the Memory

of

Munster's Illustrious and Patriotic Archbishop,

THE MOST REVEREND DR. CROKE,

One of the First Founders of the G.A.A.,

and

Patron of the Killarney Football Club,

With which the Author of this little work has had the

honour of being associated as Member and Captain.

HIS GRACE MOST REV. T. F. CROKE, D.D.
Late Archbishop of Cashel.

DR. CROKE'S LETTER.

At the founding of the Association the following letter was received from the Most Rev. T. W. Croke, Archbishop of Cashel and Emly:—

> "The Palace, Thurles,
> "December 18th, 1884.

"My Dear Sir—I beg to acknowledge the receipt of your communication inviting me to become a patron of the Gaelic Athletic Association, of which you are, it appears, the Hon. Secretary. I accede to your request with the utmost pleasure.

"One of the most painful, let me assure you, and, at the same time, one of the most frequently recurring, reflections that, as an Irishman, I am compelled to make in connection with the present aspect of things in this country, is derived from the ugly and irritating fact, that we are daily importing from England, not only her manufactured goods, which we cannot help doing, since she has practically strangled our own manufacturing appliances, but, together with her fashions, her accents, her vicious literature, her music, her dances, and her manifold mannerisms, her games also and her pastimes, to the utter discredit of our own grand national sports, and to the sore humiliation, as I believe, of every genuine son and daughter of the old land.

"Ball-playing, hurling, football-kicking, according to Irish rules, 'casting,' leaping in various ways, wrestling, handy-grips, top-pegging, leap-frog, rounders, tip-in-the-hat, and all such favourite exercises and amusements, amongst men and boys may now be said to be not only dead and buried, but in several localities to be entirely forgotten and unknown. And what have we got in their stead? We have got such foreign and fantastic field sports as lawn tennis, polo, croquet, cricket, and the like — very excellent, I believe, and health-giving exercises in their way, still not racy of the soil, but rather alien, on the contrary, to it, as are, indeed, for the most part, the men and women who first imported, and still continue to patronise them.

"And, unfortunately, it is not our national sports alone that are held in dishonour and are dying out, but even our most suggestive national celebrations are being gradually effaced and extinguished, one after another as well. Who hears now of snap-apple night, pan-cake night, or bon-fire night? They are all things of the past, too vulgar to be spoken of, except in ridicule by the degenerate dandies of the day. No doubt, there is something rather pleasing to the eye in the get-up of a modern young man, who, arrayed in light attire, with parti-coloured cap on and racquet in hand, is making his way, with or without a companion, to the tennis ground. But, for my part, I should vastly prefer to behold, or think of, the youthful athletes, whom I used to see in my early days at fair and pattern, bereft of shoes and coat, and thus prepared to play at handball, to fly over any number of horses, to throw the 'sledge' or 'winding-stone,' and to test each other's mettle and activity by the trying ordeal of 'three leaps,' or a 'hop, step and jump.'

"Indeed, if we continue travelling for the next score years in the same direction that we have been going in for some time past, contemning the sports that were practised by our forefathers, effacing our national features as though we were ashamed of them, and putting on, with England's stuffs and broadcloths, her masher habits and such other effeminate follies as she may recommend, we had better, at once, and publicly, abjure our nationality, clap hands for joy at sight of the Union Jack, and place 'England's bloody red' exultantly above the green.

"Deprecating, as I do, any such dire and disgraceful consummation, and seeing in your society of athletes something altogether opposed to it, I shall be happy to do all for it that I can, and authorise you now formally to place my name on the roll of your patrons.

"In conclusion, I earnestly hope that our national journals will not disdain in future to give suitable notices of these Irish sports and pastimes which your society means to patronise and promote, and that the masters and pupils of our Irish Colleges will not henceforth exclude from their athletic programmes such manly exercises as I have just referred to and commemorated.

> "I remain, my dear Sir,
> "Your very faithful servant,
>
> ✠ "T. W. CROKE,
> "Archbishop of Cashel.

"To Mr. Michael Cusack,
    Hon. Sec. of the Gaelic Athletic Association."

DICK FITZGERALD.

HOW TO PLAY
GAELIC FOOTBALL

(Illustrated)

BY

DICK FITZGERALD

(Captain of the Kerry Team—All-Ireland Champions)

CORK:
PRINTED AND PUBLISHED BY GUY AND CO. LTD.
70 PATRICK STREET.
1914.

INDEX OF ILLUSTRATIONS.

———

HOW TO PLAY GAELIC FOOTBALL

INTRODUCTORY.

GAELIC FOOTBALL of the present day is a scientific game. It is necessary to lay this down at the very beginning, because some people have got an idea into their heads that the game is unscientific, and they have no scruple about saying so.

There was a time, indeed, when the game was anything but a scientific exposition. This was the case some twenty years ago, when the rough-and-tumble and go-for-the-man system obtained. Then it was rather a trial of strength and endurance than an exhibition of skill. But all that is gone long since. Even as far back as the nineties, when as many as twenty-one men aside played, there were not wanting signs of development on the scientific side. Later on, when the game was confined to seventeen players aside, it became more and more a trial of skill, as in the famous Kerry v. Kildare matches, and, finally, when the number was reduced to fifteen aside, Science became the order of the day.

Can anyone say that Gaelic Football is unscientific since the memorable encounters between Kerry and Louth in May and June, 1913? Some forty thousand people witnessed each of these strenuous tussles for supremacy, and it has been said on all sides that never in the history of outdoor games in Ireland have people gone home so well pleased with what they then saw.

Assuredly no one would be found foolish enough who can now maintain that our National Football Game is not scientific.

The fact is that, given two well-trained teams coming from an area where there has been a tradition of good Gaelic football, and given fair weather conditions for the playing of the match, the game is bound to be most interesting to watch, and the better exponents of the science of the game are nearly always sure to come out on top.

In a certain sense, Gaelic Football of the present day is more scientific than any existing football game. In other forms of football, such is the constitution of the rules governing them, there is very often too much of the element of luck. In the native game, however, there is no such preponderance of luck, as the results prove, and this is to be accounted for by the fact that the rules provide the two kinds of score, viz., the Point as well as the Goal.

We cannot help dwelling upon one or two other attractive features of the Gaelic Code. Everybody knows that the tendency of outdoor games of the present day is to reduce the individual player to the level of a mere automaton. In a manner, the individual in modern games is a disadvantage to his side, if his individuality asserts itself strongly—so strongly, at least, that he tends to be too much of an individualist and too little of the mere machine. How dry is the description one often gets of those great matches, in which perfect combination alone is the only thing commended ! In them there is no hero—no great individual standing out from the whole field. If he did stand out, he would cease to be a machine, and his usefulness to his side would cease likewise.

Gaelic Football fortunately does not tend in the

direction of reducing its players to the mere machine
level. True it is that combination—and combination of
a sufficiently high standard—is much prized. Each
player is taught to see the advantage of combining with
everybody else on his side, and of playing at all times
unselfishly. But, such is the genius of the game itself,
that while combination will always be prominent, the
brilliant individual gets his opportunities times out of
mind, with the result that, after the match is over, you
will generally have a hero or two carried enthusiastically
off the field on the shoulders of their admirers.

Then, too, Gaelic Football is what may be called a
natural football game. There is no incentive in it
towards rough play. One player can hamper or im-
pede another in one way, and only one way, and that by
means of the shoulder. Hence it is that severe tackling,
rough handling, and all forms of tripping are banned.

Truly there is no artificiality about our game. There
is no such thing as the artificial "forward," "off-side,"
"knock-on," &c., rules, hedging the player about in
all his movements. When men are bound down by
almost impossible restrictions, such as those just mentioned, it is only very highly trained machines that can
adapt themselves to the playing of a game under such
conditions. No wonder is it that professionalism has
come so much into modern outdoor games, which re-
quire the players of them to devote practically all their
time to learn how to play, and consequently to make
their living thereby.

It is to be hoped that Gaelic Football will always
remain as natural a game as it is to-day; and accordingly
we trust that, while it will ever be developing on the
scientific side, it may never become the possession of
the professional player.

CHAPTER I.

Positions of the Players on the Field.

THE recognised number of players for the game is fifteen, although, under certain circumstances, it may be played by thirteen aside. In describing how the game is to be played, we must be taken as detailing the methods for the full number. At the same time we hope to say something before we close on the thirteen aside game also; for it is not wholly unlikely that the game may be confined later on to thirteen players, and on that account it is not without interest to discuss the thirteen aside game.

If we fix our attention on the placing of the fifteen players on the field, we can fancy them divided into two main sections; one defensive, the other offensive—one portion composed of backs and the other of forwards. The defence party will be made up of seven players, while the attacking force will consist of the eight remaining individuals.

Again, we must consider each section in itself and make further divisions. The defence portion will consist of a goal-keeper, in front of whom will play the three full-backs. The latter three and the goal-man form the last line of defence. Further, a tolerable distance in front of these three full-backs the middle line of defence will unfold itself, and this is made up of three players also—the three half-backs.

Kerry Football Team (1903-1904), All-Ireland and Railway Shield Champions.

Turning to the attacking force, we can fancy, in the first instance, two wing-men, one on the right wing and the other on the left. Some distance in front of the right winger will play the right scorer, and, in the corresponding place on the left, the left scorer. Thus we account for four members of the attack party.

Where are we to place the four remaining players? There is a natural berth for each of two men. One of them proceeds to take up his position at a point rather midway between the two wing-men, and the other fills in the gap, as it were, between the right and left scorers. The former is usually named the centre-forward, while the latter is called, variously, the full-forward, or centre-scorer; perhaps more accurately the centre-scorer.

We have yet two players to locate on our imaginary field. It must be said at once that these two players cannot be assigned a very definite position at all, because they are, as we shall see, "free-lances," or "rovers." However, we may place them to a certain extent. One of them will play on the right side of the field, and at a point (if we suppose our man stationary for a moment) midway between the right half and the centre half-backs, and in front of both these players. The other will play in a somewhat similar position, in front of the centre half and left half-back players. They are named the mid-field men—one right mid-field and the other left mid-field—and so called because each plays his portion of the middle of the field of play.

The disposition that we have made of the fifteen players on the field will suggest, we think, to any reader that Gaelic Football is played on scientific lines. In order to show all the positions as clearly as possible, it may be useful to make a rough diagram of the various placings

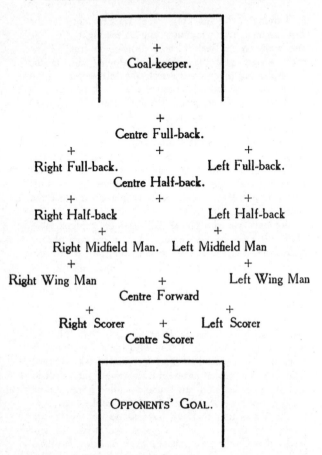

Rough diagram, showing positions of the players on
the field.

CHAPTER II.

DEFENCE.

(1) *The Goal-Keeper.*

THE Goal-Keeper, like the poet, is born, not made. Though he is pretty well secured by the three full-backs, especially by the centre-full, he has a heavy responsibility laid upon his shoulders.

The ideal man for the position should be rather tall and powerfully built. He should have a keen, quick eye, a great pair of hands, and should be a most resourceful kicker with either leg and with as much length as possible in his kicks. He should also be possessed of a fine spirit of fearlessness, combined with great coolness, and should have the capacity to do the needful with quick and unerring judgment. Nor must he be lacking in patience, for he is obliged to confine his energies within the compass of the goal area, always on the watch to stop any ball from going between the uprights. One might possibly enumerate other desirable qualities; but better not "pile it on," as folks say.

His chief duty will consist in preventing the ball being netted. As long as his backs are unbeaten, he has no fear of that disaster. But occasions will arise when it will be "up" to him to stop an opposing player, usually one of the scorers, who has outwitted the backs. What is he to do? Should he go forward and meet his man, or stay in goal and take his chance of

saving a volley from very close range? It depends.
Some would, and some would not, have him leave goal.
A really good goal-man will do the right thing under
the given circumstances, and, if he elects to go out, he
will pounce upon his opponent like a hawk. If he cannot get there in time to tackle man and ball, he will
stay at home.

Another problem arises where a high ball is coming
right underneath the bar, and the goal-keeper is about
to be charged down. If he fields the ball, he may be
shouldered, himself and ball, into the net. If, however, he does not field the leather, it will pass through
likewise. What is he to do? He must do something
to save his citadel from falling. Really, in such a crisis,
a great deal will depend upon the understanding he has
with the full-backs, and more especially with the centre-
full.

Ordinarily, the latter back can save the goal-keeper,
and it is clear that a perfect understanding should exist
between them in the face of the difficulty contemplated.
In that case the full-back should "take" the man, and
the goalie would then be free to field the ball and get
in his kick. Otherwise there is nothing left the goalman
to do but "punch" the ball away towards the side-line,
or, perhaps, if he can rely upon himself, try a fly-kick.
That is exactly what our own famous keeper, Dillon,
did on a remarkable occasion when he had to save his
goal under the circumstances here described. Dillon
kicked the ball on the "fly" and "side-slipped" his
man.

It is on account of the exceedingly awkward and
critical situations that can and do arise near goal in
every well-contested match, that one has to expect very
special qualities in the man who plays between the
sticks. He may get very little to do in comparison with

the rest of his comrades on the field, but the doing of that little under trying circumstances pre-supposes great skill, quickness, judgment, and many other things.

As a goal-man should be possessed of so many fine qualities, and as so much depends upon his making no mistakes, he should be sufficiently well-trained on all occasions. Consequently he should take his share of short sprinting, kicking for length, fielding, saving hard shots, and should, perhaps, indulge in some gymnastic exercises. He should study closely the methods of forwards, particularly the tactics of scoring men, and should know so much about them that he can divine, as it were, at any time what "move" they have in mind.

Lastly, the goal-keeper should fight always against the temptation to grow careless and dispirited when a goal is registered against him. Whether the score has come as the result of a mistake on his own part or not, he should be so minded as to play until the last whistle with the utmost confidence and cheerfulness. He must bear in mind at all times that everybody who has an intelligent knowledge of the game will appreciate the responsibility of the position he occupies in goal, and will be prepared to make every allowance for the difficulties which, of necessity, it entails.

We feel bound to mention that Dillon, our crack goal-man, reached our ideal of what a player should be in that position. Our present keeper, Mullins, coming after such as Dillon, has been singularly successful, too, between the sticks. In the early days of Gaelic Football, Fraher of Waterford had a big reputation, and Crowley of Dunmanway, Co. Cork, was held in high repute likewise. More recently we were very much struck with the goal-keeping of Fitzgerald of Kildare.

(2) *The Full-Backs.*

There are three full-backs in Gaelic Football. One plays in the centre at a reasonable distance in front of the goal-keeper, and the two others play more or less towards the wing on either side of the centre man. As those three players, together, of course, with the goal-keeper, form the last line of defence, and as any serious mistake made by them may prove fatal, it is most important that the men selected to play "full" should be possessed of good judgment and no little experience of the game. They must accordingly be safe men, "tried and true," thoroughly reliable.

It goes without saying that every "full" should have a good kick, and the more powerful the better. A long clearance is a source of great relief to a side, and it is the "fulls" who are called on most often to effect the long clearances.

Ability to kick with either foot is very important also. In order to keep the ball in play, a good left leg is almost an essential qualification for the man who fills the position of left-full. The reason is pretty obvious. Playing on the left side, he has to save against opponents who come down upon him with the big advantage of being able to use their right legs. Usually he will not get time to turn and get in his kick with his right leg, and therefore he must bring his left into action immediately. To do so with any kind of ease and safety, he should be able to kick well with that leg.

It is hardly necessary to point out that all these backs should be excellent fielders. Everyone who knows anything about Gaelic Football understands how important and useful is good fielding of the ball for every player on the playing pitch. If that is true, as it is, in the case of the players as a whole, it is much more so

Ordinary Method of Fielding the Ball.

as regards the full-backs. They cannot afford to let a single ball pass through their hands. Bad fielding on their part is usually attended by disastrous consequences.

Quick delivery of the ball is another most desirable thing in a "full." When he fields the leather, he is, as a rule, pretty certain to be tackled in possession by an opposing forward. It is then, when he is beset with difficulties, that he is expected, having slipped his adversary, to get in his kick at once. The high-class full-back will always find some means of escape from such trouble and send up-field without any appreciable delay.

Strength combined with speed will be looked for in these three backs. The centre one of the three should be, as far as possible, a strongly-built man, able to tackle any forward opposed to him. In a manner it would seem as if strength rather than speed, if we contrast the two qualities, should characterise the centre full-back.

The latter, we have remarked already, should have as perfect an understanding as possible with the goal-keeper in the matter of taking the ball or taking the man, on leaving the ball back, and, generally, in playing to save the goal. Want of this proper understanding between these two players mentioned has been the fruitful source of "soft" scores in many a match.

If the centre man should be rather strong than speedy, his companions on the right and left should be rather speedy than strong. Both are wing-backs, so to say, and have to defend against fleet-footed wingers and scorers. A good deal of speed, therefore, is very desirable in the right and left "fulls." In our All-Ireland team in Kerry we have had the good fortune of having such fast men as R. Kirwan, M. McCarthy, and T. Costello to play in those positions with rare success, while our centre men have been rather on the strong side, like Breen and J. Lawlor.

As regards the tactics to be adopted by the full-back line as a whole, it should be pretty well understood that when the right-full goes out to save, the centre-man moves into the vacancy, and the left-full drops in between the centre-full and goal. Similarly, if the left-full has to move up field, or is drawn towards the side-line, the centre man again fills in the gap and the right-full drops in between centre-full and the goal-keeper. All the while the idea is to maintain a strong and un-broken line of defence before goal.

It is almost too elementary a point to mention that the effort of all three backs must be to save rather in the direction of the side-line. As far as possible, no one of them should ever carry the ball across the face of his own goal, or, on delivery, send too much towards the centre. Their object all the time must be to get the ball clean away from the goal-area, and that will be generally towards the wing.

In getting the ball away as just described, each back must decide for himself whether he should try to find touch at once or endeavour to send the ball well up to one of the halves or one of the wing-men. The com-petent full-back must be left to himself as to what he had best do. Obviously, what is expected from a full-back is that he should clear his lines every time. He may possibly go a step further and endeavour to open up an attacking movement. That would, however, be exceptional.

What may be called quick recovery is a very com-mendable trait in a good "full," especially the right or left. Times will occur when either man will be beaten for possession, fooled in a dribble, or "taken in" in some fashion by the opposing forwards. On such occasions it is very much to be desired that the full-back in question should recover himself as quickly as possible and try to get between the attack-party and his own goal. It is wonderful what some full-backs manage to do by that habit of quick recovery.

We cannot help saying that there is great room for improvement in nearly all our full-backs up and down the country in the matter of kicking running balls. True it is that there is a tendency on the part of the greatest exponents of the game to pick up the ball with the foot, transfer to the hands, and get in a long punt. If that excellent feat can be executed with great rapidity, we must admit that it is all that can be desired. But unfortunately there are occasions when a back has not time to stop or stoop to handle the ball. The ball must then be kicked as it runs, or the situation is lost. Plainly, therefore, to be safe in such cases, a back should be able to take the running ball as it comes and get it well away.

There is another reason for our statement. From the spectacular standpoint, there is no more attractive style of kick than the neatly taken running ball. It would seem, therefore, a great mistake that this feature of the game should remain undeveloped or even neglected.

We cannot conclude this section without mentioning the names of three excellent full-backs against whom we have played. Two of them belonged to the great Kildare team of some years ago—one was Cribbon and the other Fitzgerald, both rare defenders. The third player we have before our minds is Wheeler of Wexford—a really clever footballer. The three players mentioned, with our backs, McCarthy, Kirwan and Costello, have stood out from a host of other fine "fulls" who have played the game within the past dozen years.

(3) *The Half-Backs.*

Some distance in front of the full-backs play the
three half-backs. In ordinary circumstances, when, let
us suppose, play is proceeding about the half-way, the
halves will be found operating round that quarter.
There they form the middle line of defence, as the
"fulls" with the goal-keeper form its last line, and in
that middle position they may be said to constitute the
backbone of the team.

Though they are in theory defensive, the three halves
are also rather important factors in attack, towards
which they are supposed to contribute in no small
measure. In that respect they differ from the full-backs,
who seldom take any part in delivering an attack, and
discharge, as we have seen, almost purely defensive
functions.

It is only natural to expect that the three halves should
be able to take a good deal of rough usage, and on that
account they should be pretty strong men and as hard
as nails. Fearlessness should be one of their great
characteristics, and all their play must be of the fearless
type. They should ever be quick on the ball and allow
the forwards opposed to them no time for combining, as
it were, in as far as lies in their power. The half-back
who hesitates is lost, and the half-back line that waits
more or less upon its opponents will go a long way towards the undoing of its whole side.

Of the three halves, the centre-man is the most tried.
He should be, perhaps, stronger than either his right
or left-hand comrade. A lot of gruelling work is
bound to come his way in the centre, and, in order to
get through it, he should have the heart of a lion.

The right and left halves should have a good turn of
speed. This is necessary to them, because it is their

duty to hold in check the opposing wing-men who, as we shall see, are supposed to be flyers. Needless to add, the left-half, like the left-full, should have a good left leg.

It should be part of the duty of the right-half to take every throw-in from touch on his side-line, and of the left-half along the left touch-line. The exception to what has just been said might be the case when the ball goes into touch near the end line. Then indeed it may be found more convenient to allow the right and left-full to do the needful. Clearly, a lot of time is saved in a match in which the halves on either side are deputed to throw in the ball. Furthermore, those who are delegated for that purpose can practise the art of throwing-in from touch, and so make the very most of each opportunity to do so.

In defence-play, the tactics that have been suggested to the full-backs may be adopted to a certain extent by the halves. Hence, when the right-half proceeds some distance in order to check the advance of one or two opponents, the centre-half should move into the vacancy and the left-half should come somewhat into the centre. Similarly, when the left-half is occupied on the left wing, the centre-man drops more or less into the vacancy for the moment, and the right-half should come across towards the centre.

We are suggesting rather the ideal than the real in the tactics just mentioned. The fact is that, in most passages of a game, the play is so fast and furious about the half-way, where the halves are mainly engaged, there is no time usually for one half to cross and step into the other's place. Really, each half must fight his own corner in defence-work, and, if he fails, the full-backs behind him must come to the rescue. Each half then, it would seem, should be, as far as the defence-work is concerned, very much of an individualist.

In attack, competent halves can play a very large part, and of that they should never be unmindful. They can and should feed, so to say, the attacking force in front of them. For this purpose they should advert to the necessity of being very cautious about their kicking of the ball. They must not always be thinking that a big kick will suit them as it suits the full-backs. The latter, be it remembered, are bound every time to effect a long clearance, and, in a sense, nothing more. The halves, however, are expected to afford their forwards as many chances as possible by placing the ball neatly amongst them. Therefore, whilst it is a matter of necessity for the fulls to kick for length in order to effect a good clearance, it may be incumbent upon the half-backs to kick short, with a view to the advantageous placing of the ball amongst their attacking comrades. For the plain truth of the matter is that a big kick from about the half-way is fielded usually by one of the opposing "fulls" and returned with interest. The neatly placed short kick, however, may result in the ball finding its way into the hands of some one of the forwards, who may be enabled thereby to open up a good attacking movement with every hope of success.

We may, perhaps, conclude by recalling the names of a few very successful halves. Healy in the centre, and Rice and Kenneally—the three Kerry halves—and Smith, the Louth captain, have played great games. Austin Stack, a Kerry half some years back, was also a sound player. The same was true of Florence O'Sullivan on the half-line of his days. Mehigan, the Lee captain, has been a capable half.

Fielding a rather high Ball.

CHAPTER III.

ATTACK.

(1) *General Plan.*

WE pass from Defence to Attack—from the play of the backs to that of the forwards. It is not inappropriate to take the following quotation from the Official Guide-Book of the G.A.A. :—

> "In the centre of the goal-line should stand the goal-posts, 16 feet high and 21 feet apart. There shall be a cross-bar 8 feet from the ground. . . A goal is scored when the ball is driven or played by either team between the goal-posts and under the cross-bar, except when carried or thrown* by any of the attacking side . . .A point is scored when the ball is driven or played by either side over the cross-bar and between the goal-posts, except when thrown* by any of the attacking side. . . The game shall be decided by the greater number of points. A goal shall be equal to three points."

We may add that a goal is often described as the major score and the point as the minor.

Obviously, the object which the attacking party have in view is the securing of a score, major or minor. For this object the half-backs are required to work as well as their comrades-in-arms in front of them. As we have seen, the three halves are expected not only to defend, but to help their own attack party. We may ask, then,

---

* This phrase means that "carrying" or "throwing" the ball is not allowed.

who compose this attack party, and what tactics are the latter to adopt in order to score?

There are eight players some distance in advance of the halves, and in our arrangement, which is the usual one, the eight are placed in this wise : Between the centre-half and his right-half comrade, at a short distance in front of them, is the right midfield man, and on the left, in a corresponding position between the centre and left-half, the left midfield player. Out on the wing, along the side-line and in advance of the right-half, plays the right-winger, and on the left wing ahead of the left-half, the left wing-man. If we suppose a straight line drawn across the field from the point at which one winger stands to that at which the other is situated, about midway on that line will be found the centre-forward. Some twenty or twenty-five yards in advance of the three men whose positions have been defined just now, and placed somewhat similarly, play the three scorers. In the centre plays the centre-scorer, and on his left and right, but somewhat nearer to him than are the wingers to the centre-forward, play the right and left scorers.

Two midfield men, two wingers, and a centre-forward playing, as it were, between them, and three scorers make up the attack party. What tactics are these eight players to adopt in order to score? How is the attack to be made if it is to meet with success? We have laid down that the three halves should endeavour, as far as they can, to feed the eight forwards, and, in trying to do so, keep before their minds the main plan of attack. What is this main plan which the halves must keep in mind, and which the attacking force of forwards must follow?

A very little reflection will convince one that the defence must be beaten before any score can be registered against them, and the defence is usually beaten by being "drawn," as footballers say, or deceived by some ruse or other. For, evidently, the forward who eventually scores can do so only at the moment when he gets an opening to send in a shot, and that moment arrives ordinarily only when the defence is drawn off somehow from him. In what we have just said we are simply stating the general rule according to which scores are made. There are, of course, exceptions.

It sometimes happens that one of the forwards, or even one of the halves fielding the ball pretty far out from the opponents' goal, may land it on top of the net with a huge kick. It is rare enough; but it has happened. Or, again, one of the forwards, as the result of a brilliant individual effort, may brush aside or fool two or even three backs and score entirely "on his own." These and other cases are exceptional, and merely go to prove the rule that scores come as a result of drawing the defence.

How, then, is the defence drawn? At the outset we must assume two things. The first is that six of the eight forwards—namely, the centre-forward, the two wingers, and the three scorers—must have a thorough understanding with one another. We do not count upon the two midfield men for regular and defined combination, because they are supposed to have a roving commission. The second thing to be assumed is that the six forwards in question must have had a lot of practice playing with one another in important matches, as well as in their private training. If these forwards play a good deal together, and if each one of them can be relied upon to use his head, field well, and dribble with a share of trickiness, as it were, they may be depended upon with confidence to draw the defence.

The methods to be adopted for the purpose men-

tioned should be varied. At one moment the ball may be passed out to one of the wing-men, thence passed on to the scorer immediately in front, and passed back, or "centred," as we say, to either the centre-forward or centre-scorer. That is one of the simplest ways of drawing the defence. On another occasion the ball may be passed on to the wing again, passed back directly, after a little manœuvring, to the centre-forward or centre-scorer without carrying further along the wing. That is a simple variation of the first method. Perhaps one other illustration may suffice. Let us suppose that the centre-forward has the ball at his feet. He dribbles along; pretends to pass out to the right wing. Instead of doing so, however, he "cuts in" towards midfield, and, when challenged by the backs on his left, passes out to the left-winger or left-scorer, whichever is unmarked. From thence the ball should easily be centred before goal, where the centre-scorer has every hope of getting possession and shooting successfully.

From all this we conclude that, in order that the attack should succeed, the defence must be drawn. The defence is drawn by being forced to counteract and check a clever system of "in-passing" and "outpassing" amongst the forwards opposed to them. That passing must be as varied as possible. If it were all "of a piece," or stereotyped, it would fail utterly to deceive the backs against whom it is attempted. Clever forwards will ring the changes on each form of passing so admirably that even the most experienced backs cannot be certain what is likely to happen. There is nothing more beautiful in a football match than a well-executed movement amongst the forwards, and, like all great feats of skill, it is wonderful how simple it looks to the eye of the majority of onlookers on the fence.

Fielding the Ball and keeping an Opponent off.

(2) *The Midfield Men.*

Our idea of the two men playing in the midfield in the positions already allotted them, as far as they can be placed at all, is that they should be sure fielders of high balls, full of vigour, able to tackle well, quick on the ball, and great stayers. There is no doubt about the fact that no players get so much hard work and hard knocks as those same midfield men.

It is not of vital importance that they should be either expert kickers or extra fast men. Of course speed and good kicking are very desirable qualities in them as in the rest of the team, but it is curious that some of our own very best midfield men, like Buckley, B. O'Connor, C. Murphy, and O'Shea, have not been distinguished for either quality. As they are never idle, always on the "go," as it were, they should be "lasting," so that no pace, no matter how hard, could wear them down. Then, too, as they get a lot of fielding to do, and generally in the teeth of strong opposition, their catching should be particularly good, and their grip of the ball ought to be vice-like.

A very important quality in the midfield men is quickness of movement. We have always made a clear distinction between the man who is fleet of foot and the man, not necessarily over fast, who is ready to do what is to be done. Has it not happened over and over again in football matches that a player who can travel very fast often fails to field the ball, or, having fielded it, to get in his kick, owing to a certain slowness of movement? It seems a bit of a paradox, but the fact is undoubted. We should like the midfield men, however fast or slow of foot, to be ever ready at snapping the ball, feinting, doing "the reverse," and getting the ball away. They need as much quickness as possible of that kind, for the very simple reason that every ball they get has to be fought for, and there is usually little time left them to kick.

When the ball is about to be thrown in from touch, both midfield men should keep a sharp look-out, especially so when the throw-in belongs to the opposite side. In their general play they should rather "go in" to their opponents than wait upon them. At any cost their efforts should be to get the ball, or, if they cannot secure the leather, to hamper in every legitimate manner the "other fellow." There must be no hesitancy about taking man or ball. They should also put in a lot of "spoiling" for their comrades, and spoiling is a more important item of play than either the man on the fence or the superior critic on the stand suspects.

It is just possible for the two midfield men to combine with each other. We do not suggest that combination should be an ordinary feature of their play. They are usually too far apart from each other, and it is not easy for one to signal to the other. However, it may happen that when the play is quite in the middle of the field, and both of them meet more by accident than design, they may be able to do a bit of combined work and pass from one to the other. In such a case, also, one might spoil for the other—in other words, one might be able to keep the man off while the other takes the ball. In this whole connection it is clear that the two should be accustomed to play a good deal with each other.

One bit of advice to the midfield men is not out of place or unnecessary. They should resist the tendency to play amongst their own backs when the latter appear to be sorely pressed. The backs should be allowed to do their own work, and interference with them by any of the eight forwards, the midfield men included, would be rather detrimental to a successful defence. The backs must be permitted to work out their own salvation.

Though it should not be necessary to point out that the two midfield men, inasmuch as they are a part of the attacking force, ought to support the attack everywhere, it might be well to emphasise this matter. The best laid plan of attack may be met by a clever defence. The backs may not be "drawn" after all, or they may be only partially beaten in front of goal, and effect a weak clearance. When this happens—and it does happen often enough—it is the duty of the midfield players to follow up, watch the fall of the ball, snap it if they can, and try to bring off a score. Clever midfield men will often come in for an easy score in that way, if they are fast enough to get right on the heels of their own scoring forwards, and so give the opposing backs no chance of saving fully. This is one of the many things the midfield men can do in virtue of their roving commission.

(3) *The Centre-Forward.*

The pivot of the whole attacking line is the Centre-Forward. He should be, in a sense, the star-turn of the side. He has a lot to say to the initiation of every attacking movement; he can do a great deal to continue it; very often he is the man who can best finish it off. This all follows from the fact that he is the pivot upon which the whole forward line turns. It is, therefore, a matter of supreme importance to a team to make sure of the man chosen to play as centre-forward and fill the bill competently.

We prefer a rather tall man for the position. Height counts for a good deal in a centre-forward, as so many high balls come his way, and, in fielding such balls, his height will enable him to take them times when a smallish man would not have the reach. It is apparent at once that he must be a sure fielder; and, in addition, it is very desirable that he should be an adept at trapping ground-balls with either foot. The more familiar he is with the dribbling code, the more successful he will be as a centre-forward. Accordingly, he should make his own of the art of giving and taking short passes, swerving and feinting, keeping command of the ball with his feet, and, generally, he should have thorough mastery of all the tricks of the trade. If he possesses a share of weight, it is all the better; for his weight will serve him when he is tackled, and enable him, along with his skill in "dodging," to keep possession of the ball in difficulties.

The centre-forward should be very much of an opportunist, for the simple reason that his position on the field places so many opportunities in his way. He stands, as we remember, rather midway between the right and left wing-men, and accordingly he is in the natural position to receive any ball passed in by either of them. Even when the ball travels right along either wing to the right or left scorer, he it is who most often is in place to receive the ball when either scorer centres in front of goal. Every form of wing-play, therefore, is likely to give the centre-forward an opportunity.

Again, when we consider him in relation to the half-backs, we can see how singularly well placed he is to be supplied with balls by them. The clever half, as we have observed, will try to play as much an offensive as a defensive game. Ordinarily, when the half tries to open up a movement, if he does not send on to the wing, his simplest method will be to send on to the centre-forward. He is the natural "pocket" for the ball, and a short accurate kick will easily send it to him. In that way we can understand how many opportunities may be afforded to him in front of the halves.

On account of the various opportunities given to the centre-forward in the ways mentioned, he should play a most unselfish game, and look upon himself as a great distributing centre for his comrades-in-arms round abou' him. Hence he must try at every turn to open up the game. Keeping before his mind the general plan of attack—which is to "draw" the defence—he will usually pass· out to the wing, and give the wing-men and the right or left-scorer a chance of enticing the defence away from goal. Or, again, he may make a bee-line "on his own" for goal, and thus draw one or two backs upon himself with a view to making an opening for the full scorer to whom he passes. Or, further, instead of parting with the ball to the full-scorer, as just mentioned, he may send the ball out to either winger or to the right or left scorer, in the hope that a score may be brought off by one of the men outside. In one way or another, it is his duty all the time to keep distributing the balls that reach him in as varied a manner as possible.

From what has been said, it follows that a centre-forward should be most resourceful. He must needs be possessed of great judgment and experience, quick to avail of opportunities, a first-class fielder and kicker with both legs, a tricky dribbler and an undoubtedly "heady" player. He should know all the fine points of the game, both in attack and defence, so well that, at any moment, he can perceive a weakness and avail of it. or "size up" the strength of the defence and get round it. The centre-forward should be a master tactician—a kind of General to the whole forward line, and, in a fashion, to the whole team.

(4) *The Wing-Men*.

There are two wing-men in Gaelic Football—one on the right and the other on the left. As we may recollect, the right winger takes up his position somewhere in front of the right half-back, and the left winger in a similar place in front of the left-half, while, if we reckon across the field, these two and the centre-forward are roughly in a line with each other. The two wingers also stand closer, as a rule, to the touch-line than the right and left half-backs.

Very good wing-men are a rare find. This will be understood when we consider the qualities required in the men who play in those positions. Obviously, great speed is the principal note of a really good winger, and it is few men who possess a great turn of speed. Besides pace, however, the competent winger should be an excellent dribbler who can keep command of the ball while travelling very fast. This is a difficult thing to accomplish, and here it is that very fast men fail. For they easily over-run the ball, or, kicking too hard in a dribble, put the ball too often, alas! into the hands of an opposing back.

But there is yet another quality which should be possessed by wingers, and is often missing in them. A winger is obviously a feeder for others. Rarely does he get near enough to the opponents' goal-posts in order to bring off the much-desired score. His business it is to send on the ball to somebody else. At one time it may be his best plan to pass in to the centre-forward; at another to pass on to the right or left-scorer. At all events, the wing-men must be always trying to manage matters in such a way that they will successfully give the ball to someone else. So it happens that it is of great importance for the wingers to know quite well

Picking up Ball from the Ground with the aid
of the Foot.

the art of passing the ball properly, and passing it at the right time and to the man who is most likely to get through for a score at the moment. The doing of all this demands quite a lot of skill, and it is not easy to get men who are of that type.

Quite a large number of players can be secured who can dribble a ball tolerably well and pass it intelligently, but such players lack great speed. On the other hand, it is curious that men possessed of great speed seem to learn with difficulty the art of dribbling a ball well, and are prone to the fault of passing wildly and blindly. Hence it is one of the stock difficulties in football to find men who can play on either wing with success. If a choice has to be made between the slowish player who can dribble and pass a ball properly and the fast man who is rather weak in the matter of dribbling and passing, it would appear to be better to select the former in preference to the latter. That view is confirmed in practice; for we see what a small proportion of the sprinters, whose names are household words in the running world, appear on football teams.

The duties of the two wing-men are easily defined, but not so easy to discharge. They are expected to be always on the look-out for any ball that may come their way, either from their own men or from those opposed to them. Naturally, they must expect many balls kicked on to them by their own halves who are behind them, and, consequently, they must keep well in touch with them, especially with the nearest half-back. Again, the centre-forward will often send out the ball to the wing, and his wingers must be quick enough to avail of the pass lest it should go over the touch-line, or be intercepted by the opponents. Sometimes, even, one of the midfield men may send a short pass to the wing, and the wing-man must not let the good gift go unused.

Or, perhaps, when a strong attack has been made on the opponents' goal, it may happen that the ball will be returned to the wing by the opposing backs, who may try to save towards the side-line. On such occasions, a really high-class winger will anticipate the "save" on the touch-line, get the ball from the clearance, and either send it back towards goal, or even try for a score from that position.

The task of the left-winger is harder clearly than that of the man on the right side. The former has to play against backs who can use their right legs without having to turn, whilst he himself has to depend upon his left leg, unless he can manage to turn and get in his kick with the right. As turning takes time, and the merest fraction of a second may make all the difference in the world in fast play, it is very important for the left winger to have a good left leg, with which he can kick with ease, accuracy, and a fair amount of strength.

Both wingers must be prepared, whenever they get a ball, to make an opening by passing on to the scorer in front, into the centre-forward, or by passing to somebody who happens to be in a favourable position at the moment. Before parting with the ball, however, the winger should try—after having beaten one man already, let us suppose, for possession—to draw another back away from the man to whom he intends passing the ball. Herein lies the great value of a pass. Naturally a pass to a partner who is shadowed by an opposing back will not avail much, unless that back is drawn off somehow. At the same time, of course, a wing-man may not be able to do more than get possession and kick in the direction of a partner, who then has to take his chance and fight for the ball. That plan of action will be very good under the circumstances described, and a score may eventuate.

If either wing-man is possessed of unusually great speed, his best policy will be to "run the wing" on to the right or left scorer in front of him. Only in this case he must be careful to keep control of the ball, lest he should either give an easy chance to the opposing backs of picking it up, or run himself into touch, or perhaps even over-run the ball altogether. The man who has not extra speed had better avail of every chance to pass quickly, and not take risks in a long dribble, with the prospect of being overhauled or overpowered very early in his canter.

It is scarcely worth while saying much on the duty of wing-men in the matter of watching the throw-in. What to do must be left to each winger's individual judgment. It may be no harm, however, to point out that it is not part of his duty ever to throw the ball in from touch. That is most easily and conveniently done by the nearest half-back. Lastly, the winger should be particularly careful about fielding balls on the touch line, lest he be shouldered with the ball over the line. That is a point in touch-line play which he should consider carefully.

(5) *The Centre-Scorer.*

To understand the play of the scoring-men, we had better refer once more to the diagram, giving the positions of the various players on the field. We observe that there are three scorers on the field, and these form the front line of attack. In the centre, somewhat in front of the centre-forward, is the centre-scorer, otherwise called full-scorer, or full-forward. On his right, and rather in front of the right-winger, plays the right-scorer, while on his left, in a similar position in front of the left winger, is located the left-scorer. Though these three players form very nearly the one line—

reckoning across the field—corresponding to the line
formed behind them of the centre-forward and the two
wingers, and might, accordingly, be considered together,
it seems better to analyse, in the first place, the play
of the centre-scorer, and then proceed to work out the
play of his right and left comrades, much as we have
done in regard to the centre-forward and the two
wingers.

Since the centre-scorer plays in the centre and in
front of the opponents' goal, he should possess at least
two qualities. First, as in the case of the centre-
forward, a tallish man is better than a small man,
ceteris paribus. This follows from the fact that he
plays in the centre before goal, where, very often, a
good reach for high balls tells very much. Secondly,
rather a heavy and strong man is better than a lightish
player. For, as we have seen that the centre full-back
should be, and usually is, a rather strong man, and plays
right before his own goal, the heavy centre-full will
usually be more than a match in the struggle for possession of the ball with a light centre-scorer. It would
appear, therefore, desirable to look for good height and
a fair amount of weight in the centre one of the three
scorers. If, notwithstanding, the centre-scorer be rather
on the light side, he must then have other compensating
qualities. The Irish saying applies to his case : " The
man who is not strong must needs be cunning."

It is of the utmost importance that this centre-man
should be a most accurate kicker and resourceful to the
last degree. Whether he handles the ball and tries a
punt or "drop-kick," or attempts to kick a rolling ball,
or even essays to kick a ball on the "fly," in all cases
he should be a great marksman. We do not look for
long or lusty kicks from him, as in the case of the
full-backs and others of his companions on his side.

We rather deprecate long kicking in our centre-scorer as such. What is most needed in him is wonderful accuracy at close range. Hence he should practise every kind of kick—punt, drop, place, screw, "on-the-fly," at short distances from goal—and, in that way, learn to shoot straight every time. There is no better practice for himself and his own goal-keeper than trying on the latter all the different shots with either foot from short distances before goal. The more driving force he can command, consistently with accuracy, the more successful will he be as a scorer. For it goes without saying that a good goal-keeper will have no trouble in dealing with soft shots, even those from close range. But the shot that is delivered with a good deal of force, and that travels rapidly, has a chance every time of finding its way into the net.

It is pretty plain that the centre-scorer should be more of an individualist than the centre-forward. The latter is, as we have seen, supplied with balls by his halves, his wingers and others, and is expected to distribute them rather plentifully to his companions beside him and in front of him. His business most often is to open up the game by initiating various movements all over the forward line. In the case of the centre-scorer, however, it is up to him very often to take what he can and get in a shot. He has to fight his corner against one or even two of the full-backs, try for possession, and, if he succeeds, shoot. For this purpose he must be very much of an individual player, unlike the centre-forward behind him. True, as we shall see, he can do a lot by passing unselfishly to either the right or left scorers beside him, after drawing the backs somewhat. But really his most effective work is done "off his own bat," and in spite of strong opposition.

In a sense it is more difficult to get a suitable man

for the position of centre-scorer than perhaps for any
other position on the field. On the one hand, there
is no man who is so well marked by the opposing back
as he. Playing as he is right in front of his opponents'
goal, he is faced every time by some one of the "fulls,"
usually the centre-full, or even two of the backs dog
his steps. To add to his difficulties, the goal-man is
always between the uprights with all his wits about
him, anticipating every move of the centre-scorer. On
the other hand, a great deal depends on his accurate
shooting, and every eye is upon him when he gets even
the ghost of a chance near goal. If he misses at any
time, be the chance difficult or easy, he is open to blame
for failing to bring off the coveted score. It appears so
easy of accomplishment to the lookers-on, and, if it
does not come off, a chorus of disapproval is heard all
round the grounds. Very few can realise how difficult
it is for the centre-scorer to secure the ball at all from
clever full-backs, not to speak of getting in his kick in
time before being overpowered, and shooting with sufficient force and accuracy.

We have spoken of the need there is for the centre-
scorer to be a very resourceful kicker with both legs.
We cannot omit directing his special attention to the
matter of screw-kicking. It will often happen that he
will have to field the ball with his back to his opponents' goal-post. In such cases it may be quite impossible for him to get in his kick, if he should attempt to
turn round. Turning round may simply mean his being
dispossessed of the ball. His only alternative, then,
is to screw-kick without a moment's delay. To do so
supposes no little skill, and the prospective centre-scorer
should make screw-kicking a special feature of his
practice.

The centre-scorer may be called upon to cover a

larger area than would fall to his lot in ordinary circumstances. This would arise especially when the man behind him, the centre-forward, is not up to a high standard. It may be, and does happen at times, that there is only one man on the team really able to play as centre-forward or centre-scorer. The captain of the team must choose the next best man for either position, and depend upon the expert player who can play in both places to make up for the deficiencies of his companion. Hence, when it so happens that the centre-forward is rather weak in that position, it devolves upon the centre-scorer to try and cover the latter's weakness by playing over a wider area than in the case where he has a capable centre-forward behind him. It is a difficult rôle for the centre-scorer to fill; but a really good man will go a long way to cope with such an emergency,

(6) *The Right and Left Scorers.*

We have observed that there are two other scorers—one on the right and the other on the left of the centre-scorer. Both play rather on the wing. The right-scorer takes up his position some distance in front of the right-winger, and the left-scorer somewhat in front of the left-winger. Their position cannot be more precisely determined as they fix themselves according to the swing of the play.

They must have a threefold understanding, viz., with the wingers, with the centre-forward, and with the centre-scorer. A thorough understanding is of the utmost importance in the case of these front-rank forwards. We may repeat here that, for the existence of such an understanding, one must presuppose in the players concerned an intelligent knowledge of the fine points of the game, a good deal of practice between them in hard matches, and a very keen spirit of unselfishness. One cannot expect to find a good understanding between any section of the players, especially between those of whom we are speaking, if they are lacking in the qualities mentioned. In a manner, the selfish forward, particularly if he plays to the gallery, is a positive danger. Such a man playing as centre-forward or centre-scorer, may destroy all chances of success in a closely contested match, as, in trying to play his own game, he is bound to starve his companions.

The right-scorer has his understanding with the right wing-man, and the left-scorer with the left-winger. Either scorer should be familiar with the play of his ally on the wing and anticipate every possible pass. Obviously, the scorer depends greatly on the wing-man behind him. When the winger, therefore, gets possession, the scorer stands judiciously in such a place in front as circumstances demand. He will expect either a long or a short pass, according to the run of the play, and will stand close by, or at a fair distance off, as the case may be. Plainly, if the wing-man gets clean away in a dribble, with the ball at his feet, the scorer must be generally on the alert to take a short pass at the point where the winger will be seriously hampered by the opposing back. If, however, the wing-man simply fields the ball and kicks, the scorer must take his chance and try to gather the leather from a fairly long pass in the air. Further, it may be necessary for the scorer, when he gets the ball either from a short or long pass, to re-pass the ball to the wing-man, if such a course be desirable. When the understanding is perfect between them, the right move will be made and a score may follow.

Attitude during the Giving and Taking of a Pass.

There is need of a clear understanding also between the right and left scorers and the centre-forward. In dealing with the play of the latter, we have laid down, amongst other things, that one of his principal duties is to supply his companions on the whole forward line with the ball. He is the great distributing medium for those round about him. Therefore, whenever or however a ball reaches his hands or falls beneath his feet, he calculates instantly how he can set his forwards going by passing on the ball to them. Outside the cases in which he tries to score from far out, or passes to either wing-man, he has to choose between passing either to the right or left scorer, or directly to the centre-scorer in front of him. Usually he will pass towards the wing, and this in the hope that the ball may reach one or other scorer there; for that is generally the simplest method of drawing the backs out from goal.

It is pretty evident then that, in order to make the passing out by the centre-forward effective, there should be a very thorough understanding between him and the right and left scorers. When, therefore, let us say, he dribbles the ball at his feet and seems slow to part with it, the scorer nearest him will understand that the device intended is to draw the defence towards himself, and he will expect a short pass as soon as he has enticed the backs out a sufficient distance. On the other hand, when the scorer observes that the centre-forward is not on the dribbling-ticket, but tries a long pass in the air, the former will know that there is no time to be lost about starting to gather the ball. Also, occasions will occur when the centre-forward, after passing the ball on to either scorer, may expect the latter to re-pass to himself. All this manœuvring is feasible enough between competent men who know one another's play.

Perhaps the most important understanding is that which should exist between either right or left scorer and the centre-man playing between them. When it happens that the three scorers have a perfect understanding, the opposing backs must needs be very clever to keep them out. With a really good centre-forward and three such scorers as we are contemplating, playing against capable full-backs and goal-men, a most interesting tussle is generally the outcome, with, however, the odds in favour of the smart attack.

Let us proceed now to consider the inter-play between the centre-scorer and either comrade. When the ball travels along the wing and the scorer there secures it, he is expected to manœuvre a trifle, draw a back or two upon himself, and pass to the centre-scorer. The latter may do several things in such a contingency, though ordinarily he will try to bring off a score. It may suit his book to pass out to the other scorer on the opposite wing, should that player be unmarked, or pass back to the centre-forward who may have started the whole movement. Very often it may be best for him simply to re-pass to the scorer who has given him the ball, especially where there is question of rather short passing movements, for the success of which great skill is required. Clearly, however one fashions out a movement between the three members in the front rank, perfect understanding is of the greatest importance.

Too much stress cannot be laid upon the need there is for accuracy of kicking on the part of the two outside scorers. In the last chapter, in which we discussed the play of the centre-man, we emphasised the necessity there is for him to cultivate all-round kicking ability. There we have seen how accurate he must be every time at short range. To a certain extent the same is

true of his comrades on either side of him. They
should be able to kick with the utmost precision.

Inasmuch as both scorers play rather on the wing,
one can realise how difficult it will be for them to bring
off a score from a punt, drop or drive. Great judgment
is required in measuring the angle, for the kicks from
the wing are usually of an angular character. The
question will often arise whether it will be advisable
for them to try for a score at all. On nearly all occasions they must realise that only a perfectly well-judged
kick will materialise. The moment, therefore, they
secure the ball from a pass or otherwise, they must
calculate at once whether it is best to kick from their
place on the wing, or manœuvre somehow to get the
ball passed in to the centre in the hope that somebody
there may do better. At all events, it is plain that
the right or left scorer should hesitate to shoot except,
taking into consideration his own power and accuracy
and the difficulty of the angle, he considers that he had
better try himself for a score rather than part with the
ball to another.

Of course there can be no question about the fact
that the left-scorer has a very difficult task in hand.
We have more than once directed the reader's attention
to the inconvenience of playing along the left side
against right-legged men. There is no one on the field
who has a more trying part to perform from that point
of view than the left-scorer. It is not unlikely that
one of the very best backs on the opposing side will be
playing right against him. It is rarely that a man
develops a very powerful left-leg, and yet that is just
what he wants in that particular position. The left-
scorer, who has not a particularly good left leg, will
have to turn and get in his kick with the right, and as
this turning means some delay, the result often is that

the opposing back bottles up his man, breaks up a promising movement and prevents a probable score. No getting away from the weakness of a left-scorer who cannot easily and expeditely kick with his left foot.

Speed is a very desirable quality in both these scorers. That will be clear when one remembers that the right and left full-backs opposing them are supposed to be fast men. Both scorers should be able to get up speed at once. This is a most important matter. It is somewhat amazing how often it does happen that men who can run a "fast hundred" or "two-twenty" on the track are very slow to get going on a football field. Now slowness in getting up speed would militate very much against the efficiency of either the right or left scorer, who must be very wide-awake, agile as a cat, and very ready in his movements.

Again, each of them must be expert at transferring the ball from the ground by means of the foot on to the hand, or "swooping" the ball from a low hop. Of course a man may not bother about picking up the ball either way, but simply play it on the ground. The tendency, however, in Gaelic Football is in the direction mentioned, and the hands are usually requisitioned. As this is the case, the scorers should render themselves as skilful as possible in the art of swooping, picking-up with the aid of the foot, and getting-in their kick in practically the one movement.

Scorers should not lose their heads. Indeed the competent footballer should, at all points of the game, play with great calcûlation, consistently, to be sure, with sufficient quickness and directness. Why do we dwell here on so commonplace a matter? Well, it is really astonishing how many scores are thrown away, or, rather, how many fairly easy chances are "muffed" by scorers, owing to this fatal tendency of losing their heads near their opponents' goal. One must not be too exacting in one's criticism of young players; but, unfortunately, the fault we speak of is common enough among pretty seasoned players. Nothing is more annoying in football than to find a beautifully executed movement, in which all the opposing backs have been beaten and the goal-man rendered helpless, destroyed at the last moment by a scorer who loses his head and shoots anywhere but between the posts.

Scores are lost in many ways besides the one just mentioned. We might cite one or perhaps two cases. It is not unusual to see a very accurate scorer—what is called a "dead shot"—miss a score by inches. How does this happen? This wise. The moment before taking the ball into his hands, the scorer looks at the goal-post to make sure that he has measured distance and angle. The next instant he fields the ball, but, in the effort to do so, he moves a little from the spot where he took his bearings. The result is that he, not having made allowance for that slight change of position, shoots outside his mark. Need we repeat here that this is an easily-made mistake? Another is not uncommon either. It happens in a movement where the handling, or passing, is of a rather fast nature. The scorer gets the ball finally, and tries to finish the whole movement with a swift shot. In his hurry he fails to steady himself for a moment, and the consequence is that he either puts too little force into the kick, or he kicks wide of the posts.

Amongst high-class forwards we have met in our time we might cite some names. Clifford, our fast right-winger, and Skinner, our brilliant right-scorers have been a most successful combination on the right side, while Moriarity and Doyle on the left have filled a difficult rôle capitally. Mahony, though yet a very

young player, has been a promising substitute for
Moriarity. Cahill, previous to the players just mentioned, was always grand along the left wing. Breen
as centre-scorer, though inclined to hold on to the ball
too long, was a great marksman, and had a powerful
drive. J. Rice, brother of our distinguished half-back,
has made a versatile forward. The O'Gormans, the
twin brothers of the old days, had a very happy knack
of playing into each other's hands, and were marvellous
footballers in their time. In the very early days of
Kerry football, the famous J. P. O'Sullivan, Dr.
William O'Sullivan and his brother Cornelius, also
Hayes of Killorglin, were sterling forwards, and Hayes
of Killarney was exceptionally brilliant as a wing-
scorer. Outside of Kerry, amongst the forwards that
caught our eye were Mackessy, the crack left-scorer,
Beckett, the fleet wing-man, and Richardson, a youngish player. The latter three players belong to Cork.
Rafferty, the great Kildare captain, and his comrades,
Joyce-Conlan and Scott, were great men in attack.
Campbell of Louth impressed us very much on the
wing. Rossiter, the Wexford scorer, enjoys a high
reputation in his own county. Antrim has produced in
recent years some fine scoring men, who can dribble
trickily and drive beautifully. In the West of Ireland,
the Mayo forwards have played attractive football. We
have come across so many fine forwards in the Dublin
teams—indeed, we might also apply the same remark
to their backs—that we think it would be invidious to
single out any one of them.

A Piece of Foul Play, i.e., "Covering the Ball."

CHAPTER IV.

IT has been said that Attack is the best form of Defence. As such is undoubtedly the case in every form of football, it never pays a side to weaken its attacking force. Accordingly, no matter how great the pressure of the opponents' forwards on your goal-line, do not make the mistake—you in the front rank—of thinking that you will help your own defence by leaving your places and coming to the rescue of your backs.

We are speaking of a game played under normal weather and ground conditions. In such circumstances, if a choice has to be made, for one reason or another, of playing a weak man as a back or as a forward, it appears better policy to play the weak man on the back-line rather than amongst the forwards. Why so? Well, we have already agreed that Attack is the best form of Defence, and, therefore, by keeping a good force in attack, a side stands to gain. Besides, there are other reasons which occur to anyone on a little consideration.

It is a more difficult matter than most onlookers realise to send a football sailing over the cross-bar, to say nothing of bringing off the major score. Before the happy forward gets his opportunity at all, a great deal of very clever manœuvring must precede. Be it noted at once that one "duffer" amongst the forwards may just spoil a beautiful movement at a critical moment. What should have been a score is badly muffed, and the worst of the matter is that the weak man is likely to repeat the mistake. This follows from the fact that a thorough understanding amongst the forwards is an essential condition for a successful attack.

In defence, however, a weak man cannot do nearly as much harm. It is not extremely difficult to so re-arrange a back-line as to cover the weakness of at least one member of it. Then, too, it must not be for-gotten that stopping in football is easier work than getting through, from which it follows that, by weaken-ing the attack one weakens the defence, and the op-posite is true that by strengthening the attack one strengthens the defence.

As a confirmation of what has been said, it is a strik-ing fact how difficult it is for a captain or a selection committee to secure forwards, and how comparatively easy it is to light upon backs. Of course, we must not be taken as saying that a great back is an ordinary "find," and that high-class back-play is an easy accom-plishment. This is not what we have in mind at all. But it is a frequent experience in choosing a team to have to face the problem of furnishing a good forward line. Somehow or other, one feels safe about one's backs, whilst there is generally some doubt about the composition of the attacking party.

In the matter of tactics, it is the business of the attack to try and draw the defence and get through for a score; and, on the other hand, it is the lot of the defence to guard against being drawn, and ward off possible danger. In our view it is easier for the backs to keep the opposing forwards out than for the latter to force their way in. This is part of our general statement that defence play is easier than attacking work. Even so, however, there is hardly any doubt but that a really clever, well-balanced forward-line cannot be stopped. It is interesting to dwell a little upon this.

In our arrangement of the players on the field, we have allotted seven of the fifteen men to defence work and eight for attacking purposes. There are, therefore, eight forwards pitted against seven backs. Evidently, if the eight work in the right manner, pass and re-pass successfully between them, there will always be the odd man over to score. Clever backs may and will succeed in marking that extra man. One great back in defence may be able to silence the guns of two forwards—may, in fact, break up every movement in his neighbourhood. When this occurs there is no forward left unmarked who will be able to shoot in the last alternative. That is a case where the defence is too strong for the attack; or, in other words, the attack is weak. Eight forwards should be able to beat seven backs, if they get a fair number of chances.

Let us not be taken as attaching too much importance to the fact that the number of forwards exceeds by one the number of backs. As we have stated, two of the forwards are midfield men, and since they have merely a roving commission in the middle of the field, they cannot be relied upon for certain to take a hand in every combined movement. In reality, the working out of a concerted forward attack falls chiefly, on the one hand, upon the centre-forward and the two wing-men on either side of him, and, on the other hand, upon the centre-scorer and his right and left scoring comrades. So that usually there will be six forwards against seven backs, and that means that there is one back over. Looking at the matter from this last standpoint, the backs appear to have the pull.

The advantage is more apparent than real. It is expected in every attacking movement that one of the forwards must beat one back for possession of the ball, and draw another towards himself and away from the comrade to whom he intends transferring the leather. In that manner two backs are wheeled out of the way, and it is then a tactical encounter between five forwards and five backs. In truth, it is five forwards against four backs, for the goal-keeper is more or less a fixture between the sticks, and is expected to save his goal merely. Moreover, there is the chance of one or both of the midfield men coming along in time to support the attack from the rere, and counteract, if necessary, the influence of the two defeated backs who may be trying to retrieve the situation on recovering and regaining their positions.

In the matter of kicking the ball, the backs, especially the fulls, are expected to get it away as far as possible from their own posts. The attacking forwards must do the very opposite for the most part. As their object is to drive the leather under or over the crossbar, long kicking by them will not avail, as a rule, for that purpose. The huge punt, drop, or drive may result only in an ''over,'' or a useless touch, and valuable ground may be lost thereby. The forwards must all the time endeavour to work the ball as near as possible towards the opponents' goal-area. The final effort in the manœuvre will consist in the making of a good opening for the most favourably placed member of the attack to shoot at the psychological moment.

The contrast just drawn between the backs and the opposing forwards in the matter of kicking suggests one of the big difficulties against which the latter have to contend, and brings out one of the great differences between defence and attack play. The backs simply are bound to clear their lines and the big kick is their great means of doing so. The forwards, however, have to control the ball, kick it very gently, and pass it along from one to another with the utmost ingenuity. One hard kick may result in putting the leather into the wrong hands, and the whole movement falls to the ground for the moment.   Hence we can see, after a little reflection on defence and attack methods, that the backs have less difficulties to face in warding off the onslaughts of the opposing forwards than the latter have in breaking through and scoring.

CHAPTER V.

PLAYING UNDER SPECIAL CONDITIONS.

THERE are three things which tend to make the playing of football, and, in a sense, the playing of every outdoor game, specially difficult, and these are the sun, the wind and the rain. Sometimes one may find permutations and combinations of the three elements, and the difficulties of the situation are very much increased.

We may at once lay it down as a sensible proposition that the team winning the toss should take it and play with the particular existing conditions in their favour. It is usually a big mistake not to avail of the sun or of a good breeze at one's back. Sun or wind, or both, may disappear at the end of the first half of the play, or, at all events, be less in evidence; hence it would seem foolish to take the risk of throwing such an advantage away.

It is a very simple matter for a team to play with a glaring sun at their backs, and equally simple to do so with the aid of a strong wind. It is mighty hard lines, however, on "the other fellows," who lose the toss, and are required to face such a sun or wind.

Plainly, the favoured team should proceed, from the very beginning, to pile up a score, and they should do so by keeping the ball as high as possible. A high ball travels well with the wind to carry it, and it is very hard for the opponents to field the leather, either in the teeth of the wind, or with the sun playing upon their eyes. Of course, near the opponents' goal the attacking forwards, who have the wind or sun on their side, must be careful to keep the ball under control. This is necessary, because accurate shooting is not a little difficult when the wind blows, and the advantage of it may be nullified by reckless kicking on part of the forwards.

Clearly, if it is good tactics for the fifteen, who have the wind or sun, to play the ball high mostly, it is the duty of the side that have the elements against them to keep it low. Usually it will be useful for them to play the ball towards that touch-line in the direction of of which the wind is blowing. They should also play as much of a spoiling game as possible, and hustle their opponents about as far as the rules will permit them. By some such methods they may succeed in keeping the score down and throwing their adversaries off their game.

The rain creates double trouble as a general rule. It renders the ball greasy, somewhat heavy and hard to hold, and makes the ground slippery, sticky and difficult to travel. Every experienced footballer knows this.

Ordinarily, the heavier team can move well on a sodden pitch, and, if they can utilise their weight, have a big pull over a lighter team. However, the chief thing to be considered is the fielding of the ball, and the side that can handle the greasy ball best has the advantage. On the other hand, this fielding of a wet ball can be counterbalanced to some extent, if the opposing side can manage to play ground football successfully and keep the ball low.

A general remark may be made about this whole matter of playing under special circumstances. This is that all footballers should accustom themselves in their private practice-matches to playing the game in every kind of weather. In that way only would they be able to learn how to adapt themselves to playing important matches when the elements may be most unfavourable.

CHAPTER VI.

THE CAPTAIN OF THE TEAM.

THE selection of the best man for the position of Captain of a team is a matter of no little importance. The finest players are often sacrificed if they be placed under an incapable leader. It has not infrequently occurred that an efficient captain, by means of good generalship, has pulled many a game out of the fire. When all seemed lost, such a one as we have before our mind has risen to the occasion, has suited his tactics to the circumstances, sized up the weak points in the opposition, and brought his side through with flying colours.

The skipper of a team should be, as far as possible, perhaps the oldest and certainly the best all-round player. He should have a thorough knowledge of all the fine points of the game in attack and defence, and possess an unbounded spirit of keenness and enthusiasm. The latter qualities will go a long way towards inspiring the remaining members of the team. We have said that he should be one of the oldest players, because experience counts for a great deal in important contests.

It is clear also that he should command the confidence and loyal support of his fellow-players. On the field he should have absolute control of his men, and be responsible for their formation and the tactics which they are to adopt. In this matter he should have a perfectly free hand, and a selection committee—if there be such—should be slow to question his judgment. He will give a lead to the whole team in the matter of

A Screw Kick.

prompt obedience to the decisions of the referee, and will also help to stand between the latter and the angry protests of partisans amongst the spectators. In such circumstances a timely word from him will go a long way towards preventing difficulties from arising. He must be such a one that will always give the example of good temper and fair play, and his general attitude on the field towards his opponents should be a standing rebuke to any player on his side who might be disposed to introduce unfair or unworthy methods.

It may be part of his duty, rather than that of a selection committee, in choosing his team, to put a younger player in place of an older one. This problem sometimes excites suspicion and creates difficulties. A good captain, however, of the kind we have been describing, will be able to meet it by showing on this and on all occasions that he is perfectly impartial and that no considerations of favouritism or anything else weigh with him beyond the success of his club or side.

The question is often raised as to where the captain of a team should play. Preferably we should like to see the skipper either as centre-forward or as centre half-back, and in either of those places he can do a great deal to lead the team to victory. We are aware, however, that good captains have played in other positions, and we do not pretend to give a more satisfactory solution of the question.

Finally, it may happen, for one reason or another, that the team wish to bestow the title of captain on a player who may not be able to discharge the duties in the manner described. In such circumstances we may suggest, perhaps, that it would be well to depute some other man on the side to assume command to a certain extent.

CHAPTER VII.

THE REFEREE OF THE MATCH.

IT may appear strange to say so, but it seems to be an undoubted fact that the Referee is the most important man on the field. The reason for this statement is not far to seek. For he is the one man who controls the play, the players, and, to a certain extent, the spectators.

The ideal man for the position should be possessed of many good qualities. To begin with, he should have a thorough knowledge of the rules of the game, and, what is still more important, he should be able to interpret and apply those rules, in a sensible manner, to the game in hand. In this connection, the deeper his knowledge of human nature, and the more personal experience he has had of football, the better will he be as a referee. In fact, if he brings with him the reputation of having been himself a well-known and first-class footballer, his chances of efficiency will be greatly enhanced.

Then, he should possess no small amount of resoluteness and firmness in his mental constitution. This is necessary in him; because he must be prepared, once he has given a decision, to adhere to it unrelentingly, so that no pressure on the part of the players, or on the part of the spectators, should cause him to turn back. To do so would be a blunder, and tend to mar the whole game. He must make the players feel that he will tolerate no serious breaches of rule, and must show them that, if there is any inclination on their part to adopt foul tactics, he will crush such an attitude with an iron hand. At the same time, however, he must not err on the side of severity by keeping his whistle blowing like a fog-horn at sea. He must be prepared to temper justice with mercy, and overlook, therefore, accidental infringements of the rules.

He should also be as active on the field as most of the players. Consequently he should be a youngish man, and physically fit to keep going from one end of the ground to the other. Unless he is able to follow the ball and the run of the play rather closely, he will not be in a favourable position at times to decide whether the players are keeping within the rules.

Many believe that it is advisable that the referee should be pretty familiar with the names of the players. They seem to think that a word from him to a player whom he can call by his name will go a long way towards keeping such a one in order. Our Irish temperament would appear to be more controllable in the hands of a referee who is familiar with the members of the teams.

We cannot help pleading for fair treatment towards our referees from the spectators on the side-line and on the stands. Of course, no one will expect onlookers unduly to withhold their enthusiasm and ardour on the occasion of big matches, and Irish human nature seems to revel in a good shout, whether of triumph or reproach. Assuredly, great consideration must be extended towards the man who holds the whistle, and he should be given the credit of being an impartial judge in whatever decision he gives. He cannot see everything. He may even make a big mistake, but no one should question for a moment any of his rulings. We have many good referees in the country. They deserve our thanks for the manner in which they have refereed important matches. Needless to add, the name of M. F. Crowe is honourably known in this connection throughout Ireland. J. McDonnell, of The Kingdom, and T. Irwin, of Cork, have also discharged the duties of Referee with firmness and efficiency.

CHAPTER VIII.

Some Remarks on Training.

WE intend to speak of two things in this chapter, and we will try to be as brief as possible.

In the first place, there is learning How to Play the Game. That includes quite a lot of things. A good footballer has to learn how to kick a ball properly, how to field it, how to dribble, how to pass, and how to tackle. Other items, perhaps, might be mentioned, too; but in what we have said we have included the main departments in the code. There are various kinds of kicks as we have hinted all along—the punt, the drop, the screw, the fly-kick, the place-kick, and the kicking of a running ball. Punting the ball is the most usual method of kicking, and it may be no harm for the benefit of younger players to state that the most effective method of punting a ball is to kick it with the instep instead of the toes. How to kick the ball in the other ways enumerated must be acquired on the field from a competent player. In this, as in every other art, there is no royal road, and the services of a teacher have to be called upon. Indeed, the simplest way to learn good football is to play it with competent players, and if it happens that there is a tradition of clean football in a particular district, young players will have little or no difficulty, if they have the adaptability and enthusiasm, to pick up the game.

It goes without saying that all kinds of practice matches should be useful for the purpose in hand. It would be all the better if there were enough players locally to have fifteen aside games. A fair distribution of the good players on both sides will make things a bit even, and the presence of good men on either side will help to initiate the weaker brethren gradually into the mysteries of the craft. Not a bad idea at all for practice purposes is the suggestion of five aside games, in which case the field of play can be considerably diminished. An old player on each side of the five, for instance, can be relied on to make such a disposition of his fellows that a really well-contested match may be expected to follow. In that and other such ways the older players should succeed in passing on their knowledge to the younger fry.

In the case of very young players, such as boys in schools and students in colleges, who are accustomed to work problems from a black-board, it is not a bad plan for an experienced footballer to give them demonstration lessons with the chalk. A diagram may be drawn on the board, the positions of the players indicated upon it, and a football exponent can dilate at length on the different phases of his subject. In that manner those pupils and students will learn a great deal of the science of the Gaelic Code.

A lot can also be learned by young and old players of the game from looking on at matches played by crack teams. It is obvious that each county team especially has its own peculiar style of playing, and one can learn much from those big inter-county and inter-provincial matches.

The other matter to which we wish to refer in this chapter regards what is called getting oneself into condition, or making and keeping oneself "fit." Here again we must confess that if one has a real love for the game, and wishes to play it with zest, there need be no fear on this score. We are quite well aware that books have been written on this subject, and that there are many men at the present moment whose object in life is to prepare footballers for playing through the season. Here, however, we touch professionalism, which, as we have observed, has so much invaded the realm of sport in our days. We have a decided objection to see Gaelic footballers approach the game from anything like a professional standpoint, and, on that account, we are slow to suggest any special system of preparation for the playing of the game generally. Accordingly, we will mention but a few things on this subject.

We must distinguish at once between preparing for a season and preparing for a very important match. In the former case, all that a player need do will be to lead the ordinary life, take a fair amount of the usual exercises, such as walking, some short sprinting, skipping, ball-punching, &c. Even these are not necessary for either the young player, whose muscles do not tend to get flabby, or even for more advanced players who lead an open-air life in the country and have to work at farming and other such occupations. The exercises we have referred to may be recommended to oldish players who find their feet heavy, their wind unsatisfactory, and their general vitality somewhat on the wane.

In the case of preparation for a very important match, such as an All-Ireland Final, there has been a tendency recently on the part of the opposing teams to take up a course of systematic training. In this case the men are placed under the care of one or two trainers, who are responsible for a system of dietary, a special course of exercises and massage treatment as well as a series of well-arranged practice matches. We would like to make two remarks in this connection. First, let us be taken as objecting again to any tendency towards professionalism.« It is really not altogether fair to the players themselves to be forced to go into special training for some weeks. The majority of our Gaelic men cannot afford the time or the expense to do so. Likewise, it is rather hard on the public, who are called upon to give special subscriptions to defray the heavy expenses of the players on such occasions. Secondly, there is the danger of some of the players being trained "too fine." This may happen especially in case of the younger members of the selected team, and perhaps, too, in regard to players who, as we have already said, lead an outdoor life and work hard. Of course, experienced trainers will take care that such a thing will not happen. We have had the good fortune in the Kingdom of having the volunteer services of Messrs. Collins and O'Connor in preparing our All-Ireland team, and we must acknow· ledge that they did their work sensibly and splendidly.

In conclusion, we may repeat that, in our honest opinion, it would be a great pity that, even in preparation for the biggest matches, any team should set itself to depart from the traditions that have been associated with our Gaelic games up to the present. We have, we trust, all been playing the game for its own sake, because it is OUR OWN GAME, and we should be loth to copy the methods that prevail in many of the modern games. While we say this, however, we do not wish to be taken as holding any particular team up to censure.

APPENDIX I.

THE THIRTEEN ASIDE GAME.

WE promised at the beginning of our book to say something about the playing of the game when it is confined to thirteen players instead of fifteen on each side. We have an idea that, later on perhaps, the number may be so reduced, or that it may be found convenient, for one reason or another, at least occasionally, to establish thirteen aside matches. When this state of things arises, the question is : How are the thirteen players to be placed on the field, and what change in tactics would be necessary both in defence and attack ? We will answer these questions in order, and in as brief a manner as possible. It may be well, however, for the sake of clearness, to make out another simple diagram of what we consider would be a sensible arrangement of the players under the new circumstances.

By looking at the diagram which we have appended, one will see at a glance the changes that are needed. It will be observed that the centre full-back of the fifteen aside game is removed from the defence, and that the centre-scorer is taken away from the attack.

Some might suggest, perhaps, that instead of removing these two players, it might be more appropriate to dispense with the services of the two midfield men. However, we think that the inclusion of the latter two players is necessary in Gaelic Football. Their presence in the middle of the field preserves a useful element of uncertainty in the game, because the backs opposed to them can never be sure where the two may turn up. Also, their presence in either team tends to keep the playing, especially in the centre-field, from

Strenuous Play amongst Promising Juniors.

assuming a mechanical character, and helps to preserve that attractive feature of individuality which, as we have stated at the beginning, is one of the most pleasing characteristics of our national pastime.

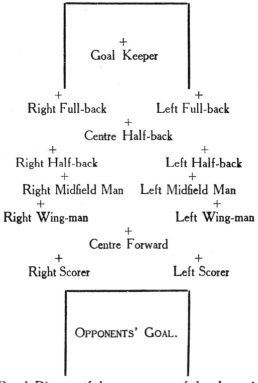

+
Goal Keeper

+   +
Right Full-back   Left Full-back
+
Centre Half-back
+   +
Right Half-back   Left Half-back
+   +
Right Midfield Man   Left Midfield Man
+   +
Right Wing-man   Left Wing-man
+
Centre Forward
+   +
Right Scorer   Left Scorer

OPPONENTS' GOAL.

Rough Diagram of the arrangement of the players in the thirteen aside game.

On the other hand, it appears to be quite natural to eliminate both the centre full-back and the centre-scorer. For these two players play near each other, and no great harm is done the defence, on the one side, and the opposing attack, on the other, when both are left out. We think that, when the experiment is made of playing thirteen aside matches, with our suggested disposition of the men, our scheme stands a very good chance of meeting with pretty general approval.

We turn now to answer the second question : What change of tactics is necessary with the limited number of players? As regards the defence, the only change advisable will concern the full-backs. If our readers will refer to what we have said about the play of the fulls, they will easily be able to construct the needful alteration of tactics. It is clear that the two fulls will have to play somewhat closer to each other, and that the same understanding which we have suggested should exist between the centre-full and the goal-keeper in the fifteen aside game needs to persist between the two players mentioned and the goal-man in the present circumstances. Hence, if the right-full goes out to save, the left-full drops in between him and goal, and vice versâ on the left side. Otherwise the play is very much the same. The methods to be adopted by the half-backs call for no further comment.

In the matter of attack, since the centre-scorer is gone, the centre-forward will have to discharge a double duty. In addition to filling the rôle required by his original position, he will need to make up for the absence of the scorer in front of him. For this purpose he will play, as the diagram suggests, more in advance of his former place on the field, and, roughly speaking, he will stand so that he will be equally in touch with the two wing-men, who will now be rather behind him, and the right and left scorers, who will be somewhat ahead of him. Making due allowance for this change, he will take care to keep up a perfect understanding with both the wing-men and the scorers. The two midfield players continue to act as before.

Finally, there are some things to be said in favour of the thirteen aside game. In many of our towns, and in most country districts, it is not easy to get fifteen good footballers. The reduction of the number would appear to tend in the direction of raising the standard of play. Again, a certain amount of ground football is an attractive feature in the eyes of the people, and the smaller number of players would undoubtedly be forced to develop that side of the game. Further, the majority of the playing pitches in the country are not over large, and very often they are insufficient to accommodate more than the lesser number. For these and other reasons, on which we need not dwell, thirteen aside matches may become more popular. However, we must leave this whole question to the consideration of the authorities that rule the destinies of our native sport.

APPENDIX II.

GROUND FOOTBALL.

MANY followers of the Gaelic Code have suggested from time to time that there is much room for improvement in our national game of Football. They complain that the game is oftentimes greatly marred by the undue frequency of fouls, and that these fouls appear to be due chiefly to the fact that the G.A.A. Rules permit the player to field the ball, *i.e.*, take the leather into his hands either "in the air" or "on the hop," while the very same rules forbid an opponent to catch the man in possession of the ball, charge him from behind, and so forth. They say that it is not in human nature to expect that a player should abstain from catching an opponent who holds the ball and looks on, as it were, at the latter getting the leather away at his ease. Further, our friendly critics would go so far as to suggest that no player should be allowed to use his hands at all, either in taking the ball "in the air" or "on the hop," and that the ball should be played entirely on the ground. In other words, they would have the G.A.A. authorities so to alter the present rules governing the playing of Gaelic Football that our matches would become so many exhibitions of what may be briefly called "Ground Football."

We may say at once that we are altogether in favour of any change that would be calculated to improve the game; or, to put this statement in another form, that would be likely to lessen the number of possible fouls in the playing of it. However, we must confess that we are decidedly of the opinion that Gaelic Football would not be improved were the use of the hands forbidden, and we believe that the G.A.A. authorities would not be acting wisely in the interests of the game were they to frame a new set of rules which would lead to the playing of merely Ground Football, as has been suggested.

Among the most important and attractive—if not absolutely the most important and attractive—features of Gaelic Football are the accurate and clever fielding of the ball, whether in the air or on the hop, transferring the ball with the aid of the foot from the ground to the hands, and getting in well-directed punts, or drop-kicks. From the spectacular point of view these are perhaps the most interesting things in the game, and, if they were absent, Gaelic Football matches would be likely to turn out very tame affairs indeed. In our Introductory remarks we have tried to indicate some of the principal points of difference between our football game and other kinds of football, and we venture to say that the comments then made are a sufficient justification of our view here that Gaelic Football would suffer vitally were Ground Football to become the order of the day in the Gaelic field.

It is undoubtedly true that fouls are of rather frequent occurrence in some Gaelic Football matches, and that the majority of such fouls arise in the manner indicated by our critic-friends. But it must not be forgotten that fouls occur in every kind of outdoor game played according to fixed rules, and more especially in games of football in which the ball travels at a comparatively slow pace, and the opposing players come into immediate bodily contact with one another at every hand's turn. Fouls cannot be entirely eliminated from football games. Indeed we are inclined to think that,

if one were to make the experiment of counting the
fouls in a given number of fairly important Gaelic
Football matches and in the same number of football
contests of a similar class under Associations other than
the G.A.A., it would be found that the fouls in the
latter will exceed those in the former case.

Again, we are convinced that the fouls mentioned are
committed mostly by unscientific players of the game.
In districts where a bad tradition of Gaelic Football
exists, we do not wonder that such fouls are of frequent
occurrence, and tend to bring Gaelic Football into dis-
repute. In such localities there appears to be an idea
abroad that the main thing for every player to do is to
"mind," "watch," and "go for" his opponent every
time, and if one cannot get the ball oneself, tackle
one's opponent anyhow, rules notwithstanding, so that
the man in possession for the moment may not be able
to get in his kick. It need hardly be said that tactics
of this kind do not make for scientific play, and, if
matches are marred by the adoption of such crude
methods, the fault should not be laid at the door of
the framers of the rule which allows a player to field
the leather, but forbids an opponent to catch the man
in possession or charge him from behind.

Furthermore, we cannot accept the statement that
Ground Football would be an effective remedy for the
trouble of frequent fouling in the matches we have
before our mind. Rather, we are pretty sure that the
class of player, who is prone to the catching of an
opponent who fields the ball in the game as it is played
at present, would be just the very last man in the world
to be relied upon to play Ground Football, were it to
come into vogue. In fact, we should be prepared to
find that such a player would still insist in the latter
case on "going for" the man rather than the ball, and

make it his objective to introduce foul methods of tackling his opponent, with the result probably that the
referee's whistle would be heard even oftener than
it has been in Gaelic Football matches played according to the existing rules.

Let us not be misunderstood in the whole matter.
We welcome as much Ground Football as possible in
our game, and we beg to be excused for adding that we
have played the ground game with as much ease as we
have played "the high game." We think that a great
deal can be done, especially in the colleges and schools,
to pave the way for introducing more and more Ground
Football into the Gaelic Code. As a matter of fact
there has been a steady tendency in this direction since
the students of the various colleges have been taking
more kindly to the National Football Game. It has
also been quite noticeable how the reduction of the
number from seventeen aside to fifteen aside has given
the players more scope to indulge in dribbling, passing
with the foot, and dispensing a good deal with handling of the leather, and it requires no prophet to foretell
that, if the number be further reduced—let us suppose
to thirteen aside—the Ground Game will be much more
in evidence.

As these are our views on the subject, we hope that
we shall not be accused of trying to decry Ground
Football. Our position in this matter is, we trust,
defined with sufficient clearness. All the while, however, we feel bound to maintain stoutly that the fielding
of the ball should ever be recognised as an essential
and most attractive feature of our game, and that the
rules which secure this attribute of Gaelic Football
should be allowed to stand in the Gaelic Code.

APPENDIX III.

GAELIC FOOTBALL METHODS APPLIED TO HURLING.

WE do not pretend to be an expert on the science of our National Game of Hurling, though we have played it from time to time, and have seen most of the great inter-county, inter-provincial, and All-Ireland matches for the past twenty years. All the while we claim to have followed the fortunes of the game with the utmost interest, and to have been closely observant of the manner in which it has been played, and we cannot help saying that, in our opinion, there is no finer outdoor sport in the world. It deserves all the encomiums passed upon it, we believe, from the far-off days, when Cucullain and his hero warriors played their great goaling matches, down to our own times, when such doughty champions as Kelleher, O'Keefe, Nolan, and the Coughlans of Rebel Cork, "Drug" Walsh, Anthony, Garrigan, and the Doyles of Moondharrig, the Boys of Wexford, Mackey and his Merry-Men from the Shannon banks, Maher, Semple and the Ryans of gallant Tipperary, have added lustre to the Hurling Code. It has always gone hand in hand with the allied game of Gaelic Football, is under the government of the Gaelic Association (G.A.A.), and has been played according to the very same rules. We venture to think that this little book, which we have written for the benefit of Gaelic Footballers, will be found equally useful in the hands of Gaelic Hurlers.

It is our opinion that the tactics that have been suggested in this work to footballers—in bringing the

Kerry Team (1913)—All-Ireland and Croke Memorial Champions—
with some prominent supporters.

leather from one side of the field to the other—may be adopted almost in their entirety by the hurlers. There is really no substantial difference between the two games, and the methods of attack and defence are much the same in both cases. Of course the hurler uses a camán instead of his foot, and the "líathróid," or ball, is lighter than the football, and, as a consequence, the game has more of the kaleidoscopic character about it. The hurler does not get as much time to calculate and look about him for the purpose of bringing off short passing movements as is the case with the footballer. But, making allowances of that nature, it might be said truly that the Gaelic Footballer and the Gaelic Hurler play very much after the same fashion.

In the matter of defence, the hurling-backs will have much the same understanding between one another as the backs in football, while the forwards will keep before their minds substantially the general plan of attack about which we have said so much. Further, it may be perhaps suggested to our hurlers that they would do well to use their feet a good deal in dribbling the ball. To our mind, the use of the feet in that way will be found very helpful to wielders of the camán in getting themselves out of difficulties, and obtaining freedom to get in their "puck." The working out of good hurling movements may be left with confidence to the competent hurler himself.

In conclusion, we will take the following quotation from Dr. Joyce's *Social History of Ireland*, in which he writes as follows :—"An episode in the story of the Táin describes how Cucullain and Ferdiad, two old friends and affectionate comrades, were forced by circumstances to fight to the death in single combat, and the fight was continued for several days. Each evening word was given for the combat to cease; they laid aside their weapons, and each threw his arms round the neck of the other and thrice kissed his cheek. Cucullain on this occasion had better medical appliances than Ferdiad; but Ferdiad had a more varied supply of food and drink; and each evening Cucullain sent his best doctor with half of his balms and healing herbs to soothe Ferdiad's wounds; while Ferdiad, on his part, sent half of all his choice food and drink to his friend. At last Ferdiad expired, and Cucullain falls on his body in a paroxysm of uncontrollable grief, from which he was with difficulty aroused up by his attendant Loeg."

That story points its own moral. We trust that the chivalrous sense of fair play which the warrior heroes, Cucullain and Ferdiad, displayed towards each other will animate our Gaelic footballers and hurlers on and off the field, and that the same spirit will pervade the minds of our fellow Gaels who come to watch their bloodless combats.